Anarchy Alive!

Anarchy Alive!

Anti-authoritarian Politics
from Practice to Theory

URI GORDON

Pluto Press
LONDON • ANN ARBOR, MI

First published 2008 by Pluto Press
345 Archway Road, London N6 5AA
and 839 Greene Street, Ann Arbor, MI 48106

www.plutobooks.com

British Library Cataloguing in Publication Data
A catalogue record for this book is available from the British Library

Hardback
ISBN-13   978 0 7453 2684 9
ISBN-10   0 7453 2684 6

Paperback
ISBN-13   978 0 7453 2683 2
ISBN-10   0 7453 2683 8

Library of Congress Cataloging in Publication Data applied for

This book is printed on paper suitable for recycling and made from fully managed
and sustained forest sources. Logging, pulping and manufacturing processes are
expected to conform to the environmental regulations of the country of origin.

10   9   8   7   6   5   4   3   2   1

Designed and produced for Pluto Press by
Chase Publishing Services Ltd, Fortescue, Sidmouth, EX10 9QG, England
Typeset from disk by Stanford DTP Services, Northampton, England
Printed and bound in the European Union by
CPI Antony Rowe Ltd, Chippenham and Eastbourne, England

Acknowledgements

This book began its unlikely life as my doctoral project at Oxford University. My foremost gratitude is to my supervisor, Michael Freeden, who in his patient and insightful way provided invaluable perspective and a great deal of useful criticism. David Miller and Elizabeth Frazer read drafts of four of the chapters that eventually made their way into this book, and offered important suggestions. Katherine Morris, my advisor at Mansfield College, was also a great source of support during the difficult and anxious process of writing.

In developing the material into this book I am grateful to have had the benefit of comments and support from Ronald Craigh, Laurence Davis, Marianne Enckel, Benjamin Franks, Sharif Gemie, David Graeber, Andrej Grubacic, Ruth Kinna, Cindy Milstein, Alex Plows, Stephen Shukaitis, Starhawk and Stuart White. So many other friends, comrades and colleagues have contributed to the ideas expressed in this book without reading my written work that I could never mention some without doing injustice to others. If you, reader, have ever exchanged ideas with me in conversation then something of the following pages is yours, as are my heartfelt thanks and solidarity.

During my research I have also enjoyed the hospitality of several autonomous spaces, whose living example of 'anarchy in action' will always be remembered: Can Masdeu (Barcelona), Centre Autonome (Lausanne), Cecco Rivolta (Firenze), CIA (Amsterdam), Dragonfly (Oxford), Equinox (Manchester) Eurodusnie (Leiden), Forte Prenestino (Roma), Les Naus (Barcelona), Les Tanneries (Dijon), La Tour (Genève), Ragman's Lane (Wye Valley), Salon Mazal (Tel Aviv) and Talamh (Lanarkshire).

Earlier versions of Chapters 2 and 6 have appeared as academic articles in the *Journal of Political Ideologies* and in *Anarchist Studies*, respectively. I thank the editors and the anonymous reviewers who contributed useful comments on these versions.

The editors and staff at Pluto Press have been of invaluable assistance in bringing this book to print, and my thanks goes to David Castle, Helen Griffiths, Melanie Patrick, Stuart Tolley and Robert Webb.

During work on this book I was supported by a post-doctoral fellowship at the Porter School of Environmental Studies at Tel-Aviv University.

Finally, my parents Ze'ev and Shifra, my sisters Noa and If'at, and my partner, Lucy Michaels, have been there for me throughout to offer their unconditional love and support. It is to them that I am ultimately indebted.

In memory of my grandfathers

Hayim Schneider (1918–2007)
Yosef Gordon (1920–2005)

Introduction

Stirling, Scotland – 6 July 2005: 2 a.m. From the 'Hori-Zone' eco-village and protest camp, where five thousand anti-G8 activists have been staying in tents for the past week, a mass exodus is in progress. The rain pours down steadily as they trek in small groups through fields and hills, heading for the A9. The plan: to prevent delegates and staff from arriving at the prestigious Gleneagles hotel, where the heads of the world's eight most powerful countries meet this morning.

It is still dark when police vans make their appearance at the camp's one exit, but by now most of the activists are long gone. Minutes later, a remaining thousand or so rush out the gate, many of them in black clothes and with covered faces. In the front is a small group with a few thick pieces of wood around seven feet long. Others wear bicycle helmets, have foam padding taped on their limbs, or carry trash-can lids as shields. Two more groups have mobile walls made of inflated tyre-liners, four in a line fastened with Gaffa tape. These are used to push back the police line, while the bloc swarms out and starts moving down the road.

Passing through the nearby industrial estate, some people build a barricade on the retreat line, others collect rocks in trollies, and another group breaks off for a moment to deface a bank and a Burger King. Pushing towards the M9 motorway as the day breaks, the march evades or fights its way through four more police lines, this time with more than inflated tyres. On the way, someone sprays graffiti on a wall: Anarchists=2 : Police=0.

Back on the A9, hundreds of people are obstructing the road along a few miles, using branches and concrete slabs or staging mass sit-downs. The cops are vastly outnumbered and outmanoeuvred, dragging one group off the tarmac only to have another block the road a few hundred metres down. Then, miles away, six affinity groups simultaneously blockade carefully-selected junctions and bridges in a ring surrounding Gleneagles, throwing the entire region into a gridlock. There is no exit from Perth and Crieff. In Muthill people lie on the ground with limbs connected through metal tubes. In Yetts o' Muckhart they use bicycle D-locks to fasten themselves by the neck to an obstructing vehicle. At Kinkell Bridge there is a mass

1

sit-down. The railway approach to Gleneagles has also been disabled – tracks raised off the ground with a compressor, tyres set aflame as a warning. Two decades of accumulated experience in non-violent direct action – only a few hours to turn Perthshire into one big traffic jam. In it, hundreds of secretaries, translators, businessmen and spin doctors are beginning one very long morning.

Earlier that week, at the 'Make Poverty History' march in Edinburgh, a leaflet was distributed where the blockaders made plain of their cause:

Make History; Shut Down the G8

The G8 have shown time and time again that they are unable to do anything but further the destruction of this world we all share. Can we really believe that the G8 will 'Make Poverty History' when their only response is to continue their colonial pillage of Africa through corporate privatisation? Can we expect them to tackle climate change when whether or not it is a serious problem is up for debate, as their own leaked documents show?

Marching is only the first step. More is needed as marches are often ignored: think back to the mega-marches against the Iraq war. The G8 need to be given a message they can't ignore. They can't ignore us blocking the roads to their golf course, disrupting their meeting and saying with our bodies what we believe in – a better world. However, we don't need to ask the G8 to create a better world. We can start right now, for example, with thousands of people converging together to demonstrate practical solutions to global problems in an eco-village off the road to Gleneagles – based on co-operation and respect for the planet.

Starting today we can take responsibility for our actions and the world we will inherit tomorrow. We can all make history.

In case someone hasn't noticed, anarchism is alive and kicking. The past decade or so has seen the full revival of a global anarchist movement on a scale and on levels of unity and diversity unseen since the 1930s. From anti-capitalist social centres and eco-feminist farms to community organising, blockades of international summits, daily direct actions and a mass of publications and websites – anarchy lives at the heart of the global movement that declares: 'another world is possible'. Far from the end of history predicted in 1989, the circulation and spread of anarchist struggles and politics – largely in advanced capitalist countries – has been a vital force behind resistance to neo-liberalism and the Permanent War. The a-word itself can be a source of pride, an unnecessary liability or an insignificant accessory. Its euphemisms are legion: anti-authoritarian, autonomous, horizontalist ... but you know it when you see it, and anarchy is everywhere.

I arrived in Europe in October 2000. The ostensible purpose was to write a PhD about environmental ethics, but the IMF/World Bank protests in Prague had just happened, the fresh buzz of anti-capitalism was palpably in the air, and I was eager to get a piece of the action. I had done some peace and environmental activism in Israel, and had read my Marx, Marcuse and Kropotkin. Now I went to a report-back meeting by activists who had returned from Prague, and within a few weeks we were organising a demo outside an Oxford lecture hall, where former IMF chief Michel Camdessus was being honoured. I soon ended up doing much more activism than studying. I became more and more involved in alternative globalisation networks, and did a fair bit of what activists snidely refer to as summit hopping. I was tear-gassed in Nice, corralled in London and narrowly escaped a pretty horrible beating in Genoa. After September 11 there were the anti-war movements and, increasingly, the line between reformers and revolutionaries was being drawn in the sand. About the same time I also realised that what I was doing was not neglecting my studies at all. I could easily construe my activism as fieldwork, and actually gear my academic work to the needs of activists. This book is the result.

Anarchy Alive! is an anarchist book about anarchism. It explores the development of anarchist groups, actions and ideas in recent years, and aims to demonstrate what a theory based on practice can achieve when applied to central debates and dilemmas in the movement today. While the content will most immediately interest anarchists and others quite familiar with the topic – to whom I would probably recommend skipping straight to Chapters 3–6, where the real juice begins – this book is also a way to learn about anarchism and explore the ideas that feature prominently in direct-action networks today. Still, the major aim is to make a contribution within anarchist theory, without having to apologise about it.

Chapter 1 offers a basic framework for thinking about anarchism, not in terms of its content, but in terms of what *kind of thing* anarchism is. I propose to understand anarchism as at least three things. First, anarchism is a contemporary *social movement*, composed of dense networks of individuals, affinity groups and collectives which communicate and coordinate intensively, sometimes across the globe, and generate innumerable direct actions and sustained projects. What is sometimes confusing about the anarchist movement is that it is so thoroughly decentralised and networked – all this activity usually happens without formal membership or fixed organisational boundaries.

Second, anarchism is a name for the intricate *political culture* which animates these networks and infuses them with content – the term being understood here as a family of shared orientations to doing and talking about politics, and to living everyday life. Some of this culture's major features are:

- A shared repertoire of political action based on direct action, building grassroots alternatives, community outreach and confrontation.
- Shared forms of organising – decentralised, horizontal and consensus-seeking.
- Broader cultural expression in areas as diverse as art, music, dress and diet, often associated with prominent western subcultures.
- Shared political language that emphasises resistance to capitalism, the state, patriarchy and more generally to hierarchy and domination.

Anarchist political language, for its part, conveys a third sense of anarchism – anarchism as a *collection of ideas*. Anarchist ideas are serious and sophisticated as well as fluid and constantly evolving. The content of central anarchist ideas changes from one generation to another, and can only be understood against the background of the movements and cultures in and by which they are expressed.

To map the ideas of the contemporary anarchist movement, Chapter 2 points to three themes that appear central to anarchist political language today. The first is the rejection of all forms of domination, a term that includes the manifold social institutions and dynamics – most aspects of modern society, in fact – which anarchists seek to uncover, challenge, erode, and ultimately overthrow. The second is the ethos of direct action, which stresses un-mediated intervention to confront injustices and build alternatives to capitalism – in destructive and defensive forms such as industrial sabotage or forest occupations, or in constructive and enabling ones such as social centres, community gardens and cooperatives. The idea of direct action is also related to the emphasis on 'prefigurative politics', or the realisation and expression of anarchist values in the movement's own activities and structures. Finally, diversity is by itself today a core anarchist value, making the movement's goals very open-ended. Diversity leaves little place for notions of revolutionary closure or for detailed blueprints and designs for a free society. Instead, non-hierarchical and anarchic modes of behaviour and organisation are cherished as an ever-present potential of social interaction here and now – a 'revolution in everyday life'.

Where do all these cultures and ideas come from? Perhaps not surprisingly, contemporary anarchism is only in small part a direct continuation of the nineteenth- and early twentieth-century anarchist movements, which had effectively been wiped off the political scene by the end of the Second World War. Instead, the roots of today's anarchist networks can be found in the processes of intersection and fusion among radical social movements since the 1960s, whose paths had never been overtly anarchist. These include the radical, direct-action end of ecological, anti-nuclear and anti-war movements, and of movements for women's, black, indigenous, LGBT and animal liberation. Accelerating networking and cross-fertilisation among these movements led to a convergence of political cultures and ideas alongside and (to be honest) way ahead of the conventional Left (whether social-democrat, liberal or Marxist). The conditions for a full-blown anarchist revival reached critical mass around the turn of the Millennium, with the global movements of resistance to neo-liberal capitalism and to the US-led invasions of Afghanistan and Iraq being the most prominent sites for anarchist activity in recent years.

While often drawing directly on the anarchist tradition for inspiration and ideas, the re-emergent anarchist movement is also in many ways different from the left-libertarian politics of 100, and even 60, years ago. Networks of collectives and affinity groups replace unions and federations as the organisational norm. The movement's agendas are broader: ecology, feminism and animal liberation are as prominent as anti-militarism and workers' struggles. In the latter area, the industrial sector and traditional syndicalism are being replaced by McJobs and self-organised unions of precarious workers (see Foti and Romano 2004, Mitropoulos et al. 2005). A stronger emphasis is given to prefigurative direct action and cultural experimentation. Another prominent difference is that the commitment to modernity and technological progress is no longer widely shared in anarchist circles, with some green anarchists explicitly promoting the assisted decomposition of industrial civilisation. These qualitative changes add up to something of a paradigm shift in anarchism, which is today thoroughly heterodox and grounded in action and an intention to win.

Although I write as an anarchist, this book is not intended to argue *for* anarchism or to convince anyone that anarchy is possible and desirable. The 'case for anarchy' has already been made exhaustively and to my own satisfaction in two centuries of anarchist literature. It has even received some remarkable if rare support in rigorous works of academic political theory (Wolff 1971, Taylor 1976, Ritter 1980, Taylor 1982, Brown 1993, Carter 2000). It would be an unforgivable waste of trees to print yet another book arguing for the validity of anarchist ideas.

Instead, Chapters 3–6 which form the main body of this book assume the basic validity of anarchism, and aim to take the debate a step further by exploring perspectives, dilemmas and controversies that only arise from within the reality of anti-authoritarian struggle for social change. These chapters explore, in turn, the topics of: internal hierarchies and power in anarchist networks; the definition, justification and effectiveness of political violence; the controversial status of technology and modernity; and the relationship with struggles for national liberation, with particular attention to the case of Palestine/Israel.

In what remains of this introduction, I want to talk about the importance and perils of 'doing' political theory as an activist. What does it actually mean to be an anarchist activist-theorist (a role open to anyone)? What tensions arise in the attempt to carry out such an enterprise among one's comrades? And, most importantly, what concrete tools and methods can be offered for facilitating the collective production of reflective political theory in anarchist networks?

PRACTICE AND THEORY

Fortunately, the activist-theorist is not alone in attempting to tackle debates like the ones just mentioned. There is little awareness outside the radical community of the explosive growth and deepening of anarchist political discussion and writing in recent years – in print, online, and most of all verbally, in everyday conversations, discussions and meetings.

The anarchist movement is, in fact, a setting in which high-quality political thinking – indeed, political *theorising* – takes place.

The substantive goal of *Anarchy Alive!* is to genuinely reflect and respond to activists' dilemmas, using a theory built on first-hand experience, on discussions with fellow activists, on a critical reading of anarchist and non-anarchist texts, and on tendentious arguments of my own. I am not so much interested in finding answers as in pinning down some of the relevant *questions* that lie at the bottom of endless and recurring debates, to explain their background, to map and disentangle them. I also occasionally make my own arguments that either take a position on a given issue, or else restructure the debate altogether by calling into question its implied assumptions and purposes.

The approach to anarchist theory taken in this book shares a great deal with the one offered recently by anarchist anthropologist David Graeber. Graeber suggests that any anarchist social theory, in addition to endorsing the initial assumption that 'another world is possible', would have to 'self-consciously reject any trace of vanguardism'. The role of the anarchist theorist is not to arrive at the 'correct strategic analyses and then lead the masses to follow', but to answer the needs of anarchists for theoretical expression on the issues that concern them, and 'offer those ideas back, not as prescriptions, but as contributions, possibilities – as gifts' (Graeber 2004: 5–12). The role of the activist-theorist, then, is not simply that of an expert observer but primarily one of an enabler or facilitator, and the role of the participants is one of co-theorist and co-activist.

Avner De-Shalit has argued for the same approach in environmental political theory. In order to be not only interesting but also relevant, he argues, a political theory should 'start with the activists and their dilemmas ... It is therefore a theory that reflects the actual theoretical needs of the activist seeking to convince by appealing to practical issues.' By bringing recurrent themes in the debates of activists to the written page, the theorist can construct a discussion where they are treated in a more patient and precise way, with attention to detail and a coherent thread of argument. The role of the theorist, on this score, is to partake in and facilitate the reflexive process of theorising among activists, functioning as a clarifier, organiser and articulator of ideas, an activity that takes place with and for activists. Her or his goal is to address, in theoretical form, the issues that activists face in their everyday organising, to assemble ideas so that they can be discussed carefully, to lay open hidden assumptions and contradictory statements, and in general to advance activists' thinking by harvesting ideas from brief and informal debates and giving them more structured and fine-grained attention. Although s/he may take sides with the broad agenda of environmental activists, 'the philosopher should not take the value of the activists' claims for granted; their intuitions, arguments, claims, and theories should also be scrutinized. However, the fact that they need to be critically examined does not affect the main point: that the activists' intuitions, claims, and theories ought to be the starting point' (De-Shalit 2000: 29–31).

Thus the process of generating anarchist theory is by itself a dialogue, which discusses real people's ideas and practices with them. Only from this connectedness can theory remain authentic and self-critical, and draw the confidence to speak – not from above, but from within (cf. Gullestad 1999, Jeppesen 2004). There are strong parallels here to the tradition of Action Research, which integrates diverse emancipatory and grassroots approaches to learning, including contributions of indigenous cultures, communities in the global South, radical pedagogues and philosophers, ecological practitioners and egalitarian, feminist and anti-racist social movements (Friere 1970, Feyerabend 1970, Birnbaum 1971, Touraine et al. 1983a, 1983b, Rosaldo 1989, Reason and Bradbury 2001). These approaches stress overtly 'engaged' methods of collaborative research, grounded in an emancipatory ethos that fosters the creation of valuable knowledge and practice among equals. Specific research methodologies take second place to the emergent process of collaboration and dialogue which empowers and develops solidarity. By providing critically engaged and theoretically informed analyses generated through collective practice, the debates in anarchist political theory offered in this book aim to provide tools for activists' ongoing reflections.

My own path has landed me among many comrades and groups, taking part in diverse local campaigns and projects, conferences and discussions, international mobilisations and mass protest events. In the UK I worked locally with the vibrant anti-capitalist and anti-war network in Oxford, and with anti-authoritarian coalitions organising for May Day actions and anti-war demonstrations, the British *Earth First!* network (which unlike its US counterpart is unambiguously anarchist) and the *Dissent!* network resisting the 2005 G8 summit. I was also an observing participant at international mobilisations including anti-G8 protests in Genoa (2001), Evian (2003) and Gleneagles (2005), and anti-EU protests at Nice (2000), Brussels (2001) and Barcelona (2002), as well as at several international activist gatherings, including the international No Border protest-camp at Strasbourg (2002), European meetings of the Peoples' Global

Action network in Leiden (2002) and Dijon (2003), and the anti-authoritarian sideshows accompanying the European Social Forums in Firenze (2002) and London (2004). As a result, this book is primarily informed by first-hand experiences on the ground and discussions with activists. To this is added a fairly extensive acquaintance with contemporary anarchist media: websites, discussion groups, blogs, films and video clips, radio programs and – finally – programmatic anarchist literature, both printed and online.

Now it should be emphasised that anarchist literature is not supposed to look like academic political theory. Much of it appears in self-published, photocopied and pirated booklets and 'zines (pronounced like 'magazines'), which may also include any combination of action reports, comics, short stories, poetry, and do-it-yourself guides to anything from women's health to bicycle repair. Many pieces are written anonymously, collectively or under a pseudonym. The pieces have very particular audiences in mind, often other anarchists. Truth be told, some of the material in the polemical section of anarchist publishing is just not very good. Jason McQuinn finds there much sectarian and vitriolic bad faith, as well as 'inarticulate ignorance … which seems to be the worst on the web, but often it is nearly as bad elsewhere' (McQuinn 2003). However, there are also many very insightful, calmly argued and well thought-out anarchist books, articles and essays out there, and the following pages make extensive use of them as a source of support or as a target of criticism.

In any event, the lack of rational discussion is certainly far from the norm in the movement, if we also count the everyday, vernacular conversations among activists, where the bulk of discussion on political matters in fact takes place. Since dedicated freedom fighters tend to be intelligent and engaged people, these conversations are usually of a very high quality. So it is extremely important for whoever wants to write about anarchism in the present tense to be part of these verbal conversations, in which surface the most relevant questions and dilemmas for anarchist theory to address, and which supply many important arguments and insights for incorporation into the theoretical work.

As for the inevitable anarchist assumptions – well, the non-aligned reader is invited to provisionally adopt an anarchist frame of assumptions and explore one version of what happens when we run with it. After all, it makes little sense to ask whether anarchists should ever use violence to achieve their ends if their ends themselves are not justified, or to wonder whether some forms of leadership in the anarchist movement are more problematic than others if horizontal organising is rejected to begin with.

In truth, the theory should not need to suffer from the fact that the theorist also thinks that 'another world is possible'. On the contrary, a self-aware, serious partiality that wants to contribute something to one's fellow activists provides a strong incentive not to gloss over difficulties or sweep tense issues under the carpet. After all, the best 'contribution' comes from a critical and disillusioned approach, which identifies and reflects on taken-for-granted rules and expectations, and raises issues which activists may not be keen to confront.

The style of anarchist political theory that I use to handle the fairly complex debates in this book owes much more to Anglo-American than to continental European methods and conventions. This is not necessarily a good or bad thing, but it does mean that the theory work offered here chiefly takes the form of analysing concepts and arguments, making distinctions and giving examples, all with the intention of driving home some point. It also means that clarity and readability are values, and that a clear policy is in place against wilfully demanding writing in general, and rare synonyms in particular. Though some passages might make some demands on the reader's concentration, I have done my best to remain in orbit around plain English rather than shooting my mouth off into hyperspace.

And now, once again: What is anarchism?

1
What Moves the Movement?
Anarchism as a Political Culture

What is anarchism? What does it mean to be an anarchist? Why? Because it is not a definition that can be made once and for all, put in a safe and considered a patrimony to be tapped little by little... Anarchism is not a concept that can be locked up in a word like a gravestone... It is a way of conceiving life, and life, young or old as we may be, old people or children, is not something definitive: it is a stake we must play day after day.
—Alfredo Bonanno, *The Anarchist Tension*

In October 2004 the European Social Forum convened in London. During that week the British capital hosted a micro-cosmos in which the tensions within the so-called 'alternative globalisation movement' were on full display. On the one hand there was the official ESF, actively supported by the Mayor of London Ken Livingstone and dominated behind the scenes by his Socialist Action group, along with large NGOs, trade unions and the Trotskyist Socialist Workers' Party. Many of the organisations involved in the ESF were operating recruiting stalls in a bid to increase their membership, informed by a strategy of building political power within the state-sanctioned realm of civil society politics, so as to challenge neo-liberal policies and global trade rules at a parliamentary and governmental level. The debates and plenaries at the ESF were largely in the format of lectures, with several speakers on the podium and an audience in the seats. The content was determined in closed meetings, and a registration fee was required to enter the event. Food was supplied by corporate caterers with underpaid staff (cf. Reyes et. al. 2005).

But elsewhere in London, numerous Autonomous Spaces were buzzing with activity. Attendance was free, workshops were less formal and everyone could organise one. The content was more radically anti-capitalist, feminist and ecological. The spaces were also different in their organizational model: decentralised, participatory and consensus-based. The participants in the autonomous spaces were very clear about their opposition to the top-down, recruiting logic of parties, NGOs and unions. Their own shared identity is produced by an ethos of active resistance to capitalism, the state, racism, patriarchy and homophobia; they endorse horizontal organisation based on a network model, largely without formal membership or hierarchies; and their struggle does not seek to take power or restructure society from above – they want to build it from below, with means that are of the same substance as the ends. As far as labels and titles were concerned, the hundreds who filled the autonomous spaces didn't really like them. But they did call themselves 'autonomous', 'anti-authoritarian' or, in explicit opposition to the top-down model of the official ESF, 'horizontal'. Notice anything conspicuously absent from this list?

THE A-WORD

There is something risky about using the words 'anarchist' and 'anarchism' to talk about a group of people many of whom *do not* normally call themselves anarchists, and sometimes actively shun the label. Words are, after all, important – and the fact that all these euphemisms are invented for the sole purpose of not saying 'anarchism' deserves closer attention.

Now there are some very obvious reasons why many of us are reluctant to call ourselves anarchists, even though we might be attracted to the word. As Bob Black put it,

To call yourself an anarchist is to invite identification with an unpredictable array of associations, an ensemble which is unlikely to mean the same thing to any two people, including any two anarchists. (The most predictable is the least accurate: the bomb-thrower. But anarchists have thrown bombs and some still do). (Black 1994: 31)

For many people the words anarchy and anarchism still automatically evoke negative images of chaos, mindless violence and destruction, not least so since libertarian ideas continue to be actively demonised through the 'anarchist scares' in the corporate media (Sullivan 2004, O'Connor 2001). Using 'anarchism' as an explicit banner when trying to engage the general public can be a liability. Anarchism has had so much negative PR that people are closed off before they give themselves a chance to listen to what activists are saying. Others, however, find power in the provocation:

I might not even choose to apply the word 'anarchism' to my own beliefs, but I think there's a value in using it, the same value and the same reasoning that has led me to call myself a Witch for all these years. And it's this – that when there's a word with so much charge attached, that arouses so much energy, it's a sign that you are transgressing on territory that the arbiters of power do not want you to tread, that you are starting to think the unthinkable, look behind the curtain ... to reclaim the word 'Anarchism' would be to wrest the stick out of hand that's using it to beat us, that very much does not want us to deeply question power. (Starhawk 2004)

However, the most common source of resistance to the anarchist title is that many anarchists do not enjoy adopting any label *at all*. People identify with many political and cultural strands, and believe that circumscribing their beliefs under any one 'ism' is unnecessarily constricting and implies (however unjustly) that they have a fixed and dogmatic set of beliefs. In the words of Not4Prophet:

Personally I am not down with any titles, tags, or designations. I've spent most of my adult life trying to find ways to do away with genres and borders and envelopes, so I think we are always better off if we don't label ourselves or allow anyone to label us. Anarchy or anarchism is really something we seek and live and struggle for, so it doesn't matter what we call ourselves (or don't) if we are in the midst of action doing it. (Imarisha and Not4Prophet 2004)

So is there really such a thing as an 'anarchist movement' out there in the present day? And what is 'anarchist' about it? David Graeber (2002) tries to overcome this tension in his own way:

I am writing as an anarchist; but in a sense, counting how many people involved in the movement actually call themselves 'anarchists', and in what contexts, is a bit beside the point... The very notion of direct action, with its rejection of a politics which appeals to governments to modify their behaviour, in favour of physical intervention against state power in a form that itself prefigures an alternative – all of this emerges directly from the libertarian tradition.

While Graeber is very right in pointing to direct action and prefiguration as core anarchist ideas, he also needs a euphemism – the 'libertarian tradition' (as in 'libertarian socialist', read: 'anarchist') – to establish guilt by historical association. This invites talk of a movement that is 'broadly' anarchist or 'inspired by' anarchism – which reifies anarchism and expects 'really' anarchist movements to conform to some pre-conceived ideal type. In contrast, I would suggest that we can indeed coherently speak about an 'anarchist movement' plain and simple – as long as we look at it through the lens of political culture, with all the richness and flexibility that implies.

The term political culture is used here to refer a set of shared orientations towards 'doing politics', in a context where interaction takes on enough regularity to structure the participants' mutual expectations. In their cultural context, political events, behaviours, institutions or processes can receive an intelligible and 'thick' description (Geertz 1975:14). The prism of political culture gives us a useful way to talk about anarchism that does not imply theoretical unity, ideological conformity or linear movement structures. As far as one-word labels go, this political culture could certainly be called anarchist.

The site in which these cultural codes are reproduced, exchanged and undergo mutation and critical reflection is the locus of anarchism as a movement, a context in which many very active political subjects can say the word 'we' and understand roughly the same thing – a collective identity constructed around an affirmed common path of thinking and doing.

As indicated in the introduction, I would suggest organising our thinking about the orientations that make for a distinctly anarchist political culture in four broad categories: models of organisation, repertoires or action, cultural expression, and political discourse.

Models of organisation

The anarchist movement, like other social movements, can be described as a network of informal interactions between a plurality of individuals, groups and/or organisations, engaged in a political and cultural conflict, on the basis of a shared collective identity (Diani 1992: 13). The architecture of the movement is that of a decentralised global network of communication, coordination and mutual support among countless autonomous nodes of social struggle, overwhelmingly lacking formal membership or fixed boundaries. This reticular model of social movement organisation has been likened to a rhizome – the stemless, bulbous root-mass of plants like potato or bamboo – a structure based on principles of connection, heterogeneity, multiplicity and non-linearity (the metaphor is borrowed from Deleuze and Guattari's discussion of knowledge – see Deleuze and Guattari 1987: 7–13). Networks do not have defined limits but rather overlap each other, and expand or contract as groups interact or part ways (Gerlach 2001). Anthropologist Jeff Juris, who conducted participatory research with anti-capitalists in Barcelona, introduces the idea of a 'cultural logic of networking' to explain how activists reproduce movement networks. Rather than recruitment, the objective is horizontal expansion and enhanced 'connectivity' among diverse movements, within flexible and decentralised information structures that allow for maximal coordination and communication. As a result,

network-based forms of political organization and practice are based on non-hierarchical structures, horizontal coordination among autonomous groups, open access, direct participation, consensus-based decision making, and the ideal of the free and open circulation of information ... network-based politics involves the creation of broad umbrella spaces, where diverse organizations, collectives and networks converge around a few common hallmarks, while preserving their autonomy and identity-based specificity. (Juris 2004: 68)

We should distinguish between the anarchist networks in the proper sense – the decentralised structure of communication and coordination among activists – and self-defined 'Networks' like *Earth First!*, *Dissent!* or *Anti-Racist Action*. The latter could equally be called 'banners' – umbrellas under which certain parts of the anarchist movement act in a particular area. A banner, in this sense, is a convenient label for a certain goal or type of political activity, which can also – though not always – be accompanied by a concrete network, in the sense that people operating under the same banner in different locations have a significant level of communication tools (meetings, email lists, websites, a newsletter). Banners are even more fluid than networks. For example, a given group of activists in Britain might operate a free vegan street-kitchen today under the *Food not Bombs* banner, meet to design a leaflet against the G8 under the *Dissent!* banner tomorrow, and confront a far-right march through their town under the *Anti-Racist Action* banner the following week.

While networks, rhizomes and banners express the movement's architecture on a macro level, it should be clarified that the bulk of ongoing activity takes place on the micro level. In this context, the most oft-mentioned constituent of anarchist organising is the 'affinity group'. The term refers to a small and autonomous group of anarchists, closely familiar to each other, who come together to undertake a specific action – whether in isolation or in collaboration with other affinity groups. The expression stems from the Spanish *grupos de afinidad*, which were the basic constituents of the Iberian Anarchist Federation during the Spanish Civil War (though the FAI was a very structured organisation, with controlled membership, and the affinity groups were generally long-lasting rather than ad hoc). Typically, an affinity group will consist of up to roughly 15 participants, and individuals within it often take on specific roles for an action (medic, legal observer, driver, etc.). The participants in an affinity group form a self-sufficient unit, plan their action down to the smaller details and look after each other on the streets. Whereas the term 'affinity group', as used by anarchists today, tends to designate an ad hoc formation, the term 'collective' is often used when speaking of a more permanent group. Collectives again have a small face-to-face 'membership', and may exist for any ongoing task: a land-based collective operating an agricultural commune, an editorial collective of an anarchist publication, a collective running a particular campaign or research activity, or a trainers' collective dedicated to teaching skills to other activists – anything from bio-diesel production to stencil-art to consensus decision-making. A collective may also act as an affinity group for a particular protest or direct action outside its normal activities.

While affinity groups and collectives represent the micro level of anarchist organising, whether ad hoc or permanent, the bulk of ongoing anarchist activity takes place on the meso level of local networks, typically in one city. The local network is a context in which many participants are used to working together, whether in an affinity group, collective or coalition. This is the venue for organising everyday activities like stalls, leafleting, small demonstrations, screenings and benefit events, as well as direct action in an affinity group. It is also an area where anarchists are most involved in coalitions – with citizen associations, youth groups, radical NGOs and even local chapters of Green and Socialist parties (though many anarchists absolutely refuse to collaborate with any political party).

On the macro level (from the regional to the continental and global), the network form is the prevalent mode of organisation. Much has been written of the contribution of the Internet to the development of the anarchist and broader anti-capitalist movements and their resulting ability to define a global terrain of solidarity (Cleaver 1998, Klein 2000). But web-based networking is only the most abstracted expression of the real-life process of forming cooperation and trust on the ground. The ties that hold anarchist networks together begin from the primary affinities of face-to-face groups and collectives, extending through a dense web of personal connections and virtual nodes to form an international context for cooperation and solidarity. This gives the patterns of solidarity in the anarchist movement a *tribal* quality. The closest affinities exists on the level of small groups and local milieus – the 'bands' and 'extended families' where there is the closest level of friendship and trust. Further affinities are created when activists from diverse places and backgrounds cooperate. This can happen in an ongoing project with occasional conferences and online communication – a prominent example being the key European anti-neo-liberal network that was created around organising the popular education caravan of Indian peasants in 1999. It can also happen during brief and intense 'plateaus' of organic network convergence, such as the coordination of an international summit protest (Chesters and Welsh 2005). A special feature of tribal solidarity is the instinctive tendency to extend it to perceived members of one's extended family or tribe. Here the feeling of identification, and the mutuality and reciprocity it motivates, is premised on shared cultures of resistance and visions for social change. In exchanges between activists from different countries who meet for the first time, familiarity is often probed through the presence of various cultural indicators of one's background and political orientation. Tribal solidarity thus exists as a potential that can be actualised selectively, destabilising the boundaries of membership and non-membership.

Repertoires of action

In terms of action repertoires, anarchist political culture emphasises a 'Do It Yourself' approach of direct action – action without intermediaries, whereby an individual or a group uses their own power and resources to change reality in a desired direction. Anarchists understand direct action as a matter of taking social change into one's own hands, by intervening directly in a situation rather than appealing to an external agent (typically a government) for its rectification. This is mirrored by disinterest in operating through established political channels or in building political power within the state.

It is important to distinguish between direct action and a related concept, 'civil disobedience'. I take the latter to mean any conscious collective defiance of the law, either for moral reasons or in an attempt to mount pressure on the authorities to respond to one's demands. Thus Thoreau: 'If the alternative is to keep all just men in prison, or give up war and slavery, the State will not hesitate which to choose' (Thoreau 1937/1849: 646). Thus civil disobedience is essentially a confrontational form of political *dialogue* between insubordinate citizens and the state, which does not challenge the basic legitimacy of the latter (since the state is expected to act in response to the disobedients' demands – changing an unjust law, for example). Often civil disobedience is accompanied by rhetoric that calls on society to live up to its professed ideals, reinforcing rather than challenging the status quo on society's basic relations and institutions.

Most commonly, direct action is viewed under its preventative or destructive guise. If people object, for instance, to the clear-cutting of a forest, then taking direct action means that rather than (only) petitioning or engaging in a legal process, they would intervene literally to prevent the clear-cutting – by chaining themselves to the trees, or pouring sugar into the gas-tanks of the bulldozers, or other acts of disruption and sabotage – their goal being to directly hinder or halt the project. However, direct action can also be invoked in a constructive way. Thus, under the premise of direct action, anarchists who propose social relations free of hierarchy and domination undertake their construction by themselves. Direct action is thus framed as a dual strategy of confrontation to delegitimise the system and grassroots alternative-building from below. The collectives, communes and networks in which activists are involved today are themselves the groundwork for a different society 'within the shell' of the old one.

Direct action also translates into a commitment to 'being the change' one wants to see in society, on any level from personal relationships that address sexism and racism to sustainable living and communal economies. This represents the extension of direct action into a 'prefigurative politics', where the movement's goals are thus

'recursively built into [their] daily operation and organizational style. This is evident in affinity groups, decentralised organisation, decision-making by consensus, respect for differing opinions and an overall emphasis on the process as well as the outcomes of activism. It is the explicit attention to organisation as a semiotic strategy and the attempt to work directly from basic values to daily practice that merits the designation of a 'culturalist' orientation; these are movements that actively symbolise who they are and what they want not just as end goals but as daily guides to movement practice (Buechler 2000: 207).

I take a closer look at this aspect in the next chapter.

Counter-cultural expression

This category includes the diverse counter-cultural trends that can be observed in the anarchist movement. Throughout the twentieth century anarchist ideas had attracted cultural and artistic movements such as Dada, Surrealism and the Beats. Today too the movement displays a mix and fusion of diverse cultural traditions, rooted in the radical ends of numerous counter-cultural movements – from punks to ravers and from hackers to neo-Pagans (see McKay 1996, McKay 1998). Many spaces of alternative cultural and social activity are associated with anarchism, including social centres, squats, show venues and festivals. The punk movement has been the most significant hotbed for anarchists throughout the last two decades, due to its oppositional attitude to mainstream society and close affiliation with anarchist symbolism, and the presence of its aesthetic in many anarchist spaces is unmistakable. Anarchists also borrow from many spiritual traditions including paganism, Buddhism and various New Age and Native American spiritualities (O'Connor 2003, Taylor 2002).

Many activists consider lifestyle choices like vegan food, queer and open relationships, or psychedelic experimentation as expressions of their values and politics. As Alex Plows points out, counter-cultures provide 'the mulch in which the seeds of radical protest are germinated and nurtured':

the development of culture, community, social networks and lifestyle choices associated with radical political ideas also form much of movement activity, political praxis, and help to sustain mobilisation in the long term, bridging activist generations ... the 'sustaining' function of movement culture and lifestyle is part of what makes a social movement able to mobilise and take other sorts of more 'political' action; definitions of 'political activity' need to include culture and lifestyle. (Plows 2002:138)

Cultural expression can serve as a shorthand designation of affiliation and connection with others. It thus plays an important role in the articulation of personal or collective identities in the anarchist movement. External appearances like styles of clothes or hair are important cultural signifiers, visible before any political conversation begins.

Also important in this context is the movement of subversive appropriation of cultural icon known as 'culture jamming'. The term was coined in 1984 by the San Francisco audio-collage band Negativland, and in its broad resonances reflects the Situationists' preoccupation with *détournement*: an image, message, or artefact lifted out of context to create a new, subversive meaning (Situationist International 1959). As a tactic of guerilla communication, culture jamming includes anything from street theatre and cross-dressing to billboard alteration and media hoaxes, whereby cultural images and symbols in the public sphere are repositioned in a way that changes their meaning in a radical direction. Naomi Klein likens culture jamming to a semiotic *ju-jitsu* that uses corporations' own strength against them, 'because anytime people mess with a logo, they are tapping into the vast resources spent to make that logo meaningful' (Klein 2000: 281).

Political language

This final heading is used to bring together those aspects of anarchist political activity which have to do with thinking, speaking and writing (as well as singing and performing). In other words, it includes the substantive content of anarchism as a political ideology. Political ideologies are not irrational dogmas or forms of 'false consciousness'. They are not mutually exclusive, and they are not organised neatly from left to right. Ideologies are paradigms that people use (often intuitively) to handle ideas that are essentially contested in political language – 'master frames' that fix the meaning, interrelationship and relative importance of essentially contested concepts in a self-contained whole (Freeden 1996). For example, it is hard to think of an ideological family which does not value 'freedom'. Liberalism, Conservatism and Socialism in all their variants, and even Fascism and religious fundamentalism, value 'freedom'. But they have vastly different versions of what freedom *is*, of what relationships exist *between* freedom and other concepts like equality and progress, and of how *central* freedom is in their arrangement of concepts and values.

Like everybody else, anarchists have their own ways of organising their understanding of politics and making sense of their own activities. The next chapter is dedicated to the content and evolution of contemporary anarchist ideology. I will be looking at three major idea-clusters that are present across anarchist discourse, and which largely define it as an ideology. The first is the resistance to all forms of domination – a phrase enveloping manifold social institutions and dynamics, most aspects of modern society, in fact – which anarchists seek to challenge, erode and ultimately overthrow. The generalisation of the target of anarchist struggle from 'state and capital' to 'domination' is what most distinctly draws contemporary anarchism apart from its earlier generations. Second, we find references to prefigurative politics, an extension of the 'constructive' do-it-yourself approach of direct action, which stresses realising libertarian and egalitarian social relations within the fold of the movement itself. The third cluster is the emphasis on diversity and open-endedness in the anarchist project, rejecting detailed prognostic blueprints for a desired future society. This lends anarchism a strong emphasis on the present tense: non-hierarchical, anarchic modes of interaction are seen as an ever-present potential of social interaction here and now – a 'revolution in everyday life' (Vaneigem 2001/1967). I return to all of these ideas below.

Along with the cultural articulation of political concepts and values, it is important to mention finally under this heading the more narrative-based elements of anarchist discourse, the movement's orally transmitted stories about past mobilisations, previous cycles of struggle, and historical episodes which are seen as an inspiration – the narratives that spin a thread connecting Greenham Common to Porto Alegre and Chiapas to Genoa (for a collection of some of these see Notes from Nowhere 2003). These stories are an important aspect of political culture which also function as a mobilising resource. As Mark Bailey points out, direct action movements today draw heavily on non-Western mythological discourses, which open up for it the possibility for 'the development of a mythology of resistance ... that is much more inclusive of previously marginalized voices than that of previous generations'. This secular mythology is ideological, generating 'a sense of solidarity and common purpose between widely disparate groups [while] highly effective in generating a celebration of "difference"' (Bailey 2005).

THE NEW SCHOOL

In the remainder of this chapter I want to look at a few more special features of the anarchist movement today. First, to continue the discussion of anarchist political language, I want to focus for a moment on a special class of written documents which are major expressions of activist discourse – documents entitled 'principles of unity', 'mission statements' and 'hallmarks' which many activist groups endorse. Such documents are not intended as constitutions or political programmes, but as rhetorical spaces in which the 'flavour' of the group's politics is represented – effectively a statement of political identity.

Similar hallmarks are often used by many different groups in a large network, such as those of Anti Racist Action and of the global Indymedia network (ARA undated, IMC 2001). Possibly the most widely circulating document of this kind is the 'hallmarks' of the Peoples' Global Action network (PGA) – a worldwide coordination of anti-capitalist groups and movements launched at an international *encuentro* organised by the Zapatistas in 1996. The hallmarks have served extensively and worldwide as a basis for actions and coalitions, and have been endorsed by many affinity groups and networks as a basic expression of their politics. The current wording of the hallmarks is (PGA 2002):

1. A very clear rejection of capitalism, imperialism and feudalism; all trade agreements, institutions and governments that promote destructive globalisation.
2. We reject all forms and systems of domination and discrimination including, but not limited to, patriarchy, racism and religious fundamentalism of all creeds. We embrace the full dignity of all human beings.
3. A confrontational attitude, since we do not think that lobbying can have a major impact in such biased and undemocratic organisations, in which transnational capital is the only real policy-maker.
4. A call to direct action and civil disobedience, support for social movements' struggles, advocating forms of resistance which maximize respect for life and oppressed peoples' rights, as well as the construction of local alternatives to global capitalism.
5. An organisational philosophy based on decentralisation and autonomy.

Now in spite of the clear resonances of its hallmarks, PGA has never been defined explicitly as an anarchist network. On the global level applicable to the PGA network as a whole, an explicit reference to anarchism would not do justice to the diversity of its participant groups, which include numerous peasant movements from Asia and Latin America who have never identified with anarchism nor with any other set of ideas rooted in a by-and-large European historical experience. In a European or North American setting, however, hallmarks like those of PGA establish the perimeters of a decidedly anarchist political space by way of elimination, so to speak. These content-rich statements exclude such a long list of features of society and ways of approaching social change, that what is left, at least in terms of public discourse in advanced capitalist countries, is inevitably some kind of anarchism. This happens entirely without reference to anarchism as a label, but the results remain the same. The third hallmark, for example, explicitly distances the PGA political space from the ones in which NGOs and advocacy groups operate, working to change the WTO and other global trade systems from within the logic of their own operation through lobbying. The laconic fifth hallmark can easily be understood as an exclusion of the centralised and hierarchical organising methods of the authoritarian left, while reserving the space for a diversity of non-hierarchical organising traditions, from the tribal-based associations of Maori and Maya peoples through Indian *sarvodaya*-inspired campaigns to the affinity-group-based structures of Western anarchists.

Documents like the PGA hallmarks fulfil three important political functions in constructing identities and solidarities in the movement. Looking inwards, they establish a frame of reference for participants that can be invoked symbolically as a set of basic guidelines for resolving disputes. Looking outwards, they attempt to express the movement's political identity to a general audience. And looking 'sideways', they define the lines along which solidarity is extended or denied to other movement actors. This comes into sharp relief when we consider that the present wording of the hallmarks follows two major revisions, which took place at the second and third global conferences in Bangalore (1999) and Cochabamba (2001). In Bangalore, the second hallmark was added in order to 'clearly distance PGA from organisations of the extreme right looking for a political space to spread their xenophobic rejection of globalisation', such as Pat Buchanan in the US. At the same conference, 'the character of the network was redefined: its previous focus on "free" trade agreements (and on the WTO in particular) was broadened, since we reached the consensus that PGA should be a space to communicate and coordinate globally not just against treaties and institutions, but also around the social and environmental issues related to them. An opposition to the capitalist development paradigm in general was made explicit' (PGA 2002, cf. PGA 1999). This change was incorporated into the first hallmark in Cochabamba, where it previously endorsed a rejection 'of the WTO and other trade liberalisation agreements (like APEC, the EU, NAFTA, etc.)'. At the same time, imperialism and feudalism were added to the list, the latter 'at the request of Nepalese and Indian delegates who remarked that it remains the immediate form of domination for many in that area'.

The next point I want to make is that approaching anarchism as political culture can help us make sense of what is probably the most prominent division within the anarchist movement proper. Graeber (2002, n.8) frames this division as one between a minority tendency of 'sectarian' or 'capital-A anarchist groups', informed by a strict ideology or political programme, and, on the other hand, a majority tendency of 'small-a anarchists' who distance themselves from strict ideological definition and who 'are the real locus of historical dynamism right now'. Who are these capital-A anarchists? The only group Graeber mentions is the North Eastern Federation of Anarchist Communists (NEFAC), an American anarchist federation inspired by the *Organisational Platform of the Libertarian Communists*. The *Platform*, created by Nestor Makhno and other anarchist exiles in 1926, calls for anarchist organisations based on Theoretical Unity, Tactical Unity, Collective Action and Discipline, and Federalism (Makhno et al. 1926, cf. Malatesta 1927). Proceeding through guilt by association, however, we note that NEFAC is a member of International Libertarian Solidarity (ILS – http://www. ils-sil.org), a global association of 'anarchist, anarcho-syndicalist, revolutionary syndicalist, and clearly anti-Statist, non-party aligned social organisations which run along libertarian principles'. On a broader view, the capital-A camp could also be seen to include the International of Anarchist Federations (IAF – http://www.iaf-ifa. org), founded in 1968, which unites anarchist federations from nine countries including Argentina, Britain, France and Italy; and the International Workers Association (IWA – http://www.iwa-ait.org), an international association of anarcho-syndicalist unions from 15 countries including the Spanish and French CNT, the German FAU and the Brazilian COB.

Now there is something to this distinction, but I think it should be taken more subtly than Graeber could have done in a footnote. To begin with, capital-A groups are hardly a minority tendency. The ILS, for example, includes the Spanish CGT, a union with 60,000 members. To be sure, in terms of numbers Spain is an exception and I do not know how active all the members are. But even without the CGT, the wider capital-A camp has many thousands of members. As for 'sectarianism', the founding declaration of ILS is quite clear:

As libertarians we all drink from the same revolutionary spring of water: direct action, self-management, federalism, mutual aid and internationalism. Nevertheless, the different flavours and currents of this spring have caused on too many occasions fractionalism, divergency and separation. We do not wish to see who has got the clearest or purest water, we believe that they are all right and wrong, pure and impure. (ILS 2001)

It is doubtful whether many members of today's capital-A camp really take their anarchism dogmatically, as if it were a 'party line'. This impression may be given by some anarchist groups' current revival of the *Platform*, but most platformists emphasise that they only 'broadly identify' with the organisational practice it advocates, 'so it is a starting point for our politics, not an end point' (Anarkismo. net 2005).

What, then, is the real difference between these groups? Aided by the approach introduced in this chapter we can provide a more fruitful explanation. The crucial difference between the two groups lies not in their having or not having a dogmatic view of anarchism, but in their political culture – their concrete activities, methods of organising and political language. While obviously participating in the decentralised networks of the broader movement, the so-called capital-A anarchists work more closely within the traditional political culture of the anarchist movement established before the Second World War. In this political culture organising typically means working in formal organisations with elected positions, rather than as individuals or in informal groups. Decisions are more often made in a debate-and-vote format rather than by facilitated consensus. Workplace organising, anti-militarist actions and publishing are more prominent than ecological and identity struggles, communal experiments and non-Western spirituality. So the difference between the two anarchisms is generational – an 'Old School' and a 'New School'. This book is primarily concerned with the latter kind of anarchism, but this is not to place it on one or the other side of an artificial division. While the distinction of genres is by itself valid, it should not be taken to mean a sectarian attitude. There certainly exists solidarity and cooperation between many old-school and new-school groups, and in some local milieus anarchists of both orientations work together regularly and smoothly (see Franks 2006).

Ultimately, the capital-A versus small-a distinction is a limited concept, which actually stands in for the issue of sectarianism itself. While sectarianism is not very prevalent in the anarchist movement, there have been tensions around the experimental re-creation of the anarchist project in recent years. The most (in)famous expression of these tensions came from Murray Bookchin's all-out attack on new trends in the movement. In his 1995 book, *Social Anarchism or Lifestyle Anarchism: An Unbridgeable Chasm?*, he announced that

The 1990s are awash in self-styled anarchists who – their flamboyant radical rhetoric aside – are cultivating a latter-day anarcho-individualism that I will call lifestyle anarchism. Its preoccupations with the ego and its uniqueness and its polymorphous concepts of resistance are steadily eroding the socialist character of the libertarian tradition... Ad hoc adventurism, personal bravura, an aversion to theory oddly akin to the antirational biases of postmodernism, celebrations of theoretical incoherence (pluralism), a basically apolitical and anti-organizational commitment to imagination, desire, and ecstasy, and an intensely self-oriented enchantment of everyday life ... a state of mind that arrogantly derides structure, organization, and public involvement; and a playground for juvenile antics. (Bookchin 1995: 9–10)

So are the new anarchists really a self-absorbed and narcissistic bunch, doing nothing more than to create escapist pockets of alternative subculture that pose little challenge to the system (cf. Feral Faun 2001)? Have anarchists abandoned the thankless but necessary work of building a mass revolutionary movement and propagating radical ideas in wider society? Unfortunately, Bookchin did not actually offer any commentary on what was going on in activist circles. His vituperative attacks were rather focused on an eclecticmix of anarchist *writers* including L. Susan Brown, Hakim Bey and John Zerzan, all of whose writings are subjected to a harangue of abuse including such savouries as 'fascist', 'reactionary', 'decadent', 'infantile', 'personalistic', 'yuppie', 'bourgeois', 'petit bourgeois' and 'lumpen'.

Bookchin's invective soon received a no less caustic retort from Bob Black, in *Anarchy after Leftism* (Black 1998). Black argues that that label 'lifestyle anarchism' is a straw man constructed by Bookchin to encompass everything he dislikes about contemporary anarchism – which seems to be all but his own views. But the real issue is deeper than Bookchin's dismissive attitude to postmodernism and the enchantment of everyday life. His approach effectively argues that there could be such a thing as an anarchist orthodoxy – a 'right and wrong' that could be used to judge new trends in anarchism, and to potentially deny their legitimacy and refuse them solidarity. Black associates this with the preoccupations of the authoritarian left, thus the call for a 'post-leftist' anarchism. Elsewhere, he argues that

Anything which has entered importantly into the practice of the anarchists has a place in the anarchist phenomenon-in-process, whether or not it is logically deducible from the idea or even contradicts it. Sabotage, vegetarianism, assassination, pacifism, free love, co-operatives and strikes are all aspects of anarchism which their anarchist detractors try to dismiss as un-anarchist. (Black 1994: 31)

This insistence on anarchism as a necessarily heterogeneous and heterodox phenomenon-in-process is what invites the condemnation of sectarianism and closed horizons against what Black calls 'Leftist' anarchists, who affix anarchism with a given meaning and deny the genuineness of other variations. In a similar vein, John Moore has called for an 'anarchist maximalism' in which everything is up for criticism and re-evaluation, 'not least when coming into contact with those icons that are vestiges of classical anarchism or earlier modes of radicalism (e.g., work, workerism, history) or those icons characteristic of contemporary anarchism (e.g., the primitive, community, desire and – above all – nature). Nothing is sacred, least of all the fetishised, reified shibboleths of anarchism' (Moore 1998; cf. Landstreicher 2002, McQuinn 2004).

The breadth and diversity of what could 'count' as anarchist expression is indeed hard to place in bounds. But this is precisely why there is such an advantage in looking at anarchism as a political culture. The concept of political culture allows us to approach anarchism from the ground up, putting organisation, action and lifestyle on the same footing with ideas and theories. We can thus separate anarchism from any expectation of a fixed dogma or precise ideology, overcoming at least some of the anxieties associated with the A-word. Finally, the richer account offered by a cultural approach to anarchism provides a grounded way to make sense of anarchist ideas – as I aim to show in the next chapter.

2
Anarchism Reloaded
Network Convergence
and Political Content

That night we sat across from each other sipping tea and singing stories, weaving the past into our present; speaking of yesterday as if it had already been entered and meticulously recorded into the history books. I felt the philosophical knife of my life before and my life after Seattle slide deep into my skin. I had broken open; I was seeing new land with views of rebellion and courage, a glimpse that will be with me through the stories of repression and time and survival. That will outlive me. I knew then that I might never have the words to tell this story, our story, a story of re-birth.
—Rowena Kennedy Epstein, in *We Are Everywhere*

In the previous chapter we looked at anarchism as a political culture, offering a basic orientation to the movement and its activities. In this chapter I want to focus on contemporary anarchism as an ideology – taking a closer look at core concepts and keywords that feature in anarchist political expression, clarifying their substance and the relationships between them. In line with the approach taken in this book, the following account is grounded in close attention to the language activists actually employ, verbally and in print, as well as to the political practice which this language reflects and influences. The discussion combines two perspectives: real-time and historical. The first is based on an interpretation of anarchist expression today, which I suggest is best approached from the outside in. On the outside are three basic markers, or first-order clusters of concepts, that define the anarchist language game. These are domination, prefigurative politics, and diversity/open-endedness – the discussion of which structures the present chapter. Within these markers, however, there is a great deal of space for creativity and indiscipline. Anarchist ideas are constantly reframed and recoded in response to world events, political alliances and trends in direct-action culture, evolving through intense flows of communication and discussion, and through innumerable experiences and experiments. The second, historical perspective explores the roots of these ideas, drawing attention to trends and developments in social movement activity over recent decades that have led to the revival and re-definition of anarchism in its present form. My central argument is that anarchism today is rooted in the intersections and convergences among diverse social movements, whose contributions to defining a new terrain of radical politics since the 1960s have accumulated to shape the present movement's culture and priorities. Analysing these processes in full would take a book on its own; my more modest purpose here is to highlight the most relevant ones, as they relate to anarchist ideology in its re-emergence.

DOMINATION AND REFUSAL

As anarchist historian George Woodcock argues, the discontinuity of the anarchist movement is its most conspicuous feature. Unlike Marxism, he says, anarchism

presents the appearance, not of a swelling stream flowing on to its sea of destiny ... but rather of water percolating through porous ground – here forming for a time a strong underground current, there gathering into a swirling pool, trickling through crevices, disappearing from sight, and then re-emerging where the cracks in the social structure may offer it a course to run. (Woodcock 1962:15)

And indeed, the periods in which the anarchist movement was at its largest and most active were ones of escalation in social struggle. The years between 1848 and 1914 were seething with revolutionary activity, and gave anarchist struggle their dynamism and sense of urgency. But two World Wars later anarchism had all but disappeared from the scene. The physical elimination of most of the European anarchist movement by the Bolshevik and Fascist dictatorships, and the repression and deportations of the American Red Scare of 1918–21, had left the international movement in ruins. Some European anarchist organs and publications were re-launched after 1945, and in Latin American countries like Argentina and Uruguay, where in spite of dictatorships and disappearances the anarchist culture and tradition knew less ruptures, the early 1950s were a peak of anarchist workers' and students' movements. But overall, it is fair to say that the anarchist presence in the political landscape after the Second World War was only a pale shadow of what it had been 50 years earlier. The post-war economic boom in Western Europe and the US saw the welfare state domesticate much of social struggle, while the

Cold War pitted Western capitalism against Eastern communism in a bi-polar international system, creating a political imagination in which the anarchist option of 'neither Washington nor Moscow' was rendered invisible. In the global South, anti-colonial struggles were for most part nationalist or Marxist, though there were clear anarchist influences on leaders like Mohandas Gandhi and Julius Nyerere (Marshall 1992: 422–7, Mbah and Igariwey 2001, Adams 2002b).

In the 1960s, however, the threads which would weave together to form the new wave of anarchism began to thicken. As from 1964, meetings of young anarchists were held in Europe, with French and Italian students, Dutch Provos and exiled Spaniards. Soon after, new social movements quite independently began promoting many anarchist values and tactics, especially in France with the students' and workers' movement of May 1968, and in the US with the anti-Vietnam War movement and the counter-culture. Although the participants in these movements for the most part did not regard themselves as anarchists, many of them were expressing basic ideas of anarchism which had come down to them 'not through direct reading, but in a kind of mental nutrient broth of remnants of the old ideologies which pervade the air' (Woodcock 1985/1962: 410ff). Thus, while explicitly anarchist groups have been involved all along, anarchism as we see it today descends from a much more diverse background of movements and ideas.

Perhaps the most prominent feature of the new anarchist formulation that emerged from this hybrid genealogy is the generalisation of the target of anarchist resistance from the state and capitalism to all forms of domination in society. Since the late 1960s, the movements at whose intersection contemporary anarchism has emerged were creating linkages in theory and practice between various campaigning issues, pointing beyond specific grievances towards a more basic critique of stratified and hierarchical social structures. With the rise of single-issue movements working on diverse agendas – economic justice, peace, feminism and ecology, to name a few – activists progressively came to see these agendas' interdependence, manifest along various axes such as ecological critiques of capitalism, feminist anti-militarism, and the interrelation of racial and economic segregation.

Accompanying the convergence of campaigning issues in the radical community was the growing emphasis on the intersections of numerous forms of oppression. Black women, marginalised in overwhelmingly white feminist circles and often facing blatant sexism in the black liberation movements, began mobilising in autonomous black feminist (or, in Alice Walker's term, 'womanist') movements heralded by the founding in 1973 of the National Black Feminist Organization and of Black Women Organized for Action (Collins 2000, Roth 2004). Autonomous black feminist movements played a particularly important role in highlighting the concept of 'simultaneous oppression' – a personal and political awareness of how race, class and gender compound each other as arenas of exclusion, in a complex and mutually reinforcing relationship.

The 1980s saw an increasing diversification of the gay rights movement in both Europe and North America, with lesbian and bisexual organisations tying feminist and gay liberation agendas, and claiming their place in a hitherto predominantly male field (Taylor and Whittier 1992, Martel 1999, Armstrong 2002). With the advent of the HIV/AIDS crisis later that decade, these agendas took a further radical turn when activist groups like the American ACT UP introduced a strong emphasis on direct action and focused on the pharmaceutical corporations keeping HIV medication at unreachable prices (Edelman 1993, Shepard and Hayduk 2002). These dynamics were carried forward under the umbrella of Queer Nation, founded in summer 1990, which emphasised diversity and the inclusion of all sexual minorities. By the mid-1990s, queer women and men of colour had founded their own organisations and radical movements had developed a holistic critique of racism, heterosexism, patriarchy and class.

The radical ecological movement draws on an especially diverse range of perspectives, since it naturally encompasses the entire spectrum of interaction between society and the natural environment. This gave rise to a holistic approach in radical ecology, which initially gravitated towards deep ecology. But the lack of an explicit critique of capitalism in deep ecology left many direct-action environmentalists unsatisfied. Throughout the 1990s, eco-radicals' growing confrontation with governments and corporations in their struggles infused the movement with a very strong anti-capitalist and anti-state dimension, through which their green was darkened, so to speak, into a recognisably anarchist black.

Contemporary anarchism is thus rooted in these convergences of radical feminist, ecological, anti-racist and queer struggles, which finally fused in the late 1990s through the global wave of protest against the policies and institutions of neo-liberal globalisation. This has led anarchism, in its re-emergence, to be attached to a more generalised discourse of resistance, gravitating around the concept of *domination*. The word domination today occupies a central place in anarchist political language, designating the paradigm which governs both micro- and macro-political relations. The term 'domination' in its anarchist sense serves as a generic concept for the various systematic features of society whereby groups and persons are controlled, coerced, exploited, humiliated, discriminated against, etc. – the dynamics of which anarchists seek to uncover, challenge and erode.

The function of the concept of domination, as anarchists construct it, is to express the encounter with a *family resemblance* among the entire ensemble of such social dynamics that are struggled against. The idea of a family resemblance used here is drawn from the philosopher Ludwig Wittgenstein. According to Wittgenstein, the general concepts we use do not possess any necessary and sufficient conditions for their definition. Rather, the items that we place under a general heading are related to one another by a set of partial overlaps, through the possession of common characteristics. Not all of the members of a family possess the entire set of such characteristics. However, our cognition operates in such a way that a continuity is established between them – in the same way we can 'tell' that someone is her father's daughter (Wittgenstein 1953/2002 §§65–7). This linkage is evident in manifold utterances, such as the following communiqué from activists in Kvisa Shchora (Black Laundry) – an Israeli LGBT direct-action group against the occupation and for social justice:

The oppression of different minorities in the state of Israel feeds on the same racism, the same chauvinism, and the same militarism that uphold the oppression and occupation of the Palestinian people. There cannot be true freedom in an oppressive, occupying society. In a military society there is no place for the different and weak; lesbians, Gay men, drag queens, transsexuals, foreign workers, women, Mizrahi Israelis [of Middle Eastern or North African descent], Arabs, Palestinians, the poor, the disabled and others. (Black Laundry 2001)

The term domination thus draws attention to the multiplicity of partial overlaps between different experiences that are struggled against, constructing a general category that maintains a correspondence between experiences which remain grounded in their own particular realities. The term domination thus remains inclusive of the myriad articulations of forms of oppression, exclusion and control by those subject to them, at countless individual and collective sites of resistance. This does not, of course, imply that the same mechanisms feature in all of these relations, nor that they operate in identical ways. Nevertheless, it is the discursive move of *naming* domination which enables anarchists to transcend specific antagonisms towards the generalised resistance that they promote. If there is one distinct starting point for an anarchist approach, it is this act of naming.

The systematic nature of domination is often expressed in reference to a number of overarching 'forms', 'systems' or 'regimes' of domination – impersonal sets of rules regulating relationships between people – rules which are not autonomously constituted by those individuals placed within the relationship (including the dominating side), prominent examples of which are the wage system, patriarchy and white supremacy (the latter two terms are preferred here to 'sexism' and 'racism' because they refer to defining features of social relations rather than to individual persons' attitudes of prejudice and bigotry). Regimes of domination are the overarching context that anarchists see as conditioning people's socialisation and background assumptions about social norms, explaining why people *fall into* certain patterns of behaviour and have expectations that contribute to the perpetuation of dominatory relations. Because of their compulsory nature, regimes of domination are also something that one cannot just 'opt out of' under normal circumstances. Women or non-white people encounter discrimination, access barriers and derogatory behaviour towards them throughout society, and cannot simply remove themselves from their fold or wish them away. The attempt to live outside them is already an act of resistance. As Bob Black expresses this, domination is nobody's fault, and everybody's:

The 'real enemy' is the totality of physical and mental constraints by which capital, or class society, or statism, or the society of the spectacle expropriates everyday life, the time of our lives. The real enemy is not an object apart from life. It is the organization of life by powers detached from it and turned against it. The apparatus, not its personnel, is the real enemy. But it is by and through the apparatchiks and everyone else participating in the system that domination and deception are made manifest. The totality is the organization of all against each and each against all. It includes all the policemen, all the social workers, all the office workers, all the nuns, all the op-ed columnists, all the drug kingpins from Medellin to Upjohn, all the syndicalists and all the situationists. (Black 1994)

On such a reading, institutions such as the state and the capitalist organisation of ownership and labour – as well as the nuclear family, the school system and many forms of organised religion – are where the authoritarian, indoctrinatory and disciplinary mechanisms which perpetuate regimes of domination are concretely exercised and normalised through the 'reproduction of everyday life' (Perlman 1969). So while what is resisted is, at the bottom of things, domination as a basic social dynamic, the resistance is seen to proceed through confrontation with the institutions through which this domination is administered. Thus any act of resistance is, in the barest sense, 'anarchist' when it is perceived by the actor as a particular actualisation of a more systemic opposition to domination. For example, resistance to police repression or to the caging of refugees and illegal immigrants becomes anarchist when it is more broadly directed towards the state as such, the latter being the ultimate source of policing or of immigration policies.

The concept of domination reflects anarchists' commitments to decentralisation in the process of resistance. It is widely believed among anarchists that struggles against domination are at their most informed, powerful and honest when undertaken by those who are placed within those dynamics (though clearly it is possible for men to struggle against patriarchy, for white folk to resist racism, etc.). Thus the impulse to abolish domination is valorised in the diversity of its enactments, explaining the anarchist refrain according to which 'the only real liberation is self-liberation' and grounding its rejection of paternalism and vanguards. The tension between the specificity of dominations and the need to articulate them in common is reflected in the (often positive) tension between unity and diversity in the anarchist outlook on struggle – the anarchist movement itself being a network of autonomous resistances. The latter retain a privileged position in expressing their oppression and defining their struggles against it, but are also in constant communication, mutual aid and solidarity with each other.

PREFIGURATIVE POLITICS AS DIRECT ACTION

The second major cluster of ideas in anarchist political expression is the ethos of 'prefigurative politics', which explains how activists think about their strategies for social change. Prefigurative politics has been defined as the idea that 'a transformative social movement must necessarily anticipate the ways and means of the hoped-for new society' (Tokar 2003), or as anarchism's 'commitment to overturning capitalism by only employing a strategy that is an embryonic representation of an anarchist social future' (Carter and Morland 2004).

Prefigurative politics thus represents a broadening of the idea of direct action, resulting in a commitment to define and realise anarchist social relations within the activities and collective structures of the revolutionary movement itself. The effort to create and develop horizontal functioning in any collective action setting, and to maintain a constant awareness of interpersonal dynamics and the way in which they might reflect social patterns of exclusion, are accorded just as much importance as planning and carrying out campaigns, projects and actions. Considerations of efficiency or unity are seldom alleged to justify a weakening of this emphasis. The development of non-hierarchical structures in which domination is constantly challenged is, for most anarchists, an end in itself.

This orientation is widely recognised as central to anarchism, as evident from an abundance of statements to that effect in the principles of unity of diverse groups and networks. The principles of Indymedia, for example, state that: 'All Independent Media Centers recognize the importance of process to social change and are committed to the development of non-hierarchical and anti-authoritarian relationships, from interpersonal relationships to group dynamics' (IMC 2001). While a local example comes from the Unbound radical bookstore in Chicago:

We don't believe in waiting until after the revolution ... if you want a better world you should start acting like it now. That is why we choose to work within a non-hierarchical, anti-authoritarian structure. All decisions are made through consensus. There are no bosses. None of us wants to have a boss, and none of us wants to be a boss. (Unbound undated)

The widespread nature of such commitments allows us to view present-day anarchist formations as 'explicit and conscious experiments, all ways of saying, "We are not just saying No to capital, we are developing a different concept of politics, constructing a different set of social relations, pre-figuring the society we want to build"' (Holloway 2003). What is encountered here is a widespread endorsement of efforts to enact anarchist transformation not only in 'society' but also in the 'processes, structures, institutions, and associations we create right now, and how we live our lives' (Silverstein 2002).

All this is simply a form of constructive direct action, which rose to prominence throughout the 1970s and 1980s. One of the primary sites for this was the nonviolent blockades against nuclear power and weapons, which drew together pacifists, early environmentalists and feminists, though not the traditional Left (Midnight Notes 1985, Welsh 2001). The Abalone Alliance, which in the early 1980s forced the Diablo Canyon nuclear power plant in California to shut down, saw a prominent involvement of women who explicitly called themselves anarcha-feminists. Through their involvement,

the anarcha-feminists were able to do a great deal to define the political culture that the Abalone would bequeath to subsequent incarnations of the direct action movement. That political culture helped to create more space for internal differences in the Abalone, and in later organisations, than there had been in the Clamshell [Alliance]. It strengthened the role of the counterculture within the direct action movement, and it opened the movement to the spirituality that later became one of its most salient aspects ... anarchia-feminism reinforced the commitment to a utopian democratic vision and a political practice based on the values it contained. (Epstein 1991: 95–6)

Direct action under its 'constructive' aspect could be seen throughout this period in the numerous self-organised urban and rural communities set up in Europe and North America. More violent direct action was also present, for example in the bombings of the Angry Brigade in Britain (Vague 1997) as well as in actions of non-anarchist (even anti-anarchist) organisations such as the Red Army Fraction and Red Brigades. From the 1980s onwards, direct action also became the primary method of political expression for radical ecological movements, as in the wilderness defence of *Earth First!* or broader social and environmental struggles such as the British anti-roads movement (Wall 1999, Seel et. al. 2000, Plows 2002).

At the same time, many activists were increasingly departing from the top-down models of organisation that characterised the old European Left as well as American groups such as the National Organisation of Women, the large anti-Vietnam War coalitions or Students for a Democratic Society (and, later, its would-be 'revolutionary cadre' the Weathermen). From the 1970s on, movements increasingly began to organise themselves in a decentralised manner without (formal) structures or leaders, inspired by critiques of political centralisation that emanated in particular from the New Left in the late 1960s and feminist circles in the 1970s (Cohn-Bendit 1968, Bookchin 1972, Lewis and Baideme 1972). Anti-nuclear blockades and sabotage actions, for example, were often organised through the cooperation of decentralised affinity groups, arguing that the movement should model the social structures it looks forward to in its own organisation. At the same time, the involvement in these actions of Quakers and feminists (anarcha- and otherwise) introduced consensus decision-making methods and 'spokescouncil' structures for coordination among affinity group delegates – until then quite alien to anarchists, but today enjoying a prominent, if contested, position in anarchist organising (Kaplan 1997). I will have more to say about consensus in the next chapter.

Meanwhile it should be emphasised that prefigurative politics is strongly attached to anarchist strategical priorities. The correspondence between vision and praxis is seen not only as a matter of values and principles, but also as necessary for achieving revolutionary goals. This comes into sharp relief against the background of the ongoing antagonism between anarchism and authoritarian, Leninist forms of socialism. Far from an antiquated preoccupation, such antagonism is alive and well in the radical milieu since Leninist parties and their front-groups continue to maintain a very visible, manipulative and often obstructive presence in anti-capitalist and anti-war movements, particularly in the UK, US and Italy (SchNEWS 2001, Munson 2005). In this context, anarchists often argue that the horrific failures of Leninism are not due to the evil particular individuals (Stalin, Mao, Pol Pot...), nor to the adverse 'objective' circumstances in which such attempts were made and which led them to 'degenerate' (cf. Castoriadis 1964). Rather, these attempts were doomed from the start due to the separation between the revolutionary process and its desired results, through the uncritical reproduction of authoritarian and bureaucratic structures within the revolutionary movement. Thus while Leninists profess a vision of 'pure communism' with no government, where people behave sociably 'without force, without coercion, without subordination' (Lenin 1952/1918), their praxis proceeds through top-down authoritarian structures, justified as the most efficient means for conquering the state which is subsequently supposed to 'wither away' (see Adamiak 1970). But one cannot build a revolutionary movement along authoritarian principles and expect that these will not have a decisive effect on the entire project. The moment one focuses merely on the seizure of state power, and maintains authoritarian organisation for that purpose while leaving the construction of a free society for 'after the revolution', the battle has already been lost. Nobody has expressed this idea more forcefully than Emma Goldman, in the afterword to *My Disillusion in Russia*:

All human experience teaches that methods and means cannot be separated from the ultimate aim. The means employed become, through individual habit and social practice, part and parcel of the final purpose; they influence it, modify it, and presently the aims and means become identical ... the ethical values which the revolution is to establish in the new society must be *initiated* with the revolutionary activities of the so-called transitional period. The latter can serve as a real and dependable bridge to the better life only if built of the same material as the life to be achieved. (Goldman 1925)

On this view, the pursuit of prefigurative politics is an inseparable aspect of the anarchist project in that the collectives, communes and networks of today are themselves the groundwork for the realities that will replace the present society. Collectively-run grassroots projects are, on this account, the seeds of a future society 'within the shell of the old' – as expressed in a famous statement by Gustav Landauer:

One can throw away a chair and destroy a pane of glass; but ... [only] idle talkers ... regard the state as such a thing or as a fetish that one can smash in order to destroy it. The state is a condition, a certain relationship among human beings, a mode of behavior between men; we destroy it by contracting other relationships, by behaving differently toward one another ... We are the state, and we shall continue to be the state until we have created the institutions that form a real community and society. (Landauer 1973/1910: 226)

If this is the case, then for social change to be successful, the modes of organisation that will replace capitalism, the state, gendered divisions of labour and so on need to be prepared alongside the attack on present institutions (though not instead, as Landauer may seem to imply). Furthermore, the nurturing spaces created by activists could facilitate individuals' self-realisation and provide them with an environment for overcoming alienation and entrenched oppressive behaviours. Thus 'the very process of building an anarchist movement from below is viewed as the process of consociation, self-activity and self-management that must ultimately yield that revolutionary self that can act upon, change and manage an authentic society' (Bookchin 1980).

Bookchin apparently forgot his own words when he wrote *Social Anarchism or Lifestyle Anarchism*. But it should be pointed out that these efforts are far from narcissistic – they can be seen as a strong form of anarchist 'propaganda by deed' (I use the term in a general sense to refer to the potentially exemplary nature of any anarchist action – not just violent ones). The most effective anarchist propaganda will always be the actual implementation and display of anarchist social relations – the practice of prefigurative politics. It is much easier for people to engage with the idea that life without bosses or leaders is possible when such a life is displayed, if on a limited scale, in actual practice rather than being argued for on paper. Hence Gandhi's assertion that 'a reformer's business is to make the impossible possible by giving an ocular demonstration of the possibility in his own conduct' (Gandhi 1915: 68). No less importantly, people would be much more attracted to becoming part of a movement that enriches their own lives in an immediate way, than they would joining a mass movement in which their desires and needs are suspended for the sake of advancing the 'thankless' work of the revolutionary organisation.

The anarchist drive towards prefigurative politics is therefore strongly related to anarchist individualism – the individualist aspect of anarchism that exists in all its forms. Anarchists often explain their actions and modes of organisation as intended not only to help bring about generalised social transformation, but also to liberate *themselves* to the greatest degree possible. On such a reading, the motivation for anarchists to engage in a prefigurative politics lies simply in their desire to inhabit liberated social relations. In the words of US anarchist publishing collective CrimethInc,

It is crucial that we seek change not in the name of some doctrine or grand cause, but on behalf of ourselves, so that we will be able to live more meaningful lives. Similarly we must seek first and foremost to alter the contents of our own lives in a revolutionary manner, rather than direct our struggle towards world-historical changes which we will not live to witness. In this way we will avoid the feelings of worthlessness and alienation that result from believing that it is necessary to 'sacrifice oneself for the cause', and instead live to experience the fruits of our labors ... in our labors themselves. (CrimethInc 2001)

This interpretation strongly echoes Situationist ideas, such as Raoul Vaneigem's famous statement that the struggle for liberation is at its core 'the struggle between subjectivity and everything that degrades it ... Choosing life is a political choice. Who wants a world in which the guarantee that we shall not die of starvation is bought for the risk of dying of boredom?' (Vaneigem 1967: 18). It also finds resonance with the insurrectionist / illegalist / eminently possibilist stream of anarchism, which is prominent in Italy and Greece and has made cross-overs to the US (cf. Bonanno 1998, Anonymous7 2001). On this approach, self-realisation goes hand in hand with intelligent destructive attack on all sources of the individual's oppression:

We fight exploitation and domination, because *we* do not want to be exploited or ruled. Our selfish generosity recognizes that our own self-realization can only be completed in a world in which every individual has equal access to all that he or she needs to realize her or himself as a singular being – thus, the necessity to destroy all authority, the entire social order, in order to open the possibility of everything life can offer. (Landstreicher 2001)

Thus personal liberation and confrontation with the oppressive social order are each seen to supply the other's motivation. The individual's own experience of their restriction within the administered world, of their position of subjugation along multiple axes of domination, and of the coercive apparatus monitoring every disobedient crossroads, supplies a direct impulse for taking action to make things otherwise. At the same time, both confrontational and constructive direct action is by itself a site of liberation since it offers the individual an opportunity to discover and express her own special power, and to inhabit qualitatively different social spaces. This reframing of anarchist goals in terms of directly experienced domination and liberation thus represents a revival of anarchist individualism, which is now articulated as a present-tense demand rather than merely a principle for some future society.

DIVERSITY AND OPEN-ENDEDNESS

The emphasis on the present tense connects to a third important aspect of contemporary anarchism – its strongly open-ended tendency. Ideologies are usually analysed in three parts – what they are against, what they are for, and how they propose to get from here to there. The first and third aspects were covered above. With the second aspect things are more complicated, because anarchists today tend to be very reluctant to spell out in minute detail what should replace hierarchical society and regimes of domination. Around the close of the nineteenth century, the anarchist movement was the site of fierce disagreements between such alternative visions – anarchist communism, collectivism, mutualism and so on. Today, in contrast, anarchist discourse lacks both the expectation of eventual revolutionary closure and the interest in utopian blueprints for a 'post-revolutionary' anarchist society. The rise of diversity to the status of a core anarchist value has resulted in an endorsement of pluralism and heterogeneity in anarchist approaches to liberation. This self-discovering attitude, based on prefigurative politics and iconoclasm, sees the imperfect, present-tense practices of the revolutionary movement itself as the primary site for realising anarchy.

Anarchists today do not tend to think of revolution – if they even use the term – as a future event but rather as a present-day process and a potential dimension of everyday life (cf. Ward 1973). While Bakunin looked forward to 'a universal, worldwide revolution ... the simultaneous revolutionary alliance and action of all the people of the civilized world' (Bakunin 2001/1866), anarchists today often explain their actions and modes of organisation as working not towards a moment of generalised social transformation, but primarily as a present-tense activity of individual and collective self-liberation. As New Zealand activist Torrance Hodgson expresses this,

The revolution is now, and we must let the desires we have about the future manifest themselves in the here and now as best as we can. When we start doing that, we stop fighting for some abstract condition for the future and instead start fighting to see those desires realized in the present ... Whether the project is a squat, a sharing of free food, an act of sabotage, a pirate radio station, a periodical, a demonstration, or an attack against one of the institutions of domination, it will not be entered into as a political obligation, but as a part of the life one is striving to create, as a flowering of one's self-determined existence. (Hodgson 2003)

Such an approach promotes anarchy as culture, as a lived reality that pops up everywhere in new guises, adapts to different cultural climates, and should be extended and developed experimentally for its own sake, whether or not we believe it can become, in some sense, the prevailing mode of society. This, then, is the remaining significant sense of utopia in contemporary anarchism: an imperfect and present-tense experiment in alternative social relations, a sustained collective effort that looks forward to proliferation as a larger-scale practice, but which can also manifest itself in fleeting moments of non-conformism and carefree egalitarianism, in temporary autonomous zones which can take manifold forms: 'a quilting bee, a dinner party, a black market ... a neighborhood protection society, an enthusiasts' club, a nude beach' (Hakim Bey 1991). Thus utopian modes of social interaction – non-hierarchical, voluntary, cooperative, solidaric and playful – are seen as realisable qualities of social interaction here and now. This view was expressed with increasing strength by anarchists from the early twentieth century on. For Gustav Landauer (1978/1911: 107), 'anarchism is not a thing of the future, but of the present; not a matter of demands but of living'.

Today's widespread commitment to diversity and individual self-realisation in the movement is traceable to the same process of anarchist reconvergence we are talking about here. As a result of the immense diversity of movements, campaigns and approaches which gave rise to contemporary anarchism, the movement itself came to be based on diverse, ad-hoc coalitions – giving rise to a pluralist orientation which disemphasises unity of analysis and vision in favour of multiplicity and experimentation. While several movements simultaneously purported to provide overarching, totalising perspectives as a vantage point for their analysis and action (as in the case of deep ecology or certain strands of feminism), their agendas' feeding into anarchism induced many activists to turn away from the requirement for theoretical unity towards a theoretical pluralism that was prepared to accord equal legitimacy to diverse perspectives and narratives of struggle. This ushered in a bottom-up approach to social theorising, and a parallel interest in manifold creative articulations of social alternatives. The anarchist movement's roots in a diversity of subcultural experiences such as the punk and New Age movements discouraged conformity and encouraged valuing diversity in the types of social and cultural orientations that could be envisioned for a non-capitalist, stateless society.

Such an orientation has evident affinities with post-structuralist thought, and indeed, over the past few years there has been a growth of interest in the correspondences between anarchist politics and the diverse intellectual currents associated with post-structuralism (May 1994, Newman 2001, Call 2002, Adams 2002a). Saul Newman describes this endeavour as 'using the post-structuralist critique [to] theorize the possibility of political resistance without essentialist guarantees', seeking fundamental critiques of authority in aspects such as 'Foucault's rejection of the "essential" difference between madness and reason; Deleuze and Guattari's attack on Oedipal representation and State-centered thought; [and] Derrida's questioning of philosophy's assumption about the importance of speech over writing' (Newman 2001: 158). Moreover, it has been argued that anarchism has had an indirect influence on the development of post-structuralism itself, seeing as major theorists associated with this current – Baudrillard, Lyotard, Virilio, Derrida, Castoriadis, Foucault, Deleuze, Guattari – were all active participants in the French May '68 events which had a strong libertarian dimension, and went on to develop their theories in their aftermath (Kellner 2001: xviii). Contemporary 'post-anarchism' thus involves drawing on post-structuralist resources to flesh out new critiques and theories with a strong anarchist leaning, coupled with an explicit critique of classical anarchism's rootedness in essentialist Enlightenment humanism and simplistic conceptions of social dynamics. It should be emphasised that post-structuralist anarchism remains an intellectual preoccupation, limited to a handful of writers rather than being a genuine expression of, or influence on, the grassroots thinking and discourse of masses of activists (which is not, of course, to detract from its theoretical importance).

At any rate, as a result of all these developments, diversity itself would appear to be a core value in contemporary anarchism, reflected not only in the aspiration for diversity in the movement, but also in the diversity of visions for alternative social relations that it has the space for. As Hakim Bey (1985b) expresses this, prescribed and fixed models for a free society only attest to their originators' 'various brands of tunnel-vision, ranging from the peasant commune to the L-5 Space City. We say, let a thousand flowers bloom – with no gardener to lop off weeds & sports according to some moralizing or eugenical scheme!' Rather than seeking theoretical unity, anarchists largely take a bottom-up approach to both action and theory, stressing creativity and plurality in the struggle against domination and the construction of alternatives.

Again the idea itself is not new, as can be seen from the following quote from Rudolf Rocker:

Anarchism is no patent solution for all human problems, no Utopia of a perfect social order, as it has so often been called, since on principle it rejects all absolute schemes and concepts. It does not believe in any absolute truth, or in definite final goals for human development, but in an unlimited perfectibility of social arrangements and human living conditions, which are always straining after higher forms of expression, and to which for this reason one can assign no definite terminus nor set any fixed goal. (Rocker 1989/1938:30)

Rocker bases his stance on the refusal of absolutes and the assertion that social arrangements display an inherent proclivity for change. For him, however, the change in question is regarded in optimistic terms – it tends towards improvement, and for this reason cannot be limited in scope. However, there is also a pessimistic side to this coin: in anticipating a constant flux of relationships between diverse and decentralised communities in a radically different social world, anarchists must also remain open to the possibility that even such societies might see the renewal of patterns of exploitation and domination, however encouraging the prevailing conditions may be for sociability and cooperation.

This type of argument does not endorse the expectation that a revolution in social, economic and political conditions would inaugurate a different pattern of human behaviour *forever* – that anarchy would now be able to flower freely under nurturing conditions, lacking hindrances to the development of human beings' cooperative / egalitarian / benevolent side. There is indeed room for doubt whether even the most favourable conditions would mean the eradication of the will to power and the creation of an eternally unproblematic arrangement of social life. The acknowledgement that patterns of hierarchy and exploitation may always re-emerge, even in societies oriented against them, means that there is a potential need for anarchist agency under any conditions. If this is the case, then a severe practical challenge is created to the notion of a closure of the revolutionary project.

The self-distancing from an anticipated closure of the 'successful' revolutionary project is very strongly apparent in modern anarchist-inspired works of a utopian nature. Ursula Le Guin's novel *The Dispossessed*, perhaps the most honest attempt at portraying a functioning anarchist society, is one prominent example (Le Guin 2002/1974). Referring to the work as an 'anarchist utopia', however, is misleading precisely for this reason, since the society it deals with is far from perfect or unproblematic. The protagonist, Shevek, is driven to leave his anarchist society on the moon of Anarres, not because he rejects its core anarchist ideals but because he sees that some of them are no longer adequately reflected in practice, while others need to be revised in order to give more place to individuality. In the 170 years since its establishment, following the secession of a mass of revolutionary anarchists from the home-planet of Urras, Anarresti society has witnessed the growth of xenophobia, informal hierarchies in the administrative syndicates, and an apparatus of social control through custom and peer pressure. All of these create a widespread atmosphere of conformity that hinders Shevek's self-realisation in his pursuit of his life project, the development of a ground-breaking approach in theoretical physics. Shevek embodies the continuing importance of dissent even after the abolition of capitalism and government. Through his departure and founding of the Syndicate of Initiative, he becomes a revolutionary within the revolution and initiates change within the anarchist society. As he says towards the end of the novel, 'It was our purpose all along – our Syndicate, this journey of mine – to shake up things, to stir up, to break some habits, to make people ask questions. To behave like anarchists!' (361)

Shevek's project renews the spirit of dissent and non-conformism that animated the original creation of the anarchist society on Anarres in the first place. As Raymond Williams observes, this makes *The Dispossessed* 'an open utopia: forced open, after the congealing of ideals, the degeneration of mutuality into conservatism; shifted, deliberately, from its achieved harmonious condition, the stasis in which the classical utopian mode culminates, to restless, open, risk-taking experiment' (Williams 1978).

The idea that diversity itself, when taken to its logical conclusion, nullifies the possibility of revolutionary closure is exemplified by the anarchist-inspired vision of an alternative society offered by the Zurich-based writer 'P.M.' in his book, *bolo'bolo*. Again the application of the term 'utopia' to this book is to be handled with care, since it not only acknowledges but treasures the instability and diversity of social relations created by the removal of all external controls on the behaviour of individuals and groups. P.M. agues that most modern utopias are in fact totalitarian, mono-cultural models organized around work and education. In contrast, the world anti-system called *bolo'bolo* is a mosaic in which every community (*bolo*) of around 500 residents is as nutritionally self-sufficient as possible, and has complete autonomy to define its ethos or 'flavour' (*nima*) – be it monasticism, Marxism or sado-masochism. Some measure of stability is afforded by a minimal but universal social contract (*sila*), enforced by reputation and interdependence. This contract guarantees, for example, that every individual (*ibu*) can at any time leave their native *bolo*, and is entitled to one day's rations (*yalu*) and housing (*gano*) as well as medical treatment (*bete*) at any *bolo*. It even suggests a duel code (*yaka*) to solve disputes between individuals and groups (P.M. 1985: 68–70). However,

There are no humanist, liberal or democratic laws or rules about the content of *nimas* and there is no State to enforce them. Nobody can prevent a *bolo* from committing mass suicide, dying of drug experiments, driving itself into madness or being unhappy under a violent regime. *Bolos* with a bandit-nima could terrorize whole regions or continents, as the Huns or Vikings did. Freedom and adventure, generalized terrorism, the law of the club, raids, tribal wars, vendettas, plundering – everything goes. (77–8)

While most anarchists might not want to go this far, the point here is that any anarchist theory which looks forward to the absence of law and authority, unfettered diversity and maximum autonomy (literally 'self-legislation') must also respond to the possibility that patterns of domination may re-emerge within and/or among them. Thus 'the price of eternal liberty is eternal vigilance', and anarchist utopianism cannot be equated with chiliasm and closure. If one insists on the potential need for anarchist agency under any conditions, then the notion of a closure of the revolutionary project loses its meaning. This makes anarchism 'an unending struggle, since progress in achieving a more just society will lead to new insight and understanding of forms of oppression that may be concealed in traditional practice and consciousness' (Chomsky 1986). At most, then, an 'anarchist society' would be one in which everyone is an anarchist, that is, a society in which every person wields agency against rule and domination. To be sure, the frequency of the need to do so may hopefully diminish to a great extent, in comparison to what an anarchist approach would deem necessary in present societies. However, one has no reason to think that it can ever be permanently removed. In sum, the inherently diverse and voluntary nature of the anarchist project leaves it necessarily open to change and challenge from within.

And this is where the real questions are found.

3
Power and Anarchy
In/equality + In/visibility
in Autonomous Politics

You are approached to answer questions for our group, make decisions and announcements. You even think it is okay to define our group to visitors, strangers. Somehow you aren't ever questioned by the group for this behavior ... It's like you think that calling yourself an anarchist makes you clean and pure and no longer subject to self examination or criticism. You've made the term repulsive to me.

—Anonymous, 'What it is to be a girl in an anarchist boys' club'

Let us put things on the table: with all the decentralisation, autonomy and the sitting in a circle during meetings, there are clearly power issues in the anarchist movement. There are individuals who consistently wield more power in a group, or are frequently found in positions of responsibility, initiating and leading actions and projects. Some people have more personal confidence, tend to speak and get listened to more often than others, or are just particularly well-read and well-spoken. There are entire groups whose coherence and activity profile have given them a very strong influence in the wider movement. Some collectives and networks have become cliquey, others are constantly disempowered by endless stagnation over 'process'. Concerns about power relations in the movement surface at meetings, during actions and in everyday conversations – still echoing the same issues that feminists, peace activists and many others have faced since the 1960s. And all the while, the most dedicated activists, overworked and burned out, get to deal with a guilt-trip over being leaders.

It is not surprising that these issues are so difficult. Anarchists and their allies are, after all, experimenting with the uncharted territory of non-hierarchical organising and social relations that challenge domination, going against the grain of our own socialisation as children, pupils and workers. Prole Cat (2004) writes:

Everywhere we turn in capitalist society is hierarchical organization ... The habits and perspectives that accompany such a social arrangement do not automatically disappear as one enters the gates of the revolutionary movement ... The leaders and the followers, the by-products of an authoritarian society: this is the raw material from which we must build the free society ... We must begin our egalitarian relations today, among our damaged selves, if we are to live in a free world tomorrow.

The discussion of power inside the movement is really the obvious place to start for anarchist political theory. It cuts to the core: hierarchy, domination, direct action, the liberation of desire – power is the stuff of these. So a central place should be given to probing the concept of power, to mapping its unequal distribution, and to making sense of the everyday dimension in which power relations are reproduced. In this chapter I want to show what a theory grounded in practice can do for us in disentangling the dilemmas and controversies around leadership and unequal power in anarchist organising. What are the basic *questions* that sit at the bottom of these dilemmas? How could anarchists best understand the functioning and distribution of different kinds of power within their own networks? And how can power dynamics on the ground come to reflect anarchist values and priorities?

This chapter begins with a discussion of the concept of power itself. As a starting point I draw on the threefold understanding of power suggested by eco-feminist writer Starhawk, distinguishing between power-to (the basic sense of power as the capacity to affect reality); power-over (power-to wielded as domination in hierarchical and coercive settings); and power-with (power-to wielded as non-coercive influence and initiative among people who view themselves as equals). My central argument is that problematic issues with power in the movement should be traced to two distinct sources: standing inequalities in power-to among activists (the 'where' of power), and the lack of transparency in the dynamic exercise of power-with among them (the 'how' of power). To clarify these problems, I trace the sources of power-to in the movement to what I call 'political resources' – material ones as well as skills and access to networks – which make for the ability to participate in movement activities. This allows us to address the first issue by suggesting concrete tools for redistributing at least some of these resources and making access to influence more equal. I then analyse the more difficult part of the debate – the tension between the overt or covert, formal or informal exercise of non-coercive influence, as suggested by the idea of a 'Tyranny of Structurelessness'. In analysing the conditions under which such power tends to be wielded in the movement, I argue that the diffuse and autonomous use of power in anarchist organising is sometimes *inherently unaccountable*, and that this situation *cannot* be remedied by formal structures and procedures. In response to this difficulty, I suggest elements of a culture of solidarity around power, one that can make its use more reflective and responsive.

THREE KINDS OF POWER

Anarchists are hardly 'against power'. This common misconception is easily shown untrue by anarchist political language, in which 'empowerment' is mentioned as a positive goal. Empowerment is seen as a process whereby people literally acquire power, whether concretely (as in having access to the resources and capacities that are necessary for creating change) or psychologically (as in having the self-confidence needed for initiative and the grounds to believe that it will be effectual). On the other hand, of course, anarchists want to 'fight the power', or at least 'the powers that be', and resist all systems of domination under which people are systematically subject to power (in the state, capitalism, patriarchy and so on). This indicates not a 'rejection of power', but a more nuanced and differentiated use of the concept. What different kinds of power are we actually talking about here?

One very useful explanation of power is suggested by Starhawk, whose threefold analysis of the term has since been taken up elsewhere in feminist writing (Starhawk 1987: 9–10, Eisler 1988, Woehrle 1992). First, Starhawk suggests the term 'power-over' to refer to power through domination. This is the kind of power 'wielded in the workplace, in the schools, in the courts, in the doctor's office. It may rule with weapons that are physical or by controlling the resources we need to live: money, food, medical care; or by controlling more subtle resources: information, approval, love.' The second category she suggests is 'power-from-within', which I will call here 'power-to'. This is

akin to the sense of mastery we develop as young children with each new unfolding ability: the exhilaration of standing erect, of walking, of speaking the magic words that convey our needs and thoughts ... We can feel that power in acts of creation and connection, in planting, building, writing, cleaning, healing, soothing, playing, singing, making love.

Finally, Starhawk adds a third form of power, 'power-with' or 'power-among'. This is 'the power of a strong individual in a group of equals, the power not to command, but to suggest and be listened to, to begin something and see it happen'. This kind of threefold division is very helpful for our purposes, because it takes us beyond monolithic conceptions of power and highlights different kinds of power with different political significances. To get a firmer grasp on the substance of these distinctions, let me take a minute to elaborate on each form of power and relate it to wider debates.

Power-over as domination

Theories of power in academic literature overwhelmingly address the concept solely in terms of power-over. Following sociologist Max Weber's definition of power as domination (*Herrschaft*), the concept is identified with the imposition of one will over another – 'the probability that one actor within a social relationship will be in a position to carry out his own will despite resistance' (Weber 1947: 152). American political scientist Robert Dahl similarly defines power as a relationship in which '*A* has power over *B* to the extent that he can get *B* to do something that *B* would not otherwise do' (Dahl 1957: 80). There are, however, different ways in which one person can be made to comply with another person's will, against her or his own will or interests. Political theorists distinguish between four different ways for power-over to be wielded – force, coercion, manipulation and authority (Bachrach and Baratz 1970: 35ff, Dahl 2003: 38–43). The difference between them is in *why* B complies.

- *Force* is being used when *A* achieves his objectives in the face of *B*'s non-compliance by stripping him of the choice between compliance and non-compliance (e.g. *A* wants *B* to exit the building so he physically pushes *B* through the door).
- *Coercion* is at work where *B* complies in response to *A*'s credible threat of deprivation (or of 'sanction'). In the face a disadvantageous cost/benefit calculus created by the threat, *B* complies of his own unfree will (e.g. *A* points a gun at *B* and demands that *B* exit the building).
- *Manipulation* occurs when *A* deliberately lies or omits information in communicating his wants to *B*. The latter complies without recognising either the source or the exact nature of the demand upon him (e.g. *A* asks *B* to check if the doorbell is working, but once *B* exits *A* locks him out).

- *Authority* is in place when *B* complies with *A*'s command out of *B*'s belief that *A* has the right to issue the command and that *B* has a corresponding duty to obey (e.g. *A* is a police officer who tells *B* to exit the building, and *B* obeys).

These distinctions are useful as a rule of thumb and I will return to them later in the book. Meanwhile, we can see how the idea of power-over helps us clarify the anarchist concept of domination. It can now be said that a person is dominated, in the relevant anarchist sense, when s/he is systematically subject to power-over. The placement is involuntary because people do not normally choose the structure of their society, their prospects in life, the social class they are born into, or the race and gender with which they are identified. It should thus be emphasised that power-over functions in the dense social context of intersecting regimes of exclusion, and is not limited to one-on-one interactions. Power-over is also manifest in 'predominant values, beliefs, rituals, and institutional procedures ... that operate systematically and consistently to the benefit of certain persons and groups at the expense of others' (Bachrach and Baratz 1970: 43). Those who benefit – usually a minority or elite group – are placed in a preferred position to defend and promote their vested interest. Thus power-over is also present when these groups create or reinforce values and institutions that limit the scope of public consideration. As Stephen Lukes points out, power-over may also be exercised by influencing, shaping or determining people's very wants, being able to secure their compliance by controlling their thoughts and desires (Lukes 2005). Indeed, deep social manipulation of people's own values and wants is a recurrent theme in popular culture as well as critical theory – from films like *The Matrix* and *Fight Club* which many anarchists seem to find appealing, to the writings of Western Marxists like Marcuse and post-structuralists like Michel Foucault. Foucault famously wrote about how power functions in the 'capillaries' of social relations – in cultural grammar, routine practices, social mechanisms and institutions – in a much more subtle and potent form than in its overt expressions in rigid hierarchy and military violence (Foucault 1980, 1988). It is thus easy to see that the word domination is more comprehensive than another concept often used by anarchists – hierarchy. While hierarchy is an apt description for the structure of many of the social relations making up domination, it does not express all of them. In hierarchical relations inequalities of status are visible, either because they are formalised (say, in the relations between a CEO and a secretary), or because one can identify their presence in a particular behaviour or utterance. But the domination of human beings is often an insidious dynamic, reproduced through performative disciplinary acts in which the protagonists may not even be conscious of their roles. Many times, the dominated person can only symbolically point to an embodied source of her or his unfreedom. These insights feed into an anarchist critique of power which goes beyond the structural focus on hierarchy, and points to new avenues for resistance.

In fact, most recent pieces that confront issues of power in the movement focus on the way in which patterns of domination in society are imprinted on interactions within it – uncovering dynamics of racist, sexist, ageist or homophobic behaviour, and asking why it is that positions of leadership in activist circles tend to be populated by men more often than women, whites more often than non-whites, and able persons more often than disabled ones (e.g. Anonymous2 undated, CWS undated, Martinez 2000, DKDF 2004, Crass 2004, Aguilar 2005). I return to these discussions later.

Power-to as capacity

Although power-over is the most readily observed *application* of power in society, it does not emerge from nowhere. The analysis of power suggested here sees power-over as a particular application, in human relations, of a more basic sense of power. This is the primitive notion lying behind all talk of power – the notion that *A* has power to the extent that s/he can produce intended effects in *B* (cf. Russell 1938: 25, Lukes 2005: 27–8). Now *A* and *B* can be persons, but if *B* is a physical object, for example a block of wood, and *A* moves it from here to there, then it still makes sense to speak of the action as a manifestation of power – *A*'s power to alter physical reality, to cause an effect or to achieve a desired result. This basic notion of power is what I call power-to, and it is clearly present in the Spanish word *poder*, which as a noun means 'power' and as a verb means 'to be able to'.

Power-over always has its source in the dominant party's power-to. Force cannot be applied without some measure of bodily strength – an aspect of power-to – even if it is just enough to pull a trigger. *A* cannot coerce *B* without *being able* to exact whatever deprivation the threat inherent in coercion specifies (or without being able to give *B* the illusion that he can do so). If a person has no power to speak, s/he cannot manipulate others. And a judge who cannot talk, read or write would not be able to actualise any authority in the courtroom – though by law he 'has' that authority. Thus we can also see that the possession of power-to is logically and temporally antecedent to its use: it is 'there' to the extent that success can be *predicted* for the possessor's attempts to influence physical objects or other persons' behaviour.

The relationship between power-to and power-over has been given a recent twist by John Holloway. Recasting the Marxist theory of alienation in terms of power relations, Holloway sees power-to and power-over as standing in a 'dialectical and oppositional' relationship. In the dynamic he portrays, the starting point is 'power-to' – understood primarily as persons' capability to change the material environment through labour. However, the reproduction of capitalist social relations consists in a constant conversion of 'power-to' into 'power-over' – the transfer of control over human capacities, which is most clearly present in the selling of labour power. This alienates humans from their capability to do and puts that capability under the rule of capital. Hence Holloway suggests a conception of social struggle centred on the notion of liberating 'power-to' from its conversion into 'power-over':

Power-to exists as power-over, but the power-to is subjected to and in rebellion against power-over, and power-over is nothing but, and therefore absolutely dependent upon, the metamorphosis of power-to ... The attempt to exercise power-to in a way that does not entail the exercise of power over others, inevitably comes into conflict with power-over ... power-to, if it does not submerge itself in power-over, can exist, overtly or latently, only as power-against, as anti-power. (Holloway 2002: 36–7)

Such an account is attractive on its own, but it has two flaws. First, it takes place on the level of society as a whole, in which capitalist relations of production are assumed from the outset. But in our case the question is not how objectionable senses of power operate in capitalist society, but what causes problematic accumulations and dynamics of power within grassroots groups and networks. It is difficult to imagine that the same type of process Holloway describes is at work in anarchist collectives. This is not to say that there is no power-over among anarchists (see below) – but it is difficult to argue that all objectionable power in anarchist groupings is generated and operates in the same way as it does in capitalist society as a whole. The second problem is that this framework presents power-to and power-over as the two sole elements in a binary antagonism, and therefore does nothing to explain forms of wielding power-to in human relations (as opposed to material labour) which are clearly *not* power-over. Imagine, for example, that I ask you for a glass of water and you give it to me. I have clearly made you do something that you would not otherwise do – but it is hardly a case of force, coercion, manipulation or authority. Hence, a third form of power is needed in order to account for the entire range of human interactions that involve other forms of influence than power-over.

Power-with as non-coercive influence

Influence without force, coercion, manipulation or authority is a very broad area of power that is normally left unexamined. But there are manifold cases in which people get each other to do things without there being a conflict of wills or interests between them – and these are still cases in which some form of power is being wielded. However, these forms of power are so distant from the central meanings of power-over that they require a separate category. This establishes the need to talk about a third, cooperative form of power, where individuals influence each other's behaviour in the *absence* of a conflict of wills or interests.

This is the idea of power-with, or power as non-coercive influence. Power-with is clearly generated by power-to, just as power-over is. The less one is able to do things (to communicate and to mobilise capabilities, skills and resources) the less one can influence others. Power-with includes many interactions in which the participants unreflectively comply with one another's requests – again if *A* asks *B* for a small favour (a glass of water, or to keep an eye on *A*'s bike), *B* will very rarely ask *why A* wants that favour. This is because *A* and *B* share cultural codes that stand at the background of their unspoken, mutual expectations. Still, *A* gets *B* to do something that *B* would not otherwise do. Or take the case of persuasion – *A* asks *B* to do something together, and although *B* initially disagrees, *A* manages to persuade *B* to go along through honest and rational argument. Again *A* clearly gets *B* to do something s/he would not have otherwise done, but surely it matters whether *B* complies despite her or his continued opposition to *A*'s will, or because that opposition has been removed by honest persuasion. In the latter case it could be argued that *B* autonomously accepted *A*'s *reasons* for doing what s/he wanted *B* to do – making the reasons themselves the cause for *B*'s action (cf. Lukes 2005: 32–3).

Now while power-with is clearly not the same as power-over, it can still be wielded unequally and/or abusively – and this is where the present discussion comes in. The vast bulk of anarchist discussions of power deals with power-over. Anarchists analyse the accumulation and ab/use of power by governments and corporations, and inequalities of power along class, race and gender lines. The entire premise of anarchist ideas for social change is that society can and should be altered 'without taking power' – without building a new apparatus of power-over that would impose different social relations from above. However, the issues anarchists face when thinking about power in their *own* groups and networks have much more to do with power-to and power-with than they do with power-over. The brief account of the different kinds of power above is helpful in mapping these issues and making the discussion more manageable.

I would now like to argue that there are actually two separate issues around power in horizontal groups. While the two often overlap and compound each other, they still derive from different sources and should be separated for the purpose of discussion before bringing them back together again. The first issue regards the unequal distribution of power-to among activists, which in turn generates unequal access to power-with. This may be called the 'static' aspect of power, and it is relatively easier to disentangle by tracing the sources of this inequality and suggesting tools for removing it. The second category, the 'dynamic' one, regards the machinations of power-with once it is being wielded. This issue is much more tangled, and to address it I shall have to go in some depth into the basic characteristics of power in action among activists, analysing the anarchist movement itself as an arena of power.

What is important to emphasise for the moment, however, is that the two issues are indeed separate. Inequality in terms of the basic ability to participate is a problem, no matter how that participation takes place or what process is used to make collective decisions. Conversely, even equally distributed influence can be abused and abusive. First, then, let me look at the issue of standing inequality, and see what insights can be had about its sources and possible solutions.

EQUALITY AND 'POLITICAL RESOURCES'

The following statement from Murray Bookchin (2003) is a good example of how uncomfortable the debate around power can get:

Many individuals in earlier groups like the CNT were not just 'influential militants' but outright leaders, whose views were given more consideration – and deservedly so! – than those of others because they were based on more experience, knowledge, and wisdom, as well as the psychological traits that were needed to provide effective guidance. A serious libertarian approach to leadership would indeed acknowledge the reality and crucial importance of leaders – all the more to establish the greatly needed formal structures and *regulations* that can effectively *control* and *modify* the activities of leaders and recall them.

What is acutely missing here is the issue of equality. It is one thing to acknowledge that leadership is a useful quality, but quite another to ask *who* leads *when*. Bookchin's statement limits problems with leadership to the possible abuse of such positions and their consolidation into unaccountable power. But this glosses over whether or not these positions are continuously inhabited by the same individuals. One may doubt, however, whether a 'serious libertarian approach' can sit satisfied with what is, essentially, a call to meritocracy. This would not only ignore equality, but also the whole range of intrinsic rather than instrumental values that anarchists find in their groups: making them nurturing spaces that facilitate the self-realisation of individuals and provide them with a self-created environment for overcoming alienation and entrenched oppressive behaviours.

A move towards more equality obviously requires some form of redistribution. But it is impossible to simply redistribute 'power'. Power comes from somewhere, and it is the *sources* of power that should be redistributed. So we need a clearer idea about the sources of power in social movements, and their currency in material and social terms. What generates the ability to influence others in movements for social change? And to what degree can (some of) these things be equalised?

In his participant's ethnography of the Manchester *Earth First!* group, Jonathan Purkis interpreted unequal influence as the result of inequalities in 'cultural capital', borrowing Bordieu's term: 'the collective amount of acquired knowledge, skills and aesthetic outlook which allows groups or individuals to produce themselves as a viable social force'. For example,

although Phil described himself as the 'convenor' of MEF! there was little doubt that he was perceived by other political groups in Manchester as the leader. This seemed to be reinforced by the cultural capital which he had at his disposal: home access to a fax machine and electronic services, personal friendships with several of the original half dozen members of UKEF!, and employment with a 'sympathetic' organisation. His stable position in Manchester ensured that, regardless of what other activists were doing, he always seemed slightly ahead. (Purkis 2001: 12)

Sociologist Mario Diani explains leadership roles in social movements as often a result of 'certain actors' location at the centre of exchanges of practical and symbolic resources ... [such as] actors' ability to promote coalition work among movement organizations' (Diani 2003: 106). In short, certain *political resources* are required for effective influence in anarchist activity, and mapping them can help us understand how influence is generated and distributed within nominally non-hierarchical groups. In activist seminars I organised on this topic, brainstorms around the idea of 'political resources' regularly brought up a familiar list of items – things like money, space, publicity, time, commitment, expertise, access to networks, status in the movement and so on. To organise our thinking around such resources, let me suggest a distinction that is important for our concerns: that between zero-sum and non-zero-sum resources. A zero-sum resource in one whose possession, use or consumption by one person prevents, excludes or diminishes another person's ability to do the same. A van is a zero-sum resource that can only be driven to one destination at a time. Money is a zero-sum resource because if I use it to buy item X, nobody can use the same money to buy item Y. On the other hand, a skill or a piece of information is a non-zero-sum resource. I can teach you a skill that I have without depleting my own possession of that skill, and I can give you information without forgetting it myself. Such resources are non-zero-sum since in their transfer we are effectively making a copy of them. So publicity can also be a non-zero-sum resource, to the extent that it is in accessible electronic format (though in this case other, zero-sum resources become the issue – computers, printers). Intangible resources like time and commitment are also part of this logic. Time is a zero-sum resource – I cannot give my time to any number of activities at once, and I cannot give you more time than you have. Because of this, the fact that people have different *constraints* on their time will mean that this resource is almost always unequally distributed. Finally, there are resources like commitment, energy, confidence, articulation and charisma. All of these are personal traits, shaped by individual circumstances: one's age, biography, experiences and so on. With these resources, although no depletion is involved in their use they are also *difficult or impossible to duplicate,* compared to skills and access to networks. A summary of these resources and their different kinds is given in the accompanying table.

	Zero-sum	*Non Zero-sum*
Easier to redistribute	**Money** (personal, fund raising options…) **Spaces** (houses, offices, allotments…) **Equipment** (vehicles, banners, puppets, tripods…)	**Skills** (writing, climbing, cooking, facilitation…) **Information** **Access** (networks, trust…) **Publicity** (electronic)
Difficult to redistribute	**Time**	**Commitment** **Energy** **Confidence** **Charisma**

This is obviously only one possible mapping – other resources that give a person influence in activist groups can be identified, and different sub-divisions suggested. But it is now easier to understand how to equalise access to power in non-hierarchical groups: doing so would mean that anyone can easily get the resources they need in order to take initiative, be effective and feel valued – as well as recognition and support in doing so. In his Food Not Bombs group, writes Criss Crass:

We began to identify positions of leadership in the group and had open discussions of power and strategized ways to share it … seeing different levels of responsibility as stepping stones to help people get concrete things done, to build their involvement, to increase their sense of what they are capable of and to develop the skills necessary for the job … [it] is also about encouragement, recognizing that people frequently carry enormous insecurities about being good enough, having enough experience, having anything worthwhile to say and doubting that anyone thinks they're capable enough. (Crass 2002)

So what concrete tools for redistribution are available for each type of resource? Beginning with zero-sum resources, we can consider two distinct forms of redistribution: sharing and collectivising. Sharing redistributes from one person to one or more other people. The person who shares subjects the portion that s/he shares to the discretion of whomever s/he is sharing it with. If I have a van, I can share it with you for a day and subject it to your discretion, with or without an explicit agreement on the purpose to which you will use it. I can also permanently share a zero-sum resource with a person or group. In this case we agree that the use of the van, which used to be subject to my sole discretion, is now subject to decision-making by other people as well. Where money is concerned, I am familiar with more than one instance in which an anarchist came into a million or two through inheritance, and used the money to set up funds that finance projects, actions and social centres.

A second version of redistribution, collectivising (or pooling), redistributes from several people as individuals to the same people as a group, subjecting the use of the resource whole to their collective decision-making, where before different parts of it were under the discretion of each individual. Again money is the most obvious example. Several groups can raise donations or funding for their joint activity separately, and then pool it. If five of us are making salaries we can move in together and set up a co-op, sharing most of our money. The same goes for spaces: personal spaces can be shared, and collective spaces can be established. If, in a given locale, the only space available for meetings or banner-making is a large-ish house owned by an activist co-op, then the members of this co-op will have disproportionate access to space, and thus disproportionate influence in the movement. One solution is for them to rent a smaller house to live in, and funnel the rest of their housing benefit to operate a social centre.

With non-zero-sum resources, redistribution looks a bit different since it means that the resource (a skill, a contact, a file or a design) is effectively duplicated from one person to others. Access to networks is a key activist resource that can be redistributed in this way. Since local activist milieus tend to be quite integrated, this type of resource is in particular need of redistribution when it comes to larger-scale activities, such as coordinating simultaneous direct actions or longer-term campaigns. It is often, however, an important condition for day-to-day work as well. Because of the highly decentralised nature of activist movements, the ability to initiate and carry out actions is strongly conditioned on the ability to communicate with individuals outside one's face-to-face setting. Access to networks can thus be thought of in terms of the quantity and quality of communication links that a person has with other activists, in particular those outside her immediate group or local area.

Communication links do not exist between groups as such. It is individuals within the groups who communicate with each other, some more than others. In his ethnography of activist networks in Barcelona, Jeff Juris (2004: 49) identifies, as the most important network nodes, 'social relayers', who process and distribute information in a particular network, and 'social switchers,' who occupy key positions within multiple networks and can channel communication flows among different movement sectors. These are key positions of power, allowing them to significantly influence the flow, direction and intensity of network activity. The wider diffusion of networking capabilities can contribute significantly to equalising access to influence in this area. On the most basic level, a person's connectivity is greatly increased by the awareness of, and access to, venues of communication with individuals from diverse groups and places. These could be regional or international gatherings, email lists and web forums. Beyond this, a familiarity with the architecture of the relevant networks (who's in touch with who, who is working on what) is also a resource that can be transferred. More substantially, however, the qualitative aspect of networking ties is determined in great measure by personal affinity, close mutual knowledge and trust. These can also be extended, for example by mutually trusting activists introducing one another to each other's equally trusted friends.

All of this might seem pretty straightforward, even trivial – until we come to the last class of resources, which opens up a whole can of worms. These are resources that are not zero-sum, but also difficult or impossible to transfer. Some, such as commitment and energy, are not even stable resources for a given individual, and are influenced by a complex combination of factors. Levels of commitment change with one's priorities, experiences and circumstances, and one's energy is often conditioned by health, disposition and mood. But the resources most difficult to come to terms with are those related to personality traits such as articulate speech, self-confidence, strong convictions, and even external appearance – all of which certainly play a role in a person's ability to influence others, especially in the intimate setting of friendship networks and fluid affinity groups. Although such resources can sometimes be acquired or consciously developed, transferring them from one person to another is a different matter. It is very strange to imagine anarchists giving each other 'charisma-coaching' and organising skill-sharing workshops in public speaking, personability and pep. What is distressing about this imagery is that it evokes the approach to such qualities in the worlds of business and state politics, where power-with operates informally alongside power-over.

Thus we seem to have come to an impasse – while a great deal of work can be done towards redistributing many material and immaterial resources, there are at least some in which equality can hardly, if ever, be achieved. But if they cannot be transferred, can the degree to which these qualities are allowed to generate power be *diminished*? Why do such qualities enjoy the status of political resources in the first place? Surely different environments for organised human action – hierarchical and non-hierarchical, formal and informal – would give these qualities different weight as far as influence is concerned.

This brings us directly to the second issue, the 'how' of power. Articulation, confidence and charisma are special not only in being personal qualities, but also because they relate most closely to power dynamics – to its actual wielding in human interaction. These qualities come to the fore when taking initiative, building trust, or convincing other people – when playing the game in the anarchist arena of power. The thing is, in anarchist networks like everywhere else, a lot depends on who you know. Much anarchist activity is organised in a diffuse and informal way, by self-selected groups in closed meetings. The presence of invisible power behind the scenes of anarchist networks has been a cause of anxiety for years. It raises serious questions about inclusion and accountability in a decentralised movement – a test-case for prefigurative politics.

THE TYRANNY OF *WHAT*?

Argentinean activist and scholar Ezequiel Adamovsky has been a closely observing participant in the movement of autonomous neighbourhood assemblies that emerged following the 2001 economic crisis in his country (see also Colectivo Situaciones 2002, Jordan and Whitney 2003). As of 2005, Adamovsky reports, participation in assemblies has massively diminished, and they network only on a very small and localized level (interviewed in Kaufman 2005). Part of the reason, he says, is that the horizontalism that characterised the emergence of the assemblies was so focused on rejection – of power pyramids and of a hierarchical division of labour – that no positive groundwork for coordination could be established. This failure led to the disintegration of some of the autonomous initiatives, as activists resorted to 'old certainties' such as building a workers' party. Others became comfortably isolated in very small circles of familiarity without the capacity to articulate the struggle with the larger society.

Mara Kaufman associates the breakdown of the *assambleas* with the lack of 'a transparent distribution of tasks and clear democratic decision-making method':

The fear of delegating responsibility becomes a kind of privileged voluntarism: whoever has the connections and time, both elements of privilege, to get something done does it. The intended avoidance of hierarchical leadership leads to an open denial of power but [allows] a nameless and invisible informal structure of power where charisma or well-connectedness becomes the defining factor for emerging leadership. In movement politics, unstructured 'open space' becomes a shady stand-in for democratic process. (Kaufman 2005)

Like another expression, 'lifestyle anarchism', the idea of 'the tyranny of structurelessness' (*TToS*) haunts the anarchist movement though its source is not animated by anarchist values at all. While what we must ultimately confront is the looser sense in which people use the expression, it is worth glancing at the original. *The Tyranny of Structurelessness* is an essay written in 1970 by sociologist Jo Freeman under the pen-name Joreen (Freeman 1970). The essay argues that the women's liberation movement has reached an impasse because feminist consciousness-raising groups have elevated the lack of formal structures and responsibilities to the level of an unquestioned dogma. This commitment to 'structurelessness', however, enables *in*formal hierarchical structures to emerge and perpetuate themselves within groups. The vacuum created by the lack of formal communication structures is filled by the existing friendship-networks among part of the group's participants. This creates a friendship-elite – a class of leaders who form an in-group, while those who are not part of it remain disempowered. To perpetuate their status, in-groups create criteria by which people in the larger group are judged, and limit their participation to prescribed roles or channels. The lack of formal structure

becomes a smokescreen for the strong or the lucky to establish unquestioned hegemony over others ... The rules of how decisions are made are known only to a few and awareness of power is curtailed by those who know the rules, as long as the structure of the group is informal. Those who do not know the rules and are not chosen for initiation must remain in confusion, or suffer from paranoid delusions that something is happening of which they are not quite aware.

Freeman thinks that unless a movement for change can overcome this problem, it will not develop but become inward looking, trapped in sterile rituals and dominated by elites. But the solution that

Freeman proposes is in no way anarchist in spirit. She suggests to accept inequalities as inevitable, but to formalise group structures so that the hierarchies they generate are constituted democratically. Since she thinks an elite is unlikely to renounce its power, even if challenged, 'the only other alternative is formally to structure the group in such a way that the original power is institutionalised ... If the informal elites have been well structured and have exercised a fair amount of power in the past, such a task is feasible.' From then on, democratic institutions are introduced; positions which incur authority and decision-making power are delegated by election, consciously distributed among many participants, rotated often, and include a requirement to be responsible to the group. Information is diffused widely and frequently, and everyone has equal access to the group's money or equipment. At the end, 'the group of people in positions of authority [*sic*] will be diffuse, flexible, open and temporary'.

Some anarchists cite *TToS* in support of their preference for formal organisations, on the model of bottom-up federations rather than diffuse networks (Class War Federation 1992, Anarcho undated). Many others are at best ambivalent about Freeman's analysis and proposals. In a targeted rebuttal, anarcha-feminist Cathy Levine insists that formalising elites is an unacceptable concession to the ossified patterns of the traditional left, which she associates with a patriarchal worldview. Rejecting 'easy answers, pre-fab alternatives and no room in which to create our own way of life', Levine emphasises the need for a radical milieu where participants are respected, nurtured and sustained, avoiding the bleak mechanisation of formal structures (Levine undated). Jason McQuinn goes on to argue that these problems are the same, or worse, in formally structured organisations:

It's much more common (because it's probably a hell of a lot easier) for 'the strong or the lucky to establish unquestioned hegemony over others' by starting or taking over formal organizations. After all why bother with blowing 'smokescreens' to hide a shaky hegemony over a small, informal group when it's easier to insinuate yourself into powerful roles in formal organizations? (McQuinn 2002; see also Michels 1999/1911)

Beyond the fact that Freeman's proposals run against the grain of anarchist priorities, the most obvious problem with implementing them today is that they would be utterly impractical. Calling for formal structures amounts to requiring the movement to entirely change its political culture, placing itself in an entirely unfamiliar mould that needs to be learned and followed against one's habits. It also means the effective stoppage of the movement's inherent fluidity in order to adapt it to rationalised structures, losing the advantages of high connectivity and rapid action afforded by decentralised, networked forms of organisation. Since any widespread change in anarchist organising would have to be widely accepted in order to happen, the stakes look very bad for the advocates of formal structures. Freeman and Bookchin, on their own principles, would have to fall in with the majority's considered choice.

More substantially, however, Freeman's analysis does not really explain the problem. People who enjoy internal positions of influence within a group or network are not necessarily friends. Identifiable leadership groups may exist, but while some of them are intimate friends, others have more of a working relationship based on trust rather than fondness. Some are happy to organise together but cannot stand each other socially. Alternately, there can be a group where all members are friends but there are *still* internal patterns of exclusion or domination. More basically, the stable, long-term elites portrayed in *TToS* would seem to require stability in the identity of the members and in the relationships between them. Otherwise, it would be hard for it to function as a forum for political coordination, especially within a larger group that it needs constantly to manipulate. But groups of friends very rarely work like that: people have different kinds of friendships with each other (best friends, good friends, mates, lovers...), creating a complex network of ties that is very rarely monolithic. Moreover, groups tend to have a very fluid nature: people burn-out, fall out with each other, make new friends, migrate a lot and so on. This does not mean that the analysis of *TToS* is *never* a reality – Freeman's analysis is clearly relevant to her own experiences in the women's movement (Freeman 1976). What is denied here, however, is the portrayal of the friendship-elite as some kind of First Cause lying at 'the' root of the problem, which tags the circumstantial as essential.

A more formal problem with *TToS* is that its analysis is clouded by the functionalist conventions of 1970s 'value free social science'. Functionalism, an approach associated with sociologists like Emile Durkheim and Talcot Parsons, handles its object of study as a system, and asks only how this system functions and how it responds to change. The only available type of value-judgement within this framework is how successfully systems fulfil their goals, whatever they are. As a result, the only problem that *TToS* can find with elites is that they hinder the effectiveness of the movement. First, the prerequisites for being part of an informal elite 'do not include one's competence, dedication to feminism, talents or potential contribution to the movement'. Second, there is not space for all good ideas: 'People listen to each other because they like them, not because they say significant things.' Finally elites 'have no obligations to be responsible to the group at large'. All the while, nothing is ever said in critique of elites as such; as with Bookchin's statement above, equality is simply absent from the agenda.

Nevertheless, the concerns that motivate Freeman, Kaufman and Bookchin are legitimate. There is a felt need to have some way of monitoring, checking and making visible the operations of influence within anti-authoritarian groups. People find it disempowering to participate in actions and projects that are steered behind their back. Being put in a situation you did not create and over which you have only marginal control – this may be the norm in environments like the army, workplace or school, but they should not be the norm in anarchist organising which wants to empower the individual.

In order to make sense of these issues in a way that goes beyond *TToS* in terms of both analysis and proposals, we need to take a closer look at how power moves and flows in the anarchist movement. Before we make any normative judgement on invisible power, we need to understand *how* it is created and encouraged. This requires us to examine the unique 'rules of the game' in anarchist organising – rules very different from those obtaining in the public sphere at large. How is power-with actually wielded in the movement? And what can this tell us about its use and abuse?

DECENTRALIASTION VERSUS ACCOUNTABILITY

The term 'decentralisation' is often mentioned as a central principle of anarchist organisation – but what does it mean in practice? To clarify, let us look at how decisions are made in large networks. Consciously or by default, it seems that the space for network-wide decisions in anarchist networks is in fact very small. Most of the activity that happens within their fold is undertaken by autonomous affinity groups, working groups and individual networkers. For example, in bi-monthly UK gatherings of the *Dissent!* anti-G8 network, decentralisation was often cited to argue for *not* making a decision on various matters at the plenary. Often a participant would say something to the effect that the plenary meeting should not micromanage the smaller groups, and that it should trust people to get on with their plans and projects as long as they are working within the principles of unity. Some of this was surely because of fatigue: large meetings are very boring affairs, and the consensus decision-making process can often make strong demands on one's patience. However, it is also clear that the activists saw decentralisation and autonomy as positive values, not just as an expedient method. Thus, when a network plenary was discussing things such as transport or legal support, people would often invoke decentralisation and relegate these decisions to a working group. Now what should be clear is that a working group on transport or legal support is not in any way a 'local' node, since it operates on a network-wide level. What it is is *a new centre of power-with*. To describe what is happening in such a situation, one could say that the plenary, a temporary 'centre' of collective power-with in the network, is 'seeding' several new 'centres'. So clearly decentralisation means not fewer centres but more. It means that there should be a process to increase the number of 'places' (face-to-face or virtual) where power gets exercised, while avoiding disproportionate aggregations of power, and/or transferring existing ones into the new locales (a principle of equality enacted on an increasing number of recipients).

However – and this is the crucial point – the transfer of such power to new centres goes unmanaged and unlegitimated. In practice, what typically happens is that by the time the plenary meets, a number of people willing to volunteer their time and effort to moving a particular issue forward will have already formed a working group, open for others to join. The plenary's 'decision' to 'decentralise' boils down to advertising an accomplished fact. One might think that, since the plenary has agreed that the creation of working groups is a good thing, this constitutes some kind of ratification. But what if the working groups simply announced their existence, without seeking to generate discussion in the plenary? Unless the purpose of the group sounded strange, or controversial individuals were involved, the announcement would likely pass without discussion (at most with a few questions for clarification). In other words, people would see the same legitimacy in the working groups whether or not they explicitly gave their consent to their existence in a plenary. Membership in the working group is also largely without oversight, since it may change at any time as people join and leave. What is distressing about these observations is that they show that decentralised processes tend to be highly *unaccountable* – which is the root of the concerns associated with ideas like *TToS*.

Accountability is the end-goal of the formal structures approach, which calls for responsibility to be clearly delegated and mandated, overseen and recallable; and for influence in the movement to be exercised as visibly as possible. Indeed, the concept of accountability has a great deal of currency from the position of movements for social change. Many activists talk about holding corporations accountable for their abuses (e.g. making Dow Chemicals pay for the Bhopal disaster), or about holding politicians accountable to the public. Anarchists, who believe that corporations and politicians should be abolished, might have less use for such a concept – but even with them it retains some rhetorical strength in the immediate term. In the case of both corporations and politicians, this is because the demand for accountability is directed towards an entity that is *more* powerful than the source of the demand. However, accountability as such does not imply a given direction for power relations. In fact, accountability most often operates hierarchically from the top down – workers are accountable to their bosses, soldiers are accountable to their officers, and so on. What does accountability, as a relationship between two agents, most basically consist in? Looking at top-down accountability and *in particular* to the kind of bottom-up account- ability that anarchists support when they say they want to 'hold corporations accountable', we should understand that all our notions of accountability are based on the idea of exerting certain behaviours from agents through *demands backed by sanctions*. So *A* is accountable to *B* if and only if *B* has the ability to impose sanctions on *A* in case of *B*'s dissatisfaction with *A*'s activities. And this is where the problems begin. For sanctions are impossible to use in a consistent way in decentralised networks. The discussion of decentralisation above reveals that, while often addressed as a value, decentralisation is also a *default functional principle* of anarchist organising. I would now like to argue that this is because of the 'elephant in the room' so often ignored during discussions of anarchist organisational processes: the absence of enforcement.

The concept of 'enforcement' introduced here is meant as a particular variant of coercion. The latter, as we mentioned above, is the extraction of compliance through a threat of deprivation. Enforcement, on the other hand, is coercion which has two additional features. First, it is rationalised and institutionalised. Enforcement is coercion that follows formal procedures and guidelines, such that both the victim and the perpetrator know what behaviours are expected from them. It is usually a form of coercion against which society considers it illegitimate and/or illegal to defend oneself, that is, it is attached to a legal/rational form of authority (Weber 1958). Second, it is coercion where the threat is permanent. The means and protocols for enforcement are constantly available to the enforcer. The coercer, on the other hand, may have to 'invent' their own means and strategy for coercion. Both of these aspects differentiate enforcement from sporadic or diffuse coercion.

It should be clarified in passing that while anarchists would clearly object to enforcement, they do not have to take the same position on coercion as such. If someone attacks me, today or in an 'anarchist society', I will certainly coerce them to stop. Social transformation will also likely involve some forms of non-defensive coercion, against owners for example. Even in the hunter-gatherer and horticultural communities that many anarchists look to for cues on non-hierarchical living, there exists the use of 'diffuse social sanctions' – shunning, marginalisation, exclusion – whose application or threat coerce sociable behaviour to some extent (Barclay 1990). In fact, anarchists use the same form of diffuse social sanctions – gossip, refusal to work with certain people, or public displays of distrust. Social sanctions are threatening to the degree that it is costly for a person to pollute their relations with other members of a group or, ultimately, to leave it. Marginalisation as a result of falling out with a bunch of anarchists may not seem very costly – compared to the threats issued by the state, or even to diffuse sanctions in a tribal community, where one's survival may depend on cooperation. However, the cost is neither zero nor insignificant – it could only be so if there were no purpose in participating in the movement. For example, there is often a large degree of overlap between activists' political milieu and their social one, with one's comrades being the bulk of one's friends. An individual thus also faces the cost of drifting to the periphery of their social milieu, losing friendship ties and opportunities for social interaction with like-minded people outside the activist circle. This cost is larger, the more of one's friends are activists, and smaller to the degree that individual friendship ties that were created through activism can continue.

The point, however, is that whereas diffuse social sanctions are indeed coercive, they are hardly something on which an edifice of *enforcement* could be built. Social sanctions, taken on their own, do not yield to the permanence and rationalisation entailed by enforcement.

They are by nature only possible to employ in a sporadic and diffuse way. And aside from social sanctions, the available sanctions that can be exercised in a networked social movement are next to nil. Anarchists have no army or police, nor any economic sanctions to mobilise against one another. When it comes to the rub, activists hardly have a way to make someone do something s/he strongly refuses to do, or to prevent someone from doing something s/he strongly wants to do. The lack of appropriate sanctions, then, makes enforcement not only undesirable for anarchists in their politics, but structurally impossible. This is important; because where there is no enforcement to begin with, there can only be anarchy. Human relations in activist networks will follow anarchist patterns almost by default, since enforcement is inevitably absent from its structures.

Perhaps this is only possible in the thin air of dislocated network politics, and such a model is untested in the more messy ground of community living, food production, etc. I am not asking whether this absolute non-enforcement can or cannot work in an anarchist *society* and apply to all areas of life (I think it can, to the degree that there is ease of mobility between communities, making the cost of secession low). But what cannot be denied is that as far as the contemporary movement is concerned, decentralisation and autonomy are not just values but also facts on the ground. They are there because the impossibility of rationalised, permanent enforcement stands the entirety of anarchist activities on the basis of voluntary association.

Once we shift our understanding of anarchist process in this way, we are able to shift the mistake that most clouds our thinking over process – the continued couching of the debate in the language of democracy. It is true that there are major parallels between some of the values animating activists' collective process practices and those which feature in the more radical end of democratic theory – especially concepts of participation, deliberation and inclusion (Cohen 1998, Gould 1988, Young 2000). However, there is still a fundamental difference between the coordinates of the debate. Democratic discourse assumes without exception that the political process results, at some point, in collectively binding decisions. That these decisions can be the result of free and open debate by all those affected does not change the fact that the outcome is seen to have a mandatory nature. Saying that something is collectively binding makes no sense if each person is to make up their own mind over whether they are bound by it. Binding means enforceable, and enforceability is a background assumption of democracy. But the outcomes of anarchist process are inherently impossible to enforce. That is why the process is not 'democratic' at all, since in democracy the point of equal participation in determining decisions is that this is what legitimates these decisions' subsequent enforcement – or simply sweetens the pill. Anarchism, then, represents not the most radical form of democracy, but an altogether different paradigm of collective action.

The confrontation with non-enforceability reveals that the status of a 'decision' in anarchist organising is fuzzy, and can easily be seen as a matter of consultation and arrangement. The consensus decision-making process that anarchists widely employ is not only a cultural relic handed down from feminists and Quakers. It is also, for all decentralised movements, the default option that makes most sense. Much has been written about the mechanics of consensus decision-making, about its difference from unanimity, and about its intrinsic qualities, such as non-adversarial and patient discussion, valuing everyone's voice and concerns. The provision for 'blocking', or qualified veto, is said to express respect for the individual, and the facilitated discussion process is widely promoted as encouraging creative overcoming of differences or coexistence despite them (Coover et al. 1977, Butler and Rothstein 1998, Herndon 2001). But there is another point to be made about the important *functional* role that consensus plays in producing collective action under circumstances of unenforceability. In groups and networks thoroughly predicated on voluntary association, compliance with collective decisions is also voluntary. Consensus is the only thing that makes sense when minorities are under no obligation or sanction to comply, because consensus increases the *likelihood* that a decision will be voluntarily carried out by those who made it.

Such a perspective also enables us to look differently at the function of spokespeople, delegates or representatives in the anarchist movement. If we assume that what representatives decide among themselves will then *have* to be followed by those they represent, then we will obviously want to ask who gave these representatives their mandate, and what is its nature and scope. We would perhaps consider it good practice for 'spokes' to arrive at the meeting with a 'starting position' based on earlier consensus in their own group, and to have some guidelines from their group as to how flexible they can be. We may also be strict and expect that for such a decision to be legitimate, it would have to be ratified by the local groups. All of these would indeed make the decision more democratic, but only because they would be mitigating the basic problem of enforced decisions.

Anarchists, however, are not doing very well at all at being 'democratic', because delegates to spokescouncils are rarely given a specific mandate, nor do they get elected. Usually those who have the time and money to travel to a meeting do so, and at the meeting itself nobody even checks which local groups are represented. However, the spokespeople can have no way of having their decision enforced – and thus they require no legitimacy. At most, a spokescouncil is a useful mechanism for banging heads together – generating 'decisions' for which the spokespeople can *anticipate* that the individuals not present will voluntarily follow. A spokescouncil's consensus will be practicable to the degree that the spokes are being literally 'representative' of the rest of the moment. This means not that they are appointed to make decisions on someone else's behalf, but that they think like others think, and are likely to raise and resolve the issues that others would raise. Again, the resulting consensus is of practicable utility simply because it generates not a decision but what essentially remains a proposal, while ensuring through discussion a high *likelihood* of voluntary acceptance from other people not present in the meeting, because their concerns will have already been anticipated in the shaping of the proposal for decision.

These observations cast a grave doubt on the possibility of truly 'accountable' relationships becoming the norm in the anarchist movement. But the difficulty is even deeper than that. Sanctions or no sanctions, *B* certainly cannot hold *A* accountable in any meaningful sense *if B does not know about A's actions*. What the entire issue really boils down to is the *invisibility* of influence in anarchist networks. The dilemmas we are confronting here stem from the power-with that anarchists use invisibly, behind the scenes – where those affected may never know who made things this way, and how they conspired to do it. The demands for formal structures are, at the end of the day, demands for visibility. But what happens when invisibility is inevitable? More importantly, what happens when it is politically *valuable*?

THE PLENARY AND THE CAMPFIRE

In this final section I want to talk about two major problems with visibility, which finally exclude all talk of formal structures and force us to look for another way to address issues around the wielding of power-with in the anarchist movement. The first problem is that in some cases visibility is *impossible* – namely in actions that require secret planning although they will inevitably affect people who did not participate in their preparation. The second problem is that there is an important sense in which anarchists would be drawn to *positively value* the existence of invisible power within the movement, based on a feminist critique of the demands of public forums for influence.

Many times a small group of activists may wield, at least for a given time, a great deal of influence that is inherently unaccountable because it has to be wielded in secret. When illegal actions are being planned, anarchists may or may not agree with the outcome – but they cannot honestly expect the organisers to be transparent about the process. The activities of Reclaim the Streets (RTS) in its heyday are a poignant example. RTS originally formed in London in 1991, close to the dawn of the anti-roads movement, but entered its most prolific phase in the mid 1990s through the organisation of mass, illegal street parties. Harnessing the energies of the recently criminalised rave subculture to an environmental anti-roads and anti-car agenda, RTS organised parties that rendered vast areas car-free for the day, creating self-organised spaces of party and protest – a combination that would carry on in anarchist mass actions. The parties drew thousands of people, and fused together several agendas: the reclamation of urban space from the hands of developers; a critique of the automobile culture and climate change; and the drive to create spontaneous, unregulated 'Situations' or, in more recent terminology, 'Temporary Autonomous Zones', which display a qualitative break with normality (cf. Situationist International 1959, Hakim Bey 1985). The RTS project reached its climax on 18 June 1999, the first 'global day of action' against capitalism coinciding with the G8 summit in Köln, Germany, when thousands of dancing people caused massive disruption in the City of London and simultaneous actions were held in over 40 cities from Vancouver to Tel-Aviv. As John Jordan recounts, 'the road became a stage for participatory ritual theatre ... participatory because the street party has no division between performer and audience, it is created by and for everyone, it avoids all mediation, it is experienced in the immediate moment by all, in a spirit of face to face subversive comradeship' (Jordan 1998: 141). We might accept that an RTS party is 'participatory' once it has started. But it is highly questionable whether this also applies to the organisation of the event. The parties were, after all, staged entirely by a small core group of RTS activists, working full-time from an office in a London suburb and devising the plans to minute detail. The thousands who participated in the parties would turn up at a designated meeting place without having any idea of what was about to happen. As Jordan (143–4) recounts, in one scenario

thousands of people emerge from Shepherd's Bush tube station, no-one knows where they are going – the mystery and excitement of it all is electrifying. Shepherd's Bush Green comes to a standstill as people pour on to it ... up ahead a line of police has already sealed off the roundabout ... The crowd knows that this is not the place: where is the sound system, the tripods? Then, as if by some miracle of collective telepathy, everyone turns back and disappears around the corner; a winding journey through back streets, under railway bridges and then up over a barrier and suddenly they are on an enormous motorway and right *behind* the police lines ... The ecstatic crowd gravitates towards the truck carrying the sound system which is parked on the hard shoulder ... The crowd roars – we've liberated a motorway through sheer numbers, through people power!

No 'miracle of collective telepathy' took place here. There were always activists from the RTS core group who took on leading the crowd to the tarmac, in a carefully planned tactical manoeuvre which none of the thousands of attendants knew about in advance. The idea that a handful of activists could wield so much influence over a crowd, however willing, has given many anarchists cause for alarm, and was raised in numerous other events (see for example Anonymous3 2000, Friends of Phil and Toby 2003, Squirrellife 2004). It is important to emphasise that nobody was coerced – you did not *have* to turn up at the event or stay there. However, once you were there you were basically putting yourself in a situation where you did not have the space to control what was going on around you. Police attacks, injuries and arrests were not an uncommon feature of these events, and organisers who created the situation have been accused of behaving like irresponsible cadres. However, could they have acted otherwise? Putting together a successful street party (or a summit blockade for that matter) seems to be inherently incompatible with visibility. To begin with, technically, a discussion of the operation among a large number of people, each of which would of course have to have their say, would be time-consuming and endless. Second, and most obviously, the realities of police surveillance and potential repression that surround the planning of these actions rule out any public process. It is important to remark that the RTS model is also power-sharing, because it is easy to imitate. RTS groups were started throughout the early 2000s in many cities around the world, adding nothing to the power of the original RTS group. However, the tactic *itself* is inherently incompatible with visibility. Someone else can adopt it, but in doing so they are only creating another invisible process.

The point, however, is that despite these dynamics it is clear that the RTS experiment was immensely valuable. By developing such an innovative, inspiring and meaningful form of direct action, this small group of people politicised a large amount of people, and helped make the anti-capitalist movement a global phenomenon. So the fall-back position for supporters of visibility would be to say that, while there are unfortunate limitations to visibility, the ideal itself should not be given up. However, this cannot overcome the second issue – namely, that sometimes invisibility is not merely a matter of expedience, but politically meaningful in itself.

Imagine Emma, an activist who lives in a town which has a strong and vibrant anarchist milieu. She has a great deal of experience and commitment, many friends, and is a very empathic and caring person. She also has a lot of energy and many useful ideas for actions and projects. However, Emma is also very uncomfortable speaking at large public meetings. She believes that this is the result of deep-seated emotional patterns that derive from her socialisation as a woman, and finds confirmation for that view in the experiences of many other woman activists. Speaking in a large group of people makes her feel uneasy and anxious – something she has noticed that men do not suffer from nearly as much. When she has something to say she takes a lot of time to think it through, often speaking only if she sees no one else is saying it, despite the fact that she knows her ideas are worthwhile and that the others respect and value her. As a result, Emma says she much prefers to offer her ideas to people informally, in personal or small group conversations. When she has a good idea for an action, or some strong opinion about how some resources should be allocated, she prefers to speak about it with people she trusts, informally, by the campfire as it were. She prefers to float an idea and see how it rolls along in the local milieu, rather than arguing for it in a large meeting. Since her ideas are often very well thought-out, and since people trust her, Emma has in fact a great deal of power. She is clearly an invisible leader.

Emma's behaviour is clearly not an accountable way to exercise power. None of her influence is transparent or visible to those she does not want to see it. On the other hand, anarchists who have a strong critique of patriarchy will find it very hard to censure the path

Emma has chosen to empower herself. Like many women (and other members of disempowered groups), Emma is going to use power invisibly or not at all. To expect that she strive to 'get over' her emotional patterns and feel empowered at meetings would be not only patronising, but sexist, because it brackets the conditions of patriarchy that engender these patterns. What I am getting at is that the ideal of visibility privileges 'the Plenary' – the public theatre of power-with – while excluding 'the Campfire' – the venue for its informal wielding behind-the-scenes. But making the Plenary the only accepted way to put things into motion is very problematic. Returning to the discussion of resources in the previous part, it can be seen that exercising power-with in the Plenary requires precisely those resources which are most difficult to share – public confidence, articulation and charisma. Not only that, often these resources *only become* ones that generate inequality in such formal and assemblary venues of decision-making. Because it is so difficult to share this resource, and because its current distribution strongly reflects patterns of domination in society, the only way to equalise the access to the influence it generates is *to minimise its relevance as a resource*, to reduce the volume of instances in which it matters to have it.

While anarchist networks may well be a supportive environment for self-deprogramming and empowerment, as matters stand it is unfair to say to a woman 'you have to get self-confidence' as a condition for participation. Why does she have to make a special effort to change in order to participate on equal footing just because she is a woman in a patriarchal society? At the same time, privileging the Plenary erases and de-legitimises the manifold forms of using power that women have developed in response to patriarchy, and the ways in which many people find it most comfortable to empower themselves. As a result of these considerations, I think anarchists are bound to acknowledge that this invisible, subterranean, indeed *unaccountable* use of power is not only inevitable in some measure (because of habit and secrecy), but also needs to be embraced, since it coheres with their worldview in important respects.

The quest for accountability, then, arrives at a dead end. Such an agenda inevitably ends up challenging the legitimacy of any invisible power, which is not only a practical necessity but also has intrinsic political value from an anarchist perspective. Where, then, does this leave anarchist concerns about invisible power?

Any resolution of these issues would have to meet two basic requirements. First, it could never take the form of a model that seeks to artificially redesign movement practices, running against the cultural logic of decentralised and autonomous organising. Rather, any change in the anarchist use of power-with would have to be itself a *cultural* change, which can proliferate organically in a diffuse process. Unlike structures and protocols, only cultural change can reach beyond the public theatre of power and influence habits and attitudes in anarchists' everyday activities. Second, and more ambitiously, any modification to how people reflect upon and wield power in anarchist organising would have to be viewed not as a restriction on freedom but as its expression. Rather than discouraging empowerment in informal venues, it would make people *more* encouraged and excited to create, initiate and do – only perhaps in a different way. Precisely because the entire edifice of anarchist organising is built on pure voluntarism, any change would have to be actively desired rather than seen as a concession.

For these reasons, I would suggest that the only way to resolve this particular set of anarchist anxieties would be through a *culture of solidarity* around the invisible wielding of power in the movement. Solidarity expresses a relationship between persons, and within and between groups, that is based on a feeling of mutual identification. Cohen and Arato (1992: 5) define solidarity as

> the ability of individuals to respond to and identify with one another on the basis of mutuality and reciprocity, without calculating individual advantages, and above all without compulsion. Solidarity involves a willingness to share the fate of the other, not as the exemplar of a category to which the self belongs but as a unique and different person.

Therefore, inasmuch as solidarity modifies behaviour it does so as a positive motivation, not as a limiting duty. Solidarity can be amplified and actualised in activists' choices about their use of influence, and it can also be actively promoted. A culture of solidarity would encourage activists to wield power reflectively rather than tripping on empowerment; to make actions participatory and/or easily copyable whenever possible; and to encourage consideration for the anticipated needs and desires of those whom one's actions will inevitably impact unaccountably. Solidarity in the dynamic wielding of power-with would also have to meaningfully intersect with the redistribution of political resources discussed earlier. By itself, the practice of redistributing resources requires a cultural orientation that makes it a matter of habit rather than book-keeping, and solidarity in the use of power could naturally be added to this. The way to promote such cultural change – an act of power in itself – is not so much through verbal propaganda but through propaganda by deed. People can initiate change in their own organisational practices, taking initiative to create habits of resource-sharing and of reflective and considerate use of informal power, displaying that agenda and hopefully inspiring others to follow suit. If these practices catch on, then resource-sharing and solidarity will have become something that people keep in mind by default. Such a resolution is clearly partial and imperfect, but at least it is something that can actually happen, unlike a 180-degree turn away from informal organising that extinguishes the Campfire of initiative.

4

Peace, Love and Petrol Bombs
Anarchism and Violence Revisited

It is better to be violent, if there is violence in our hearts, than to put on the cloak of non-violence to cover impotence. Violence is any day preferable to impotence. There is hope for a violent man to become non-violent. There is no such hope for the impotent.

—M. K. Gandhi

Anarchists hardly discuss political violence anymore. And really it's a bit strange to be revisiting the debate on anarchist violence while in the Middle East scores of people are killed weekly by car-bombs, firearms and plain old machetes, from Darfur through Palestine to Iraq. Suddenly a bunch of sticks and stones doesn't seem like that big a deal. And so, what generated the most impassioned controversies early on in the anarchist revival has largely been abandoned and laid by the wayside. Not that any resolution or clarity have been achieved on the matter. If anything, it was so confusing and emotionally charged that many activists are by now sick to death of the subject. So anarchists have agreed to disagree, among themselves and with their hesitant allies in the wider global justice movement. The frustrating debate has been replaced with a call for 'diversity of tactics': everyone from the black bloc to the Christian pacifists, from the Clown Army to the padded White Overalls, should have the space to carry out their plans as they think right, without stepping on each other's toes or denouncing each other afterwards. Calling for diversity of tactics certainly has its practical use. For one thing, it relieves activists of the requirement to attempt reaching an impossible consensus over tactics at any given mass action. But this does not always work, and the lack of elbow-space at some protest events has caused more than a little trouble and perceived betrayals of solidarity. More fundamentally, the uneasy compromise has come at the price of stifling very real tensions which are still seething under the surface, however hard we try to look away.

This is why I think another stab at the issue is worthwhile. The purpose of this chapter is to explain why questions around violence are so difficult, to disentangle them in some measure, and to offer markers for reopening a rational debate on the topic. I begin by reviewing recent anarchist discussions of violence and the events that prompted them, emphasising two points. First, that the dilemmas in question result in large part from the fact that anarchism – a movement with an obviously violent past – has re-emerged after a long period of hibernation into an activist environment in which an ethos of principled non-violence has in the meantime taken hold. Second, that this surrounding ethos has skewed the debate such that many anarchists have internalised its outright taboo on violence and failed to make the decisive and crucial separation between two very different questions: what violence *is*, and whether violence can be *justified*.

Then, isolating the question of definition, I enter into a critical engagement with some academic literature and end up arguing that an act should be considered violent if it generates an embodied sense of attack or deliberate endangerment *in its recipient*. This definition serves to clarify some chronic sticking points, most importantly those concerning the violent status of property destruction. I then approach the core of the debate – the question of justifying anarchist violence. Here I consider (a) concerns on the inconsistency between violence and the anarchist ethos of prefigurative politics; (b) difficulties with stock anarchist rhetoric justifying violence; and (c) inherent limits to any enterprise of justification based on the obvious but correct rule, 'avoid violence as far as possible'. The reader should not expect any hard and fast conclusions here. I am not going to end up arguing either 'for' or 'against' violence. My more modest goal is to clarify the exact nature of the dilemmas that each individual and group will inevitably have to face in making their own decisions about violent action. In closing, I offer some comments on violent activity's capacity to both empower and disempower, on the status of revenge as a motivation for violence, and on the necessary conditions for any anarchist reconsideration of armed struggle.

A MESSY DEBATE

There is a striking difference between the context in which violence was discussed in the historical anarchist movement and that which structures debates today. When anarchists in the nineteenth and early twentieth century talked about political violence, they were typically referring to one of two scenarios: mass armed insurrection, or assassinations of heads of state and capitalist bosses. Today, in contrast, the primary context for discussion is the use of non-lethal violence during protests: scenes of property destruction and confrontations with police on the streets, in particular during demonstrations against summits of government leaders and international economic organisations. Violence of this kind has accompanied the chain of mass mobilisations that followed the anarchist movement's 'coming-out parties' in 1999 – the June 18 Carnival Against Capital and the November 30 blockades of the World Trade Organisation in Seattle. Of these events, perhaps the most emblematic was the weekend of anti-G8 protests in Genoa in July 2001, where one protester was killed, and hundreds injured in street fighting and a police raid on the Diaz school where activists were sleeping.

What caught the public eye in many of these events was the activity of overtly anarchist black blocs. A black bloc is an ad hoc tactical formation in which affinity groups and individuals cluster together, wearing mostly black and often covering their faces – both to protect themselves against identification and to maintain a symbolism of anonymity as promoted by the EZLN (Marcos 1998). The tactic originates with the German anti-fascist scene and first appeared in the United States during the protests against the Gulf War in 1991. At mass protests, black blocs typically engage in attacks on symbolic corporate targets such as banks, fast food outlets and gas stations, and often also in confrontations with police which range from building barricades or pushing through police lines to throwing stones and even petrol bombs (see Katsiaficas 1997, Flugennock 2000, Bray 2000, Black 2001, One Off Press 2001, Wu Ming 2001, Anonymous4/5 2003, Gee 2003, Van Deusen and Massot 2007).

Yet even the heaviest street fighting does not involve anarchists taking up arms, as they would and did a hundred years ago. Non-violent revolution was, at the time, a non-concept. Tolstoy's libertarian Christian pacifism, the first quasi-anarchist doctrine of non-violence, was a unique exception to the rule (Tolstoy 1990); the 'revolution' – if there was such a thing – was almost universally seen as a fairly bloody affair. It should be emphasised, however, that the difference lies not in the levels of violence used by anarchists alone, but by egalitarian movements across the board. Indeed, the revolutionary aspirations of Marx, Lenin and Luxemburg involved mass insurrectionary action as much as those of the anarchists. It was only in the second half of the twentieth century that a principled commitment to non-violence came to the fore in the worldviews of progressive social movements.

But this happened during a period when anarchism had already largely disappeared from the scene, and it was in its absence that civil rights and anti-war movements popularised the notion of non-violent action in public discourse, inspired by figures such as Mohandas K. Gandhi and Martin Luther King. Later, the movements at whose intersection contemporary anarchism reappeared were either squarely rooted in this new tradition of civil-rights pacifism – as in the case of the women's anti-nuclear movement – or focused on self-endangering tactics without too much attention to questions of violence – as in the case of direct-action environmental defence.

The result was that the anarchist movement reawoke into an environment where a culture of non-violent radicalism had achieved a hegemonic status. A tension was therefore inevitable. On the one hand there was the anarchist movement's violent past, and a sizeable number of activists up for urban confrontation. On the other hand there was the taboo on political violence, unquestioned by most alternative globalisation activists, whereby peaceful protest was taken to be the only legitimate form of political contestation.

This atmosphere strongly influenced the contours of the debate during the first years after Seattle. Ceding ground to the prevailing ethos of non-violence, many anarchists responded to denunciations of their protest behaviour by attempting to minimise the presence of 'violence' in their tactics. In Seattle, for example, the marches and sit-down obstructions of WTO delegates were undertaken under strict non-violence guidelines. However, on the first night of the blockades, an anarchist black bloc trashed a number of banks, store-fronts of clothing chains associated with sweatshop labour, a McDonald's outlet and other corporate targets, though avoiding direct confrontation with police. After the protests, one of the affinity groups participating in the attacks issued a statement that claimed:

We contend that property destruction is not a violent activity unless it destroys lives or causes pain in the process. By this definition, private property – especially corporate private property – is itself infinitely more violent than any action taken against it ... When we smash a window, we aim to destroy the thin veneer of legitimacy that surrounds private property rights ... Broken windows can be boarded up (with yet more waste of our forests) and eventually replaced, but the shattering of assumptions will hopefully persist for some time to come. (ACME collective 2000)

Propaganda by deed through property destruction is thus presented as a non-violent act, since it is directed at inanimate objects which cannot experience pain. Simultaneously, the tag of 'violence' is transferred to capitalism, symbolised by the object of destruction. The purpose of ACME's rhetoric is to cast the weight of violent protagonism away from themselves and on to capitalism. This amounts to a *tu quoque* argument (Latin for 'you too' or 'look who's talking') which minimises the significance of anarchist actions in comparison to the much more frequent and large-scale violence perpetuated by the existing order. It forces statist critics to own up to their own support for some forms of violence (say, the legal violence of armies or police forces), diverting the discussion away from violence and on to the legitimacy of the latter institutions.

The credibility of such arguments, which seek to deny or minimise the violent status of anarchist actions, was challenged in strong terms in an influential pamphlet from the period, 'Beyond the Corpse Machine' (Ashen Ruins 2002). The author argues that while violence must never be romanticized or fetishized, anarchists have fallen under the sway of a reactionary rhetoric of non-violence 'clouded by Statist assumptions and middle class fears'. The prevailing ethos of non-violence thus constructs an inescapable grammar, whereby it is enough to *call* something violent (however defined) in order to make it automatically *unjustified*. In their uncritical stance towards the ethos of non-violence, he argues, anarchists are in fact extending credence to the quietism and respect for the social peace associated with the statist left (both liberal and communist) – which 'may as well be the [values] of the capitalist and the politician for all the difference it makes'. Anarchists, however, should not be afraid to rock the boat:

Instead of claiming that smashing a window isn't violent – a point that average people reject out of common sense (and therefore makes me wonder about the common sense of some anarchists) – why don't we drop the semantics and admit that, yes, it's very clearly violent and then make a case for it? Do we consider the Israeli bulldozing of Palestinian homes non-violent? If, on the other hand, smashing a window is merely a symbolic act, but not violent, what message are we trying to send? With smashing a window thus set as the absolute limit of appropriate dissent, aren't we really making the absurdly contradictory point that this violent system must be opposed through a variety of tactics, up to and including smashing a window (which is not violent, by the way). But no further. Is this the limit, then, of our resistance? What a sad comment on our motivations, if non-violence is the furthest frontier of our rage in the face of this corpse machine, America.

Ashen Ruins' critique of this attitude is part of a broader point connected to the so-called 'insurrectionary' current in contemporary anarchist thinking, which recalls Bakunin in its emphasis on an ever-present potential for revolutionary uprising (cf. Bonanno 1998, Anonymous7 2001). It typically includes the claim that there is a broad-based undercurrent of often violent (and non-violent) revolt in advanced capitalist societies, present in prison life, in sporadic violence against police in poor communities, in vandalism, 'anti-social behaviour' and other types of activity rationalised as criminality. The unstated presumptions of this revolt are seen as anti-authoritarian since they are spontaneous and resistant to institutionalised organisation. Ashen Ruins calls on anarchists to depart from this logic and to respond to undercurrents of revolt with active solidarity, which he sees as crucial to a truly revolutionary praxis. All the more so since the liberal and communist 'left' is both afraid of and unable to understand this undercurrent, because of its endorsement of a discourse that codes violence in terms of a cultural taboo, strongly connected to a fear of the uncontrollable, the abnormal and the criminal, and reflecting the ultimate interest of its middle-class proponents in preserving their social position rather than risking action for a classless society (cf. Churchill and Ryan 1998).

These reflections are strengthened by the analysis of sociologist Zygmunt Bauman, who interprets such attitudes towards violence more generally as part of the hegemonic social discourse of modernity. Bauman argues that the discursive attachment of violence to abnormality and criminality serves to overshadow normalised and legitimised instances of violence which can be just as serious. Thus people will often say that a police officer is only 'violent' if she oversteps her mandate and uses 'excessive force', but not so if she acts as the law expects her to (which can easily include using a truncheon or live ammunition). Bauman traces this paradox to a particularly modern ambivalence about might, force and coercion. He argues that the humanising pretences of the Enlightenment are at work in portraying modernity as a process that removes violence and brutality from social relations. But this belief needs to be rationalised against the fact that violence has not been abolished but only redistributed. Torture, public execution and indiscriminate violence by legal armed forces may have been removed from modern Western societies, but they continue to be employed by proxy in the post-colonial world, while within Western societies they have been replaced by forms of violence that are far more sanitized, though often no less cruel – lethal injection, prison brutality, chemical weapons for crowd dispersal, and so on. To maintain the belief that violence in social relations is receding, the word 'violence' itself comes to be coded on one side of dichotomies such as legal–illegal, legitimate–illegitimate, normal–irregular. The former is attached with a positive indicator – e.g. punishment or the enforcement of law and order – while the other is censured *as* violence, expressing shock, reaction to the unexpected and the fear of the uncontrolled (Bauman 1991: 143–6).

I would endorse these insights, and argue that any discussion of violence that is aware of the wider discourses around it must be wary of uncritically falling into them. This requires decisively separating two axes of discussion: violent/non-violent and justified/unjustified. The consequences of this separation will be seen in the discussion below.

Meanwhile, it should be mentioned that frictions around violent protest turned out to be the last straw that split the uneasy anti-globalisation coalitions that had proliferated since Seattle. Many grassroots and direct-action groups, most of them not self-identified as anarchists, were already sitting uneasily with NGOs, unions and political parties because of their reformist agendas, hierarchical forms of organisation and political opportunism. Now, as the mass media sensationalised anarchist violence in the wake of every protest, many NGO figureheads and communist spokespeople chimed in, complaining that the anarchists were 'distorting the message of the protests'. As a result, a breach of solidarity was perceived in many grassroots and direct-action groups. Especially after Genoa, many activists who would not normally condone violence saw the stock denunciations of the anarchists as an expression of gross insensitivity and lack of solidarity with hundreds of traumatised and imprisoned activists, playing along with the G8 leaders' and corporate media's obvious divide-and-conquer strategy of separating 'good protesters' from 'bad protesters' (cf. Moore 2003: 368–9). As a result, many grassroots activists now began refusing to denounce anarchist violence, eroding the position of the ethos of non-violence in their discourses. This was replaced by the call for diversity of tactics – a measure taken in order to move beyond seemingly irreconcilable debates and towards cohesion and solidarity in the horizontally-organised, direct-action end of the alternative globalisation movement, which now felt abandoned and isolated. Starhawk's action reports, collected in *Webs of Power* (Starhawk 2002), provide a good illustration of this progression. Writing after the International

Monetary Fund/World Bank blockades in Prague (September 2000), she puts herself squarely on the principled non-violence side of the dichotomy with statements such as 'this is a violent system [but] I do not believe it can be defeated by violence' and, 'as soon as you pick up a rock ... you've accepted the terms dictated by a system that is always telling us that force is the only solution' (58). But after the Quebec City FTAA protests (April 2001) the picture is different. In the article 'Beyond Violence and Nonviolence' she acknowledges the validity of arguments for 'high confrontational' (though no longer 'violent') struggle, and maintains that couching the debate in the terms she herself earlier used is constricting, at a time when 'we're moving onto unmapped territory, creating a politics that has not yet been defined' (96). By Genoa (July 2001), Starhawk is prepared to declare her sisterhood with the black bloc-ers, who represent 'rage, impatience, militant fervor without which we devitalize ourselves' (123). The attempt here is explicitly to transcend the use of the word 'violence' – which is also invoked by the phrase 'non-violence'. It is intended to silence what Starhawk sees as a politically crippling debate, because of the loaded nature of the word itself.

The word violence was also effectively swept under the carpet by the third global conference of the PGA network in Cochabamba, Bolivia. In September 2001, the conference plenary agreed to strike the phrase 'non-violent' from the network's fourth hallmark that originally called for 'non-violent direct action and civil disobedience', inserting the wording on 'maximising respect for life'. According to one participant (El Viejo 2002):

The problem with the old formulation was first that the word 'Non-violence' has very different meanings in India (where it means respect for life) and in the West (where it means also respect for private property). This basic misunderstanding has proved quite impossible to correct in media – or indeed in the movement itself. The North American movement felt that the term could be understood to not allow for a diversity of tactics or even contribute to the criminalisation of part of the movement. The Latin American organisations had also objected to the term ... [since] 'non-violence' seemed to imply a rejection of huge parts of the history of resistance of these peoples.

The conference had opened on 16 September 2001, when it was still unclear what would happen to social mobilisation after the attacks on the Pentagon and World Trade Center. The wars in Afghanistan and Iraq, however, certainly generated renewed protest, only this time against the backdrop of extremely violent actions by the state. In such a situation, complaints about violent protest were felt to be wearing thin in the public discourse, and it seems that many activists no longer felt themselves obliged to defend their actions as non-violent. When asked about violence during George W. Bush's upcoming visit to Rome, Luca Cassarini, a leader of the non-anarchist *disobedienti* (formerly the 'White Overalls') replied: 'If a criminal of the calibre of Bush is given the red carpet treatment, then rage is the right reaction' (BBC News, 28 May 2004), adding that 'compared to a hundred thousand civilian deaths in Iraq, a few broken windows are hardly what will bother the Italian public'. At the same time, forces on the mainstream left who would denounce anarchist violence were caught in an uncomfortable position: how could they do so while supporting parts of the armed Palestinian or Iraqi resistance movements, without being portrayed as no more than 'Not In My Back Yard' pacifists? Their only available response would be to argue that Palestinians and Iraqis were resisting an illegal occupation, and that the US and Israeli armies are not the same as a legitimate domestic police force – a point with which anarchists would obviously disagree.

At this juncture, then, it would appear that the taboo over violent protest has been somewhat eroded, not so much by anarchists as by the frequency of warfare. With it, arguments which seek to preserve the 'non-violent credentials' of anarchist actions are losing their relevance. This, along with the inherent difficulty of the debate, may explain why it has been abandoned. But there are still issues to be clarified, and new perspectives to be offered. To do so, I would now like to enter into a critical engagement with some of the major discussions of violence in academic literature. Through the process of clarifying their weaknesses, I will be able to offer what I believe is a more genuine answer to the initial question in the debate: What *is* violence?

RECONSIDERING OUR DEFINITIONS

Violence is a concept with which it is famously difficult to come to terms. As Argentinian anarchist writer Eduardo Colombo points out, the word has an especially expansive semantic field:

Violence is not a unified conceptual category. The most general content of the word refers to an excessive, uncontrolled, brutal, abusive force. The violence of rain, wind, fire. If one wants to coerce someone by force, one does him violence. But one can coerce by other means – threat, *bons sentiments*, deceit. A body or a conscience is violated. But one also does oneself violence to overcome one's anger. One has a violent and devouring passion for a woman or for liberty. Violent are despotism and tyranny. (Colombo 2000)

Because of this complexity, a first step we must take towards making the debate more manageable is to segregate away the metaphorical uses of the word, narrowing down our discussion to the senses of violence relevant to the present issue: those which refer to interaction between human beings. Now in this realm, one distinguishing feature immediately presents itself; in all its uses that refer to human interaction, violence is universally thought of as something bad, as a disvalue. It is trivial that, all other things being equal, less violence is better than more. Even where violence is widely thought to be justified (e.g. self-defence against a life-threatening attack), it is intuitively seen as something bad, albeit that it is intended to prevent something worse. The controversy over the definition of violence is precisely about where we *allocate* this negative normative charge. What is it about violence that is by definition bad, even if justifiable? The first two definitions that I will be dealing with here are problematic precisely because they mistake the negativity of violence for its defining feature, instead of it being of a *property* of that feature.

Robert Paul Wolff defines violence, in its 'distinctive political sense', as 'the illegitimate or unauthorized use of force to effect decisions against the will or desire of others' (Wolff 1969: 606). Force alone is clearly not violence – consider a doctor setting a dislocated shoulder – and thus political violence is force proscribed by a source of political legitimacy, i.e. the state. Now since, as a philosophical anarchist, Wolff thinks that the legitimacy of state authority cannot be in any case established, he concludes that its proscription of uses of force can never carry any moral weight. Wolff concludes that the concept of political violence is nonsensical, since lacking a valid source of political legitimacy it is impossible to distinguish between legitimate and illegitimate uses of force. As a result, 'no coherent answers could ever be given [to familiar questions] such as: when is it permissible to resort to violence in politics; whether the black movement and the student movement should be nonviolent; and whether anything good in politics is ever accomplished by violence' (602).

There are two problems with this definition. First, the use of physical force is hardly the only type of action that can qualify as violent. It would mean, at odds with ordinary usage and belief, that systematic emotional abuse is not violent. A definition of violence which pays no attention to non-physical actions fails to address central senses of the term. Second, and more fundamentally, the definition is indeed nonsensical. It entails that no act of force by a legitimate authority (if such could exist) could ever be considered violent. According to such a definition an execution, unlike murder, is simply not a violent act (Wolff's example). It also implies that in a gunfight between guerrillas and military forces, both of whom are doing the exact same thing, only the former's actions are violent while the latter's are not. Wolff wants these fallacies, because he is deliberately steering towards a nonsensical definition that he can dismiss as nonsensical. He is not really demolishing the concept of political violence, but only a tailor-made concept defined by its negative status as such.

What Wolff is really getting at is a more general argument, similar to those offered by Ashen Ruins and Bauman above. The concept of violence, he says, 'serves as a rhetorical device for proscribing those political uses of force which one considers inimical to one's central interests' (613). The dispute is irredeemably mired in ideological rhetoric, designed to halt, slow or hasten change in the existing distribution of power and privilege in America – depending on the class position of the observer. Established financial and political interests identify violence squarely with illegality and condemn all challenges to the authority of the state and property rights. Middle-class liberals encourage some illegal dissent and disruption (rent strikes, sit-ins), but only so long as it does not challenge the economic and social arrangements on which their comfortable position is based. For reactionary white constituencies, 'violence' is any threat from the outclass – street crime, ghetto riots and civil rights marches. Whereas for the black outclass and its sympathisers in the liberal wing, the meaning of 'violence' is typically reversed to apply to the police not rioters, to employers not strikers, etc. Wolff's definition may be a useful springboard for advancing such a critique, but it takes us nowhere towards a better understanding of the concept.

Another political theorist, Ted Honderich, seeks a definition that is sufficient for discussing the moral dilemmas of political violence for the 'left'. An act of violence, he stipulates, is 'a use of considerable or destroying force against people or things, a use of force that offends against a norm' (Honderich 1989: 8). The same two problems are present here: the arbitrary exclusion of non-physical acts, and the fact that the definition does not allocate the disvalue of violence to anything, only states that it exists – a norm is offended. The immediate question is, of course, Whose norm? But Honderich sidesteps this question. He states that the forms of violence he wants to consider cover 'such things as race riots, the destruction by fire and bomb of pubs and shops, kidnapping, hijacking, injuring, maiming and killing', as well as riots 'despite their non-rational momentum'. As a result, the deciding factor for defining 'political' violence is that it is directed against the government. So for all relevant purposes, he says, a 'norm' is simply substitutable for criminal law. Thus *political* violence is a use of force as above, inasmuch as it is 'prohibited by law and directed to a change in the policies, personnel, or system of government, and hence to changes in society' (151).

Honderich thus offers another tailor-made definition of political violence which ends up being identical to Wolff's. The substitution of illegality for a norm, introduced to define an act as *political*, ends up also being what defines it as *violent*. But such a substitution is unjustified since Honderich, like Wolff, does not think that state authority enjoys any moral status *a priori*. As a result illegality cannot by itself be the deciding factor on whether something is violent – a different source of the concept's negative charge, independent of political considerations, inevitably needs to be stipulated.

Both authors do so, but only under their breath. Honderich later refers to the cost of violence as 'distress' (195) – intuitively an unpleasant feeling or situation, perhaps temporary, and not necessarily physical. While Wolff states that beyond the 'distinctive political' concept of violence which he has rejected, the word could also be 'construed in the restricted sense as bodily interference or the direct infliction of physical harm' (1969: 608). And indeed, harm as the central criterion for defining violence is central to a third attempt at definition that I want to discuss, this time coming from the field of critical criminology.

Peter Iadicola and Anson Shupe (1998: 15) criticise theories of violence which narrow the domain of studied violence to deviant behaviour that is incidental to the social order, while bracketing violence that is used to maintain that order (which is seen as legitimate and necessary). Such traditional approaches to the study of violence, which the authors call 'order' approaches, also stress culturally relative definitions of violence, alongside an assumption that violence is inherent rather than learned. On the other hand, the 'conflict' approach they suggest to violence is informed by a Marxist-oriented emphasis on conflict as endemic to class, gender and ethnic divisions in the population. A conflict approach to violence recognises that the distinction between violence as crime or as punishment is politically partisan and should be rejected. Here, then, the distinction between violence and illegality is decisive, avoiding the central problem with the previous accounts.

Iadicola and Shupe thus offer a definition of violence as 'any action or structural arrangement that results in physical or nonphysical harm to one or more persons' (23). Here, then, the negative charge of violence is allocated to *harm*. The authors further define (a) personal violence as 'violence that occurs between people acting *outside* the role of agent or representative of a social institution' and (b) societal violence, divided into (b1) institutional violence – 'violence by individuals whose actions are governed by the roles that they are playing in an institutional context'; and (b2) structural violence – harm caused 'in the context of establishing, maintaining, extending or reducing the hierarchical ordering of categories of people in society'.

Structural violence can be exercised, then, both for and against hierarchy. The authors note that, according to their definition, actions or structural arrangements that cause harm must be wilfully perpetuated, reproduced or condoned to be considered violent (so harmful accidents are excluded). However, violence occurs whether harm is the primary intention of an action or only its foreseeable byproduct. Furthermore, on this definition an act of violence may be justified or unjustified; it may harm either physical or psychological well-being (or both); and it may or may not be recognized as 'violence' by the perpetrator and/or the recipient. The authors need this final clause in order to avoid cultural relativism, and include all cases of racist and sexist violence, however normalised they may be in a society.

While this definition of violence alleviates many of the concerns attached to the earlier, legitimacy-based definitions, several issues remain. First, it should be clarified that while the definition may avoid cultural relativism, it does not avoid relativism altogether. This is not necessarily a problem, but it should be acknowledged here that a more strict anti-relativist stance around violence – one that says that the fact that an act has caused harm can only be established subject to verification by a non-partisan participant – is not sustainable. At its base, the authors' reference to their definition as 'universal *as opposed to* relative' is misplaced because it fails to distinguish between total and bounded relativism. Bounded relativism argues that it is impossible for individuals to completely step outside themselves and enter a neutral vantage point, or another person's shoes, and make fully objective observations about human existence. However, the presence of culturally or even biologically shared human contexts marks out the boundaries within which there can be such a thing as truth, and therefore protects us from the extremes of radical relativism. Such a bounded relativism is capable of granting *some* subjective truths an independent status, when the demand for external verification conflicts with other, more basic or important considerations.

One such consideration is the elusive nature of psychological harm. Studies on Post-Traumatic Stress Disorder point out, for example, that a person may sustain psychological harm, without displaying any unambiguous symptoms thereof. With or without symptoms, connecting psychological harm to a particular incident is not always straightforward – a victim may have suppressed details of a traumatic event in his or her own memory, sometimes as far as 'erasing' the event altogether, thus retaining the harm without being able to trace it to a cause. For reasons such as these, psychological harm by its nature stands at an unfair disadvantage to physical injury in terms of its verifiability. With it, the observer needs to perform a more extended exercise in interpretation in order to substantiate that violence has occurred.

Moreover, the complaint of the victim of violence is often what prompts the very act of interpretation and, no less often, is the only input on which the interpretation can be based. Imagine that *A* and *B* are divorcees who have just exchanged some harsh words. *B* says she has suffered psychological harm because on two occasions *A* used language that she perceived as abusive and threatening. However, the words were abusive only in the context of some very idiosyncratic, perhaps embarrassing sensibility, that only she and *A* are aware of (and which *A* was prodding on purpose). An external observer, to whom *B*'s sensibilities are entirely alien, might fail to understand how the words could possibly be abusive. Here, Iadicola and Shupe's definitions would indicate that the only way to determine that *A*'s action caused *B* psychological harm is to *believe B that she actually felt what she says she felt*. If the demand for universality is uncompromising, then as a subjective utterance *B*'s complaint on its own cannot enjoy any credence.

So much for bounded relativism. There is, however, another important anomaly. Imagine *A* throws a punch at *B*, and misses. No harm has been done, but surely the act is violent. In case psychological harm might be stipulated, assume also that B has been in many fights before – maybe A missed because B was skilled enough to dodge the blow. At any event, B can conceivably walk away from the exchange without having sustained any psychological harm – but still the exchange can only have been violent. This calls into question the very status of 'harm' as the appropriate defining characteristic of violence.

Consider also recent footage from the anti-G8 blockades in Stirling, Scotland (resist.nl 2005), depicting a scene described in the opening pages of this book. A black bloc is moving down a road and approaching a line of riot police, officers in padded armour carrying large, transparent plastic shields. The protesters intend to break through the line, and make for the nearby motorway. Shouts are heard, a few objects are thrown, miss, or hit the policemen's shields. Then a group of protesters uses a makeshift battering-ram made of large inflated tyres to push through the centre of the police line. Others are throwing more objects, using intimidating language, and cheering. One person strikes an officer's shield with a golf club. If the footage is faithful to reality, and inasmuch as the policemen are trained for such situations or have been in them before, then it is hard to see where any physical or psychological harm is being done to persons in this particular exchange. Nevertheless, the protesters are very obviously being violent. Why?

What is really happening here is the enactment of a set-piece violent exchange in which both sides know what variables are at work. The protesters and police have both considered, and probably drilled, this eventuality. Why did the police allow the protesters through? One could imagine that a commanding officer would give the order to stand down in such a situation, following contingency guidelines issued to him in advance. He is effectively responding, in a way prescribed in advance, to the cost–benefit calculus imposed by the protesters' actions. For example, he could have judged that it was impossible to contain the protesters at this place and time without mounting a counter-assault, which would be more costly (in terms of potential injury to officers or even to the police's public image) than to call in a larger force that would try to confront the protesters elsewhere. However, what is just as likely is that the policemen are acting of themselves, on the basis of the same cost–benefit calculation but only inasmuch as it is sublimated in their training. They are generating a spontaneous, self-organised response to the protesters that can only end up letting the latter through.

In both cases, the protesters have exerted from the police a behaviour that is against their interests – they have *coerced* them. This is clearly a case of power-over, but not enough in itself to establish violence. Where this exchange is violent is in the *currency* of the convincing communication: masked faces, offensive force, verbal abuse. It is violence because although the policemen may be neither harmed nor afraid, they do feel (at least to some degree) *attacked* and/or *endangered*. This is, to be sure, a unique situation: bodily harm would easily be involved if the police were not so padded and shielded. This is not the typical situation in which we form our notions of violence. But it does isolate their basic source, which is every person's embodied experiences of violence on the *receiving* side. Such a concept of violence centrally involves a sense of manifest vulnerability, and the infringement (violation) of one's immediate physical space. The horrible thing about torture is the forced bodily and mental intimacy with the torturer.

Let me suggest, then, that *an act is violent if its recipient experiences it as an attack or as deliberate endangerment*. This definition encompasses all the forms of violence mentioned by Honderich as 'political violence' (which are also the relevant ones for anarchist preoccupations), as well as violence in the personal(-is-political) sphere. Like Iadicola and Shupe's definition, the present one may be extended to an account of institutional and structural violence. As a definition of violence that builds on individuals' shared embodied experiences, it clearly includes emotional and psychological forms of violence, which we also experience bodily. Taken alone, it makes no political distinctions: it covers both the protester being clubbed and the policeman subjected to a volley of Molotovs; the prisoner led to execution and the tyrant dying with a bullet in his chest. Unlike Wolff's definition, violence is not necessarily bound up with the application of physical force, only with the bringing about of an embodied experience of violation – often deliberately, but sometimes without great sensitivity to what the recipient is experiencing. It can avoid cultural relativism since our intimate experiences of violence in everyday life are largely of a common pool. Differences certainly exist among individuals, social classes and cultures in terms of the average frequency and intensity of violence in one's life, but the raw experience of violation seems to be very broadly shared. Even a person who has had a relatively sheltered biography can draw the connection between their own experiences of violation and those of individuals who are subject to it more frequently and/or intensely.

On this definition, credence must be given to the victim reporting her or his experience, but that an attack or endangerment have occurred will usually still be verifiable against reasonable interpretations of bodily symptoms and/or known circumstances. This is still bounded relativism, but it is certainly better than basing one's definition of violence on legitimacy, when the latter is acknowledged to be a matter of 'superstition and myth' (Wolff 1969: 610). It seems preferable to have things hinge on shared embodied experience than on successful brain-washing.

While the great majority of actions perceived as an attack or danger also cause harm, there are also types of harm that are not thus perceived and are therefore not violent in the sense suggested here. What I have in mind is harm as a foreseeable byproduct of an action, where the perpetrator and the victim are not known to one another – what Iadicola and Shupe do include in their categories. This would mean that it is not violent if a pharmaceutical company distributes drugs that it knows may be harmful but does not care, resulting in the deaths of children. This is harmful, and certainly unjust, but it is only rhetorical or swear-word violence, not the real thing. Likewise, property destruction that is not witnessed, and causes nobody to feel attacked, is not violent *even if* it harms someone's livelihood. This, however, does not mean that property destruction is never violent. I am referring to the violation that people often experience in the *context* of public anarchist actions of property destruction. The frame of thinking needs to be broadened here to consider the violence of the situation, not of any particular instance of an arm lifting a crowbar. A situation as a whole can be violent whether violation is the goal or the byproduct of any particular action that happens within it – what matters is whether it involves humans experiencing it as an attack or anticipating it as a danger *while it is happening*. If anarchists trash a gas station in the dead of night, or at a midday protest when the station is closed while the neighbours are out in the street giving water to the protesters and partaking of looted food (as happened during the 2003 G8 protests in Lausanne, cf. Anonymous6 2003) – then the action is not violent. But if the kid behind the counter at a Shell gas station feels attacked and in danger when anarchists begin smashing it up during a demonstration, then that act is indeed violent, even if the anarchists reassure us (and the kid behind the counter) that nobody was even dreaming of hurting him. Similarly if a passer-by thinks that the anarchists are about to attack him, it is also inevitably a violent situation. In neither case does this necessarily mean that the violence is unjustified or unacceptable, only that it is there. Now we can move to the core of the debate: the justification of violence.

LIMITS TO JUSTIFICATION

In discussing the justification of anarchist violence, we should begin by setting the terms of the debate. What needs to be clarified from the outset is *who is justifying what to whom*. We may easily assume that it is an *anarchist* who wants to justify a *violent action* (as defined above). With the question *to whom* there is larger difficulty. On the one hand, if the listener is another anarchist, then the discussion may become too dependent on shared views, and thus self-referential, prone to uncritical thinking and potentially blind to the concerns of people outside the movement. On the other hand, if the listener does not share any values with the anarchist, then the discussion itself is pointless – if one thinks anarchist goals are by themselves unjustified, then no means to achieve those goals can be justified, violent or not. In order to keep the debate within controllable parameters, then, let us take the middle road and assume that an anarchist is trying to justify a hypothetical or intended violent action to an ally outside the movement – a person who may identify with the anarchist's general goals, but not so much that s/he will accept anything.

Such a person would have serious problems with the first kind of argument that I want to examine, one that denies that a debate over justification is to be had altogether. What I have in mind is the a-moral celebration of instinctual violence sometimes forwarded in post-leftist and (more typically) primitivist anarchist writing. Such an attitude rejects moral discourse as such, since it is taken to be a vestige of hierarchical civilisation and domestication, a construct standing in the way of instinct and wildness which are seen as the original and repressed mode of human existence. Such an attitude sees violence against the existing order as valid *a priori*, because it expresses an unmediated realisation of desire and affords a connection to the individual's animality. For Gimli (2004):

Reconnecting with our wild selves through violent conflict with our oppressors is one essential, and often overlooked, aspect of the rewilding project ... No other species relies on institutions to settle disputes or 'protect' them. Breaking down these institutions and taking responsibility for our own lives is not only key to anarchy, but also part of deconstructing society back into the wild. ... The examples of this process are limitless, but share a common characteristic:

complete disregard for the legal, moral, and physical boundaries of claimed authority ... every smashed piece of technology, every punched TV reporter, every burnt bank ... every wounded soldier, every knee-capped executive ... every castrated rapist, every beheaded king ... and every dead cop is the derivative of a rewilding act.

Now there is something disingenuous about Gimli's argument. Acts like torching a bank, destroying a laboratory or assassinating a politician may arouse a sense of wildness and immediacy when they are carried out, but they are not really 'wild' since they require careful planning, timing and calculation. One's 'feral self' can hardly read a map, prepare a detonator or drive an escape vehicle. Using wildness as a blank cheque for acts that are, in fact, the product of a distinctly civilised self is an easy way to dismiss dilemmas that should not be so ignored.

More materially, however, the major problem with such arguments is that they foreclose the debate itself. Unreflective, wild violence is by definition something that cannot be rationally discussed since it belongs to the realm of the irrational. Setting things in these terms has very little significance unless one already accepts the background discourse to which they are attached – which is not even shared by the majority of anarchists. And while anarchists may have good reasons to think that moral categories are oppressive and constructed to the benefit of dominant groups, this does not exclude discussions of violence that have some common ground against which justification can be tested.

Moving on to concerns that can be rationally discussed, our next step is to address what is probably the most prevalent point of contention, namely, the argument that violence is inherently inconsistent with anarchists' own values and principles. April Carter (1978: 327–8) reviews two typical versions of this argument. Here is the first:

Anarchist values are inherently and necessarily incompatible with the use of violence, given anarchist respect for the sovereignty of the individual and belief in the unqualified rights of each individual. No anarchist society would sanction one execution, let alone mass executions or wars on other societies ... if anarchists distrust political fictions that justify the denial of actual freedoms, they must distrust more a style of [instrumental, 'Leninist'] thinking which justifies the most final denial of freedom – death.

This argument is attractive at first sight, but ultimately fails because it relies on a vast stretching of principles. If this argument is right, then anarchists are also supposed to rule out purely defensive lethal violence against life-endangering assault. But not only anarchists would say that even the supreme right to life may have to be violated by killing an otherwise unstoppable homicidal aggressor. Even if anarchists really thought in terms of individual sovereignty and rights (which are taken from the language of Enlightenment liberalism), they would hardly believe them to be 'unqualified'. No individual, for example, is thought to have the 'right' to exploit or abuse another person, and doing so is not part of the anarchist notion of freedom, which is socialist and communitarian. Attaching anarchism to necessary pacifism on such absolutist terms does not work.

The uncritical expectation of purism on behalf of anarchists also colours a second version of the argument (Carter 1978: 333–4). Anarchists' principles, it can be said, lead them to reject centralisation and parties,

shunning contamination with politics in all its conventional forms, refusing to endorse even progressive parties or to take part in elections, however crucial the possible outcome ... when it comes to violence, however, many anarchists are prepared to use a little violence to prevent greater violence by the state, or even a lot of violence to try to achieve the anarchist vision of society. It would seem that the logic of this approach is that it is worse to cast a ballot than to fire a bullet ... the utopianism of anarchism logically entails also the utopianism of pacifism, in the sense of rejecting all forms of organized violence.

This is again a straw man. Anarchists *do* often cooperate with non-anarchist organisations, NGOs and even political parties such as the Greens on particular campaigns and mobilisations. In the 2004 US elections there were some anarchists who took the strategic decision to cast a ballot for John Kerry, in compromise of their principles, and not for any positive reason but only in order to avert what they saw as the much greater evil of a second Bush term. Anarchists, then, should not be expected to be purist to the point of ridicule – there remains a room for compromise, the debate being over where to draw the line. Since they do not claim to be fully consistent in their rejection of state politics, the parallel expectation of pure non-violence also falls away.

The salient issue which these two arguments orbit, but do not touch, is the one of prefigurative politics. Can violence ever be coherent with strategies that are an embryonic representation of an anarchist society? Unlike other revolutionary movements, anarchists explicitly distance themselves from the position that the end justifies the means. They cannot say that violence, on whatever level, would be justified just because it helps achieve a free society. Rather, they believe that means and ends should always be of the same substance. The argument thus tends to take the following, straightforward form: 'Anarchists want a non-violent society. Anarchists also believe that the revolutionary movement should prefigure the desired society in its means and ways. Therefore, anarchists cannot use violence to achieve a non-violent society'. This argument again seems very logical, but it fails on several counts. Beginning with the first premise, it is simply untrue that anarchists desire a 'non-violent society' and nothing else. If lack of violence were the only issue, then one might expect anarchists to equally desire a hypothetical totalitarian state, in which the threat of Draconian sanctions is so effective that all citizens obey the law and the state consequentially does not need to ever actually use violence. The point, of course, is that anarchists want a stateless, *voluntarily* non-violent society. Given this, it should first be emphasised that the type of violence anarchists are *primarily* concerned with abolishing is violent enforcement or institutional violence – an area in which complaints about prefiguration are irrelevant since anarchists certainly do not promote or use these forms.

As for non-institutional, sporadic and diffuse instances of violence, it is misleading to say that anarchists want a society from which they are simply absent. Again, they seek a society from which they are absent voluntarily. If an anarchist society were to be purely non-violent, it could only be so because all individuals choose to refrain from violence. But precisely because of its voluntary nature, the non-violence that anarchists promote for their desired society can only exist within the terms of an all-sided concord. As indicated by the discussion of open-endedness in Chapter 2, the proposed goal is an elusive one and by no means failsafe: violence would still exist, even in a world without states and armed groups, if someone chose to perpetrate it. In the present tense, the prefigurative realisation of such an anarchist model of voluntary non-violence is clearly impossible, since the state rejects such a set-up and consistently resorts to violence. Because of the state's preparedness to resort to violence, the anarchist model of non-violence by universal consent simply cannot be enacted in the present tense. It could be argued, then, that at least when it comes to violence, the idea of prefigurative politics can only be enacted *within* present-day anarchist settings – that is, in the striving for social relations free of violence within the movement itself, incorporating peaceful conflict resolution, mediation or – in case of unbridgeable differences – secession.

Finally, it can be argued that anarchist violence against the state *is* precisely prefigurative of anarchist social relations. This is because anarchists would always expect people, even in an 'anarchist society', to defend it (violently if necessary) from any attempt to reconstitute social hierarchy or impose it on others. Thus violent action taken against the (re)production of a hierarchical social order is as appropriate now as it will be in a stateless society.

So much for responding to claims that violence can *never* be justified by anarchists. But the onus is still on anarchists to argue that violence *can* ever be justified, and to specify what justification would entail. In the remainder of this section I want to take a critical look at a number of arguments that anarchists typically use to this end, which are by no means free of problems.

When speaking of violence, anarchists tend to draw all manner of distinctions. They distinguish between the violence of individuals and the organised violence of groups; between unprovoked and defensive violence; between violence as an act and violence as the property of an institution; and (obviously) between the violence of the state and revolutionary violence. The latter is said to be justifiable because it is qualitatively different to that of the state – in its type, the spirit in which it is used, its extent and targets. April Carter reviews such distinctions between state violence and the archetypes of lethal anarchist violence – the assassination of an individual tyrant and insurrectionary armed struggle. Anarchist violence in both cases, she points out, relies on limited technology, is a 'heroic' form of violence involving direct risk to those who take part (unlike the judge or general), and can be limited in its extent and discriminate in its targets (unlike the indiscriminate killing of most warfare). When it comes to justification, however, the use of such distinctions is a bit dubious. It 'justifies' some violence by way of its qualitative segregation away from forms that anarchists reject, without specifying why the distinction is important. That people are outnumbered and under-armed does not automatically justify their actions, even if their ends are just. Such distinctions are, at their base, simplistic 'just war' rhetoric intended to draw the discussion in directions that are convenient for anarchists.

Another example for such an argument of convenience is the extension of the logic of self-defence – a very common excuse for anarchist violence. Today, many anarchists legitimise throwing stones, bottles and Molotovs at riot police as an act of self-defensive violence, defence not only of their own bodies but of a liberated urban space (whether a temporary one during a protest or a more permanent one like a squat facing eviction). The argument is an attractive starting point because it begins from a form of violence that is almost universally legitimated. Self-defence, however, is a dangerous source of justification because it can easily be stretched in a very problematic way:

The slave is always in a state of legitimate defence and consequently, his violence against the boss, against the oppressor, is always morally justifiable. [It] must be controlled only by such considerations as that the best and most economical use is being made of human effort and human sufferings. (Malatesta 1921)

This stretching of the concept of self-defence to justify any and every 'pre-emptive strike' smacks of dishonesty. It depends on equating capitalism with slavery, erasing the distinction between metaphorical slavery and the real thing, which still exists today in large parts of the world (see ASI 2005). The exploitation of the worker, who has no choice but to sell her or his labour power under structurally unjust conditions, is very different from that of the chattel slave, who is extended *no* rights and who may face direct bodily violence if s/he does not work or tries to escape. Papering over this difference is intended only in order to tag any agent of capital or the state as a slave-holder, a convenient way to dehumanise 'class enemies' for the sole purpose of making the violation of persons more palatable.

The valuable point, however, is in the second sentence of Malatesta's argument. Surely violence against the oppressor is not morally justifiable 'always', but only if there is an effort to minimize human effort and suffering (or, as some would have it, to 'maximise respect for life'). To justify a specific violent act, then, we would inevitably need to think about its overall consequences. Here, it is possible to return to Wolff. He proposes that while the political sense of violence he constructs is nonsensical, 'moral philosophy in general' can in fact deal with justified and unjustified violence. Here, 'the obvious but correct rule is to resort to violence when less harmful or costly means fail, providing always that the balance of good and evil produced is superior to that promised by any available alternative' (Wolff 1969: 608). With the appropriate modifications to how violence is defined, this rule seems commonsensical. It seems uncontroversial that it is better to try and liberate oneself, if possible, by non-violent methods rather than to exalt violence as the default form of revolutionary action. Can this 'obvious but correct' rule finally give anarchists some useful criterion for deciding whether to resort to violence at any given juncture?

Unfortunately, despite the straightforward nature of this rule it leaves open two grave difficulties. The first is how exactly 'resorting to violence' is framed. For in fact, this term may be seen to cover almost all available courses of political action including, most importantly, legal ones. This is because any appeal to, or pressure on, the state to back one's goals is, implicitly or explicitly, an attempt to solicit its violent capabilities to one's side. To take an historical example: while the American civil rights movement is often credited with the use of non-violent means, the abolition of legalised segregation in the United States was in fact accomplished through what was clearly a series of violent state interventions, most notably sending in the National Guard to oversee the desegregation of schools in southern states (Meyers 2000). Likewise, in wilderness protection, legal action is clearly a violent means: receiving a court injunction against a logging company means that the latter is to withdraw from timber harvesting, otherwise it will be forced to do so, or punished for not doing so, ultimately involving the armed might of the government. State intervention in such cases may not actually amount to bodily interference or the direct infliction of physical harm, but these acts of violence are always in place as a threat, and can in principle be enacted if the threatened party does not comply earlier. Thus in choosing legal means we do not determine that violence will not be introduced into the situation: we only entrust the decision on whether this will happen to the state. Such considerations seem to put a very stringent limitation on what can be considered 'non-violent action', restricting it only to the most passive forms of intervention.

The second difficulty comes from the fact that a framework of justification necessarily depends on the success of violent actions. Violence might be justified if it achieves some purpose, but it is certainly never justified if it fails. According to Wolff, we are to resort to violence only provided that the balance of good and evil that comes about as a result is superior to that created by any other course of action. But the kind of calculations this calls for are extremely difficult to carry out. Success is very hard to judge in retrospect, let alone to predict. To begin with, it is impossible to foresee with any certainty the results of a violent action (or any other action for that matter), since the factors that come into play are too numerous and contingent. A violent action may or may not involve injury to persons other than the intended target; it may or may not give rise to increased state repression; and it may or may not achieve the desired results. Since there is scant historical evidence to put the case one way or the other, it is doubtful whether any stable criteria can be established for judging whether a certain course of action is more harmful or costly than another. Discussing five possible scenarios of political violence motivated by an egalitarian agenda, with different degrees of success and different upshots of state repression, Honderich concludes that the probabilities for a lower balance of distress after the event 'will be close to their critical level ... for the most part we cannot judge the relevant probabilities with the precision needed for rational confidence. Certainly judgement between alternatives is necessary, and almost certainly there is a right judgement. That it can be made with rational confidence is unlikely' (1989: 196–7).

This is, I am afraid, as far as the discussions of violence and justification can reach. No fully secure answer can be given to prevalent anarchist dilemmas around violence, such as whether it 'sends a radical message' or 'just alienates the public'. The final and *insecure* judgement-call on whether to engage violence can only remain, at the end of the day, in the hands of the individual. However, the framework offered here does disentangle the debate, and offers some clear markers for such decisions. All that can be prescribed beyond this is clear-headed consideration, avoidance of easy rhetoric that only serves for self-assurance, and a new form of 'diversity of tactics' under which the debate over violence is not silenced, but undertaken in a constructive manner that takes full account of the gravity of violating human beings.

EMPOWERMENT, REVENGE AND ARMED STRUGGLE

The final section of this chapter is dedicated to three further issues concerning violence, which follow on from the previous discussion.

The first is related to the ethos of prefigurative politics discussed above. This ethos may introduce a further requirement for justifying anarchist violence beyond the striving, however imperfect, to minimise it – namely that the use of violence should also be a worthwhile experience in its own right. We can ask, specifically, whether the experience of violence can by itself be liberating, empowering and radicalising for those involved.

In his participant's analysis of two anti-capitalist riots in 2003, Tadzio Mueller (2004) distinguishes between the 'collective effervescence' of spontaneous but tactically effective violent moments, and the disempowerment associated with the stale reproduction of ritualised confrontation. An example for the first type of event is a confrontation he witnessed at a blockade against the Evian G8 summit. The blockade, near the French town of Annemasse where many of the activists had been camping, was supposed to be symbolic and non-confrontational. It was set to take place on the main route into Evian – which the police had already decided, in anticipation of protests, not to use for transporting any delegates or support staff (they were instead driven to Lausanne and ferried across Lake Geneva). The event was organised, under strict non-violence guidelines, by the ATTAC coalition – which despite its militant-sounding name is in fact a reformist group lobbying for taxation of financial transactions. However, events took an unexpected turn as the march approached the point of blockade, and received an unprovoked tear-gas attack:

After initially retreating about 50–100 metres and recovering from the initial shock, a number of masked activists, not affiliated with ATTAC, began building a barricade, while others threw stones at the police. Soon, one of the activists who had expressed her anxieties during the march passed me carrying an armful of wood for the barricade – which had by now been set alight – exhorting me to join the effort: almost the whole march participated.

In this situation, activists without an experience in confrontation were able to draw on a new and alien action repertoire. As a result, they later reported experiencing a moment of rupture through which certain things that were 'impossible' prior to the riot had now become possible. Such effervescent riots, Mueller says, are empowering because they can produce sudden changes in the established mindset of activists, which last beyond the event and have effects beyond the circle of immediate participants, thanks to the diffusion of their stories in movement networks. On the other hand, during the Thessaloniki EU summit a few months later, virtually everyone had arrived in town expecting a massive riot. For weeks activists had been stockpiling Molotovs, slingshots and shields. The street fighting began almost as soon as the march left the university campus, stones and firebombs were thrown, tear-gas was fired and shops were burned. Within a few hours it was over, and the protesters returned to the safe haven of the university. Many participants felt that the whole event had been staged. Analysing this event, Mueller notes that it was not merely as the result of rote repetition that the militants in Greece kicked off, it was a 'rational' response to the structure of the field of militant activism, embodied in a militant habitus which generated a massively violent, but thoroughly expected riot ... in spite of all the nihilist graffiti and radical posturing on the squatted campus, all that happened was a mere (re-)enactment and reproduction of traditions, habiti, rituals, and power structures – from this perspective, the riots were more conservative than radical.

As Sian Sullivan further argues, there are also serious feminist issues with such unreflectively militant environments, since they

valorise physical strength, machismo (in relation to other men as well as to women), and emotional passivity ... one which is akin to that also represented by the machismo of a male dominated, body-armoured riot police. Given reports of sexual harassment made by women at the anarchist encampment at Thessaloniki ... it indeed is tempting to see an emerging dynamic in militant factions whereby 'worthy' political violence is transmuted and normalised 'back' into the banal and disempowering violence of everyday sexism. (Sullivan 2004: 29–30)

So violence may indeed be intrinsically valuable, but only if through it people experience self-liberation and a radicalising effect. I would go further to suggest that it is precisely the search for this kind of effervescence – especially the desire to recapture the founding ruptural moments of early mobilisations such as Seattle – that has played a significant part in motivating continued summit protests. However, as is evident from the examples, the potential for rupture stands in inverse proportion to how anticipated it is. The surprising and unexpected nature of such moments is what gives them their special quality. The search for rupture through violent action is therefore likely to be self-defeating, and can easily lead to ritualised and predictable patterns which provide no vitalisation. This is not to say that no new moments of rupture can happen – only that they cannot be engineered.

A second issue I want to discuss is the question of revenge. Can it be considered a valid motivation for violence within an anarchist framework? To examine this question I want to look at two examples of revenge-motivated anarchist actions in order to tease out the source of the tension at hand.

The first example is the shooting of King Umberto I of Italy by the anarchist Gaetano Bresci. In 1898, during protests in Milan over high bread prices, soldiers opened fire and killed hundreds of unarmed protesters who ignored the order to disperse from in front of the city palace. King Umberto later decorated the general who gave the order to shoot, complimenting his 'brave defence of the royal house'. For this symbolic act Bresci, an Italian-American immigrant, resolved to kill the king. He crossed the Atlantic, and on 29 July 1900 he approached the king while he was on a visit to Monza and shot him three times. Umberto died of his wounds, and Bresci was caught and sentenced to hard labour. A year later he was found dead in his prison cell, probably murdered by the guards.

Bresci's act was clearly motivated by revenge, as were many earlier anarchist assassinations, which created a great deal of controversy in the anarchist movement of the time. Emma Goldman, for her part, dedicated several articles to defending Bresci's action and her choice of words says a lot about the problematic status of revenge for anarchists. She argues that anarchist assassins have been extremely gentle and sensitive souls who were driven to desperate action by the indignation they felt in the face of grave social injustices:

High strung, like a violin string, [souls] weep and moan for life, so relentless, so cruel, so terribly inhuman. In a desperate moment the string breaks. Untuned ears hear nothing but discord. But those who feel the agonized cry understand its harmony; they hear in it the fulfilment of the most compelling moment of human nature. (Goldman 1917)

A similar tone is heard from London anarchist poet and polemicist Louisa Bevington (1896). Sometimes, she says, an individual anarchist

feels it impossible in his own case not to abandon the patiently educational for the actively militant attitude, and to hit out, as intelligently and intelligibly as he can, at that which powerfully flouts his creed and humanity's hope, making it (for all its truth, and for all his integrity) a dead letter within his own living, suffering, pitying, aspiring soul.

This is all a bit tragic and Victorian isn't it? Excuses that victimise the perpetrator are not necessarily a credit to a cool-headed, carefully planned assassination like the one Bresci carried out. The problem is that revenge led to individual assassinations with a serious price for the perpetrator and the movement while they were highly unlikely to achieve any lasting social change. Unlike most cases of violence, this course of action can usually be ruled out with rational confidence. The murder of leading politicians, businessmen or armed personnel does not attack the structure of the system in which they are embedded – it only removes a person from a role, not the role itself. There are exceptions to this rule, like taking out a true autocrat on whose person the edifice of government actually depends (someone like Hitler). But otherwise it would appear largely pointless and irresponsible. The question here is whether revenge can be rationally accepted as a justification for calculated action, without 'pleading insanity'. Sometimes it would appear it certainly can, as in the following example of an action often taken against corporate and government figures:

Date: Tue, 27 Jan 2004 12: 36: 26 -0800
From: Biotic Baking Brigade @bbb bioticbakingbrigade.org>
Archived: http: //biotech.indymedia.org/or/2004/02/2254.shtml
Subject: Biotech Baking Brigade Pies Bayer Biotechnician

On 21st January Paul Rylott – top GM scientist at Bayer Cropscience delivered a stirring speech on how to manage consumer response to biotechnology, at a conference on Managing and Predicting Crisis in the Food Industry. As he took his place in the queue for his buffet dinner a polite call of 'Mr Rylott?' brought him face to face with a chocolate fudge cake (skipped and stale) covered with the sweaty rotting whipped cream and the shout 'That's for GM!' before the assaulting party fled.

Some leaflets were given out to the surprised and immobilized crowd and all those protesting left before the cops arrived.

This is part of a national UK campaign against Bayer and against GM commercialization. Actions taken place have included junk mailing, sabotage including lock glueing, spraypainting, window breaking, golf courses destroyed, office occupations, noise demonstrations and trespasses.

On the definitions proposed above, pieing is certainly violent – Rylott no doubt experienced it as an attack. It is also clear that the anarchists are motivated by revenge ('That's for GM!') and that they derive undeniable satisfaction from exacting it. I would suggest, then, that what is disturbing about Bresci's act – unlike that of the Biotic Baking Brigade – is not the motivation of revenge, but only the fact that it does more harm than good. Revenge can indeed be a valid motivation for violent actions, but if we are not to trump any strategical considerations, we should notice that the violence by no means needs to be lethal in order to satisfy our vengeance. Pieing, after all, is nothing but a simulated political assassination. Besides aiming to ridicule and humiliate the victim, the attack also plainly has the intention of intimidating him. He lives to know that the pie could just as well have been a knife or a bullet. A substitute, perhaps, but just as fun.

This leads, finally, to some exploratory remarks on an issue that anarchists will need to consider sooner rather than later – lethal violence in the context of armed insurrection. Such a discussion is clearly impossible without imagining some broader revolutionary scenario, which is inevitably speculative. Still, some things can be said with relative confidence, at least regarding the North.

One should begin by noting that the state's utterly disproportional military might, and powers of surveillance and social control, mean that it simply cannot be defeated in outright battle. Anarchists will probably never get their hands on what it takes to fight against tanks, mines, aeroplanes and so on. This means that, under any foreseeable circumstances, a precondition for any revolutionary social transformation is that most members of the police and army forces *desert* or *defect*. This, further, would seem to only be plausible in the context of an already existing popular mobilisation that is very broad-based and very militant, and which is capable of winning over even serving members of the state's armed wing. So the first conclusion is that while mass insurrection may still be successful under some conditions, it also requires very sustainable foundations in the population

On these considerations, armed struggle seems to be for now a self-defeating prospect. However, what anarchists may consider in this speculative context is the possibility of creating the appropriate conditions for its success. The current swelling of anarchist ranks means that, while there will certainly continue to be a presence on the streets, more energy is also becoming available for pro-active exploits beyond maintaining the public presence of dissent and raising the social costs of state and corporate excesses. The strategic outlook already prevalent among anarchists is that the road to revolution involves the proliferation of urban and rural projects of sustainable living, community-building and the development of skills and infrastructures. But while this is usually couched in terms of 'hollowing out' capitalism, it can also be considered as the creation of a sustainable social base for more militant activity, up to (possibly) insurrection. In such a situation, armed struggle would be undertaken, not by isolated groups of desperadoes, but by communities which have already carved out a significant space of autonomy within hierarchical society. This could happen either in defence from a final, violent attempt of the state to recuperate those

5

Luddites, Hackers and Gardeners

Anarchism and the Politics of Technology

Many of these kingless people rode horses and some wielded iron implements, but this did not make [the Hyksos] any more civilised than the copper-using ancestors of the Ojibwa on the Great Lakes; the horses and iron became productive forces, they became Civilization's technology, only after they became part of Leviathan's armory.
—Fredy Perlman, *Against His-story, Against Leviathan!*

There is a curious ambivalence in contemporary anarchists' relationship with technology. On the one hand, anarchists today are involved in many campaigns in which the introduction of new technologies is explicitly resisted, from bio- and nanotechnology to technologies of surveillance and warfare. At the same time, among social movements in the North anarchists have been making the most extensive and engaged use of information and communication technologies, to the degree of developing their own software platforms. Our archetypical anarchist could pull up genetically modified crops before dawn, report on the action through emails and independent media websites in the morning, take a nap, and then do a bit of allotment gardening in the afternoon and work part-time as a programmer in the evening.

In this chapter, I would like to look beyond this ambivalence towards the critiques and theories that can form a broad-based anarchist politics to technology. This means asking two basic questions. First, can we articulate a critique of technology that is coherent and theoretically sustainable in its own right, while being harmonious with central anarchist political concerns? Second, what types of political action does such a critique point to, once we take into account the broader strategic perspectives that many anarchists already endorse?

I refer to my goal as a 'broad-based' anarchist politics of technology because the major difficulty in approaching the topic is its almost automatic conflation with a particular strand of anarchist thinking, namely anarcho-primitivism. At its base, anarcho-primitivism is a certain outlook or mentality that enjoys significant currency among anarchists, most notably in the North-western United States but also in many other places. This current clearly has strong roots in environmental direct action – as evinced by the titles of prominent publications such as Green Anarchy (US) and Green Anarchist (UK) – and has received elaboration in a number of well-known books and essays (e.g. Perlman 1983, Zerzan 1994, Moore 1997, Watson 1998; Jensen 2000). With inevitable oversimplification, one could say that the most prominent features of an anarcho-primitivist outlook are:

- Very strong political, ecological and spiritual antagonism towards industrialism, technology and hyper-modernity.
- Love of the wild, eco-feminist consciousness and earth-based / non-western spirituality.
- A 'maximalist' anarchist critique of hierarchical civilisation, and of its His-story of domination and destruction from the beginnings of domestication, agriculture and the state.
- A re-appreciation of hunter-gatherer societies as sites of primitive anarchy – egalitarian, peaceable, leisurely, ecstatic and connected to natural cycles.

Although I am personally very sympathetic to this approach, it is very difficult to take it as the starting point for the discussion of technology I want to develop here. Specifically anarcho-primitivist critiques of technology are so thoroughly integrated with the other elements just mentioned, and the current as a whole has generated so much controversy within anarchist circles, that it is impossible to use it as a basis for a broad-based approach. As a result, part of the purpose of this chapter is to free the discussion of technology from its entanglement with anarcho-primitivism – not by rejecting such ideas but by remaining largely neutral towards them. As a result, the discussion in this chapter should be relevant whether or not one endorses an anarcho-primitivist approach.

In what follows, I begin with an overview of the ambivalent anarchist relationship with technology, past and present. I then elaborate a critique of technology based on the abundant output of surprisingly critical literature on technology by non-anarchist writers. Contemporary scholarly discussion is in fact unified around the position that technology expresses hierarchical social relations and fixes them into material reality. There is a widespread understanding that technology is to be approached not as a matter of individual devices but as a socio-technological complex – interlocking systems of human–machine interfaces that fix human behaviour, sustaining and enhancing inequalities of wealth and power. I also look at the more clearly anarchist critique offered by Basque activist-hacker Xabier Barandiaran, and examine the applicability of all these insights to the emerging field of nanotechnology.

Where mainstream critics ultimately fail, however, is in their respective agendas of technological democratisation, and their ultimate reconciliation to technological modernity as a process that can be managed and controlled, but not fundamentally contested. Insisting on the validity of the latter option from an anarchist perspective, I examine how the critique presented here can be actualised in three different areas. First, I argue that many technologies which have an inherently centralising and profit-driven nature can only elicit an attitude of abolitionist resistance from anarchists, amounting to a new form of Luddism. I then discuss anarchists' attraction to the Internet as a decentralising and locally empowering technological platform, but argue for a disillusioned approach that is mindful of the opposite qualities of the computer and communications infrastructures that enable such a platform to function. Finally, I look to areas in which anarchists would be drawn to adopt and develop alternative approaches to modifying the natural world, emphasising Permaculture and lo-tech innovation as parts of the 'constructive' facet of an anarchist politics of technology.

ANARCHISTS AND TECHNOLOGY

As mentioned in the outset, anarchists' relationship with technology is highly ambivalent, containing both rejection and endorsement. A hallmark of the rejectionist aspect is anarchist resistance to genetically modified (GM) crops, which flowered throughout the 1990s. The first recorded trashing of GM crops occurred in the US in 1987 when *Earth First!* activists pulled up 2,000 genetically modified strawberry plants (SchNEWS 2004: 171). The first European trashings were in Holland in 1991. By 1993, when a demonstration of 500,000 peasants in Bangalore ended with the physical destruction of seed multinational Cargill's head offices in India, anarchists in the North were well aware of the much larger picture of militant campaigning against GM crops by peasant movements in Latin America and South Asia, providing opportunities for international solidarity around the issue. German autonomists squatted fields to prevent GM crop trials, leading to the cancellation of a third of them and many more being destroyed. In the UK, anarchists have played a large part in the over 30 groups comprising the Genetic Engineering Network, engaging both in campaigning and in direct action. Over several years, groups of 'crop-busters' conducted nightly raids to destroy trial crops of GM maize, sugar beet and oilseed rape, until in 2004 the Blair government dropped its plans for commercial growing of GM crops in the UK.

But the resistance to technology is much wider than GM. Looking back at two of contemporary anarchism's main 'progenitor' movements in the 1980s, we can notice that the direct-action feminist movement was strongly involved in resistance to nuclear technology, first energy then weapons, and that the direct-action environmental movement also had clear issues with technological progress – in genetics, chemicals and transport to name a few. More recently, there has been active anarchist involvement in campaigning against . the introduction of biometric Identification Cards in the UK, and French anarchist squatters have resisted the construction of a nano-science centre in Grenoble. Anarchist political culture also displays a strong attraction to low-tech, 'simple living' lifestyles, including the promotion of small-scale organic farming and of cycling as an alternative to car culture.

On the other hand, there is a multitude of examples for the contemporary movement's integration and even development of technological systems. Anarchists make extensive use of email and mobile phones in their communication, and Internet websites are used to publicise and coordinate events, often including an online discussion forum. The movement has a number of electronic media hubs, including the global Indymedia network, whose collectives often hold web-based meetings and have a functioning process for consensus decision-making online. The Internet also serves as an immense archive for the self-documentation of social struggles.

However, anarchists have taken a step further by more thoroughly integrating – and even developing – information and communication technologies. The collaborative authorship software used on Indymedia was invented and continues to be developed directly by activists. There is also prominent anarchist involvement in the free software movement. Many anarchists are talented programmers, mostly using GNU/Linux operating systems and other open-source applications to develop software for use by social movements. In Europe such activists currently operate over 30 HackLabs, community spaces with computers and Internet access which also act as hubs for political organising.

Historically speaking, anarchists' attitudes towards technology display a similar ambivalence, oscillating between a bitter critique driven by the experiences of industrialism, and an almost naive optimism around scientific development and its enabling role in a post-capitalist society. Rooted in the nineteenth-century working-class movement, anarchist activists and writers were well aware of the displacement of workers by machines, and of the erosion of producers' autonomy as household and artisan economies were displaced by a production process in which the machines themselves dictate the pace, stages and outcomes of work. Proudhon, for one, seems to have had little sympathy towards technological advance:

Whatever the pace of mechanical progress; though machines should be invented a hundred times more marvellous than the mule-jenny, the knitting-machine, or the cylinder press; though forces should be discovered a hundred times more powerful than steam, – very far from freeing humanity, securing its leisure, and making the production of everything gratuitous, these things would have no other effect than to multiply labor, induce an increase of population, make the chains of serfdom heavier, render life more and more expensive, and deepen the abyss which separates the class that commands and enjoys from the class that obeys and suffers. (Proudhon 1847: Ch.4)

At the same time, many anarchists saw industrial progress as desirable and beneficial, as long as social relations were transformed. Kropotkin, despite his groundbreaking contributions to scientific ecology and his sympathy for the medieval commune, cited 'the progress of modern technics, which wonderfully simplifies the production of all the necessaries of life' as a factor reinforcing what he saw as a prevailing social tendency towards no-government socialism (Kropotkin 1910). His belief in the ability of technology to improve workers' conditions led him to state that after the revolution 'factory, forge, and mine can be as healthy and magnificent as the finest laboratories in modern universities', envisioning a proliferation of mechanical gadgets and a centralised service industry that would relieve women of their slavery to housework, as well as making all manner of repugnant tasks no longer necessary (Kropotkin 1916: Ch.10). This approach was echoed more recently by Murray Bookchin in his wildly techno-optimistic *Post-Scarcity Anarchism* (Bookchin 1974).

After the First World War, well-known anarchists such as Malatesta, Goldman and Rocker continued to advocate a liberated industrial modernity, albeit under workers' control through their own economic and industrial organizations. In Rocker's formulation, 'industry is not an end in itself, but should only be a means to ensure to man his material subsistence and to make accessible to him the blessings of a higher intellectual culture. Where industry is everything and man is nothing begins the realm of a ruthless economic despotism' (Rocker 1989/1938). Overall, anarchists saw mechanised industrial processes as dominating under capitalist conditions, but not inherently so, and were confident that the abolition of the class system would also free the means of production from their alienating role in the system of private ownership and competition.

Most past anarchists, then, shared the basic attitudes towards technology that continue to pervade official and everyday discussions of the topic today. The desirability of technological progress is taken for granted, and technology is understood as neutral – an amalgamation of tools and applications that can be used for good or bad ends, but have no inherent moral or political content.

POWER AND THE MACHINE

At the margins of society's prevailing technological optimism, there have been critical voices spotlighting the increasing technological mediation of nature in modern society and the alienation it generates. In *Technics and Civilisation*, Lewis Mumford (1934) traced the historical development of technology from the Middle Age clock, arguing that moral, economic and political choices have shaped technological society, ending in what he saw as a spiritually barren civilisation, based only on productivity. Against the notion of inevitable machine dominance, however, Mumford suggests that the 'esthetic' of the machine, based on observation directly from nature and the balancing of functionality against form, can be absorbed and used to good ends in a rational, grassroots-communist society geared towards 'Handsome bodies, fine minds, plain living, high thinking, keen perceptions, sensitive emotional responses and a group life keyed to make these things possible and to enhance them' (399). Three further major works appeared in the 1960s. As a continuation of his philosophy of Being, Martin Heidegger (1977/1962) argued that the essence of technology was not in devices but in the 'unconcealment' to humans of all beings whatsoever as objective, calculable, quantifiable and disposable raw material ('standing reserve'), which is valued only insofar as it contributes to the enhancement of human power. Thus the real danger of technology for Heidegger was the process by which the machines alter human existence and draw it away from a deeper experience of Being. 'The essence of technology, as a destining of revealing, is the danger', he wrote. 'The rule of enframing threatens man with the possibility that it could be denied to him to enter into a more original revealing and hence to experience the call of a more primal truth' (333). In *The Technological Society*, Jacques Ellul (1964) proposed a 'sociological study of the problem of *Technique*' – the latter being a term for the sum of all techniques, of all means to unquestioned ends, the 'new milieu' of contemporary society. All individual techniques are ambivalent, intended for good ends but also contributing to the ensemble of Technique. Unlike Mumford, Ellul through that the artificial milieu had become autonomous and unstoppable. A similar fatalism was expressed by Marcuse, who in *One Dimensional Man* (1964) argued that technological advancement, contrary to traditional Marxist expectations, had created affluent capitalist societies characterised by public docility and an unlimited ability to domesticate dissent.

Anarchists are aware of these works, and Ellul in particular is often cited by primitivist writers. However, each of these accounts is packaged in its own, very specific set of philosophical commitments and biases, each of which is too narrow to serve as a basis for a broad-based anarchist politics of technology. Mumford's mythologised history, Hedegger's ontology, Ellul's existential theology and Marcuse's neo-Marxism all inform their treatment of technology as inexpendable baggage. Recent critiques, however, assume a more succinct analytical approach and offer a better place to start.

Anarchists would probably be surprised to learn that contemporary, mainstream academic writing on technology is highly politicised. Among contemporary writers on the politics of technology 'little needs to be said concerning the "neutrality" of technology. Since the social-political nature of the design process has been exposed by Langdon Winner and others, few adhere to the neutrality of technology thesis' (Veak 2000: 227). The neutrality thesis has been rejected since it disregards how the technical or from-design structure of people's surroundings delimits their forms of conduct and relation. As Winner (1985: 11–12) argues, 'technologies are not merely aids to human activity, but also powerful forces acting to reshape that activity and its meaning':

As technologies are being built and put into use, significant alterations in patterns of human activity and human institutions are already taking place ... the construction of a technical system that involves human beings as operating parts brings a reconstruction of social roles and relationships. Often this is a result of the new system's own operating requirements: it simply will not work unless human behavior changes to suit its form and process. Hence, the very act of using the kinds of machines, techniques and systems available to us generates patterns of activities and expectations that soon become 'second nature'.

This type of analysis politicises the discussion of technology on a deeper level than usual. Political issues around technology, if they are ever brought up, are almost exclusively framed as matters of government *policy*, and brought in only as an accessory to debating the cost–benefit analysis of particular technologies, or their environmental side effects. To politicise the debate at its base is to argue that technologies both express and reproduce specific patterns of social organisation and cultural interaction, drawing attention 'to the momentum of large-scale sociotechnical systems, to the response of modern societies to certain technological imperatives, and to the ways human ends are powerfully transformed as they are adapted to technical means' (Winner 1985: 21).

Technologies fix social relations into material reality. This can be seen in how modern society has come to depend materially on the pervasive stability of large-scale infrastructures, whose dimensions are found in 'systemic, society-wide control over the variability inherent in the natural environment' (Edwards 2003: 188). Such an environment requires a high level of 'technological fluency' in order to function in all social interactions, from the habitual to the specialised – effectively making it a prerequisite to membership in society. Infrastructures, for Paul Edwards, 'act like laws: They create both opportunities and limits; they promote some interests at the expense of others. To live within the multiple, interlocking infra-structures of modern societies is to know one's place in gigantic systems that both enable and constrain us' (2003: 191). While infrastructure breakdowns are treated either as human error or as technological failure, few 'question our society's construction around them and our dependence on them ... infrastructure in fact functions by seamlessly binding hardware and internal social organisation to wider social structures' (190).

Winner gives several examples of technologies employed with intention to dominate, including post-1848 Parisian thoroughfares built to disable urban guerrilla, pneumatic iron molders introduced to break skilled workers' unions in Chicago, and a segregationist policy of low highway overpasses in 1950s Long Island, which deliberately made rich, white Jones Beach inaccessible by bus, effectively closing it off to the poor. In all these cases, we can see technical arrangements that determine social results in a way that logically and temporally precedes their actual use. There are predictable social consequences to deploying a given technology or set of technologies.

On the macro level, new technologies must be integrated into an existing socio-technological complex, and as a result are imprinted with its strong bias in favour of certain patterns of human interaction. This bias inevitably shapes the design of these technologies and the ends towards which they will be deployed. Because of the inequalities of power and wealth in society, the process of technical development itself is so thoroughly biased in a particular direction that it regularly produces results that favour certain social interests.

One does not need to be an anarchist to see that the constraints created by the existing socio-technological complex and its infra-structures have a specifically exploitative and authoritarian nature. Workplace technologies from the robotised assembly line to the computerised retail outlet subordinate workers to the pace and tasks programmed into them, reducing the workers' opportunities to exercise autonomous judgement and to design and run the production process by themselves. The capitalist bias of modern society is also abundantly present in the mindsets shaping technological development. Today in every developed country, corporations exert a great deal of influence on every stage of the technological research, design and implemen-tation process. In each country, industry spends pound billions on research and development – whether in-house, through funding for universities, or in public–private partnerships. Academia is also encouraged to commercialise its research, in a combination of funding pressures created by privatisation and direct government hand-outs. As universities look to generating lucrative spin-off companies, it makes perfect sense to them to consider the commercial relevance of research paramount. It should also be unsurprising that a society biased towards hierarchy and capitalism generates the entirely rational impetus for the surveillance of enemies, citizens, immigrants and economic competitors. In such a setting, technologies such as strong microprocessors, broadband communication, biometric data rendering, and face- or voice-recognition software will *inevitably* be used for state and corporate surveillance, whatever other uses they may have (Lyon 2003).

When it comes to policy-making on technological development, official corporate representatives often sit in committees of bodies such as the UK academic Research Councils which allocate huge amounts of funding. Unofficially, there are industry-funded lobby groups (the British Royal Society's recent donors included BP [£1.4 million], Esso UK, AstraZeneca, and Rolls-Royce), as well as a revolving door between the corporate world and senior academic and government posts relevant to science and technology policy (Ferrara 1998, Goettlich 2000). Former British science minister, Lord Sainsbury, has substantial investment interests in companies that hold key patents in biotechnology. The 2005 Reith Lecturer was nanotechnology pioneer Lord (Alec) Broers, who is President of the Royal Academy of Engineering, Chairman of the House of Lords Science and Technology Committee, former Vice-Chancellor of Cambridge University and for 19 years a senior research manager at IBM.

Under such conditions it is not surprising that the decision on the viability of a technological design 'is not simply a technical or even economic evaluation but rather a political one. A technology is deemed viable if it conforms to the existing relations of power' (Noble 1993: 63). Technological development, then, structurally encourages the continuation and extension of Western society's already pervasive centralisation, rationalisation and competition, the state and capitalism. On this reading, there is 'an ongoing social process in which scientific knowledge, technological invention, and corporate profit reinforce each other in deeply entrenched patterns, patterns that bear the unmistakable stamp of political and economic power' (Winner 1985: 27). In other words, the hypothetical question about whether technology can ever be in the 'right' hands is trumped by the obvious point that, in a hierarchical society, it is and has always been in the 'wrong' hands.

While the argument so far draws attention to the existing socio-technological complex into which new technologies are inserted, there is an even stronger sense in which a technology is 'political'. According to this argument, many technologies have an *inherent* political nature, whereby a given technical system by itself requires or at least strongly encourages specific patterns of human relationships. Winner (1985: 29–37) suggests that in some cases, it may be argued that the adoption of a given technical system either actually requires or is strongly compatible with the creation and maintenance of a particular set of social conditions. This can happen in the system's immediate operating environment, and/or in society at large. In some cases this is eminently clear. Consider the case of a nuclear weapon: its very existence demands the introduction of a centralised, rigidly hierarchical chain of command to regulate who may come anywhere near it, under what conditions and for what purposes. It would simply be insane to do otherwise. More mundanely, in the daily infrastructures of our large-scale economies – from railroads and oil refineries to cash crops and microchips – centralisation and hierarchical management are vastly more efficient for operation, production and maintenance. Needless to say, in the hegemonic discourse on technology efficiency trumps any other consideration.

On the other hand, it can be argued that some technologies have inherent features that encourage decentralisation and localism. Solar and wind energy, for example, would appear to be highly compatible with a decentralised society that engenders local energy self-reliance. This is because of their availability for deployment at a small scale, and because their production and/or maintenance require only moderate specialisation. The question of whether any particular technology has such inherent political qualities, and if so, whether these encourage centralisation or decentralisation, is a matter for both factual and political debate that needs to be resolved separately for every given case. Winner, for his part, concludes that 'the available evidence tends to show that many large, sophisticated technological systems are in fact highly compatible with centralized, hierarchical managerial control' (1985: 35).

What the socially derived and inherent political qualities of technologies add up to is what Winner calls the 'technical Constitution' of society – deeply-entrenched social patterns that go hand in hand with the development of modern industrial and post-industrial technology. This constitution includes a dependency on highly centralised organisations; a tendency towards the increased size of organised human associations ('gigantism'); distinctive forms of hierarchical authority developed by the rational arrangement of socio-technical systems; a progressive elimination of varieties of human activity that are at odds with this model; and the explicit power of socio-technical organisations over the 'official' political sphere (47–8).

The critiques of technology offered by Winner, Edwards and others already provide very useful markers for anarchists. They are far removed from the widespread beliefs about the neutrality of technology and the unquestioned acceptance of progress, and clearly indicate the hierarchical and exploitative nature of the socio-technological complex. However, something further needs to be said about how technological rationality codes domination and hierarchy into the politics of everyday life. In an explicitly anarchist theory coming from the HackLab scene, Xabier Barandiaran (2003, my translation) suggests a core distinction between 'technique' as 'the particular application of a piece of knowledge to a predetermined problem', and 'technology' as 'the *recursive* application of a series of techniques and mechanisms to a space of reality'. As opposed to technique (which includes tool use), technology 'generates, delimits and structures a real space (electronic, scientific, social...) since it is a recursive application in which the result of the application returns to be (re)utilized on the same space; which in turn is submitted to those techniques and mechanisms, etc'. Barandiaran identifies four moments in technological systems. These are not linear stages but moments in a retroactive cycle, a 'metamachine' where outputs are re-utilised as inputs:

1. *A code is generated*: This is the scientific moment and relates to knowledge and to the creation of understanding and discourse. The generation of a code involves digitisation (separation of continuums into discreet units – many of them binary and normative – good/bad, correct/incorrect etc.), the selection of elements or components, taxonomies (classifications) of those elements, creation of conjoined procedures for control, analysis and manipulation (diagnosis, measurements, etc.), and the abstraction of a series of relations and rules of calculus among the signs that define the code (mathematical equations, structural causals, generative rules, instructions for manipulation etc.). The code orders and operationalises (permits an organised operation of) a domain of reality (social or material) for the construction of machines in that domain.

2. *Machines based on the code are built*: Once created, the code (or piece of knowledge) permits the design of machines that produce order, control, objects, or diverse changes – social, biological, physical, etc. The codes are also utilised for objectifying or codifying diverse phenomena (organisms, material, minds, collectives, markets, events, etc.) in the form of machines and submitting them to manipulation, control and order. A machine is the abstraction in code of the transformations that a user exercises on an operand (forces on the movement of a wheel, castigation or soothing on the conduct of an individual, or a filtration system on the flow of information on the web).

3. *The machines are realised/implemented*: These machines are realised or implemented in artefacts, institutions, devices, symbols, products, factories, etc. When the system or phenomenon is anterior to the machine (to its description in a codified domain), the machine is utilised to pre-decide its operation, control it or manipulate it. In this way phenomena come to be machines already when we begin to interact with them on the basis of their compression into machines.

4. *The machines are inserted into a technological complex*: Recently created machines are inserted into a complex context of other machines and social processes: in the conjunction of social institutions, in the market, in quotidian life, etc. ... transforming that environment but at the same time being transformed and re-utilised for that complex ecosystem of machines and codes, of devices and practices, that are *technological systems*. In many cases the final technological complex reinforces the knowledges and the codes by which it is supported, since it permits a more effective manipulation of that domain (reducing it, as many times as it is possible to control, with that code). Some machines have been operating in reality for so long that they have produced orders and structures that we consider normal and normalised, others irrupt violently in those contexts producing refusal or illusions around the changes they bring about.

Based on this analysis, Barandiaran suggests understanding phenomena such as biotechnology as technological processes which:

establish or discover a code (the genetic one) and a series of manipulation and control procedures to build machines for the production of genetically modified food, for control of genetic illnesses, genetic banks, etc. Machines that adapt and socialize themselves through the interfaces of the market and other legal machineries (such as biotech patents) sustain and assure a relation of forces in that technological domain. (Barandiaran 2003)

Through this schema Barandiaran 'technologises' the familiar post-structuralist critique of power relations in society. Domain (*dominio*) is inherent not only in technological design and implementation but in the activity of codifying that sustains the entire recursive process. This account's reliance on the conjunction between power and knowledge recalls Foucault, in whose directed studies of social processes Barandiaran reads an expression of how 'diverse forms of knowledge (psychiatry, teaching, criminology) develop a series of codes with which to classify and objectify human beings and their conduct (mad/sane, successful/failing, criminal/non-criminal)'. On the basis of these codes are developed 'devices or disciplinary "machines" of caution, normalising sanction and scrutiny (surveillance as well as medical, pedagogical, and legal examinations) and institutions that apply them (the psychiatric hospital, the school, the prison)'. A technological disciplinary regime is thus constituted, generating power relations that structure the permitted and un-permitted and produce forms of subjectivity and individuality.

An important perspective to be added to this social critique of technology is derived from a historical analysis of technological waves. The theory of the wave-motion of the global economy led by technological development (Kondratieff 1984/1922) is a matter of common currency. Contemporary scholars chart a history of consciously manufactured technological waves separated by narrowing time-lapses, beginning with Portuguese and Spanish navigation advances in the fifteenth century, followed by the wave led by printing in the seventeenth, steam and iron around 1800, steel and electricity later that century, heavy industry at the beginning of the twentieth century, the successive waves of automobile, atomic and semiconductor technologies throughout that century and, most recently, the waves of biotechnology and nanotechnologies (Spar 2001, Perez 2002). Reviewing the impacts of successive waves, Pat Mooney concludes:

History shows that, at least initially, every new technological wave further destabilizes the precarious lives of the vulnerable ... Those with wealth and power are usually able to see (and mould) the technological wave approaching and prepare themselves to ride its crest. They have the economic flexibility to survive, as well as the protection afforded by their class. But a period of instability (created by the technological wave) washes away some parts of the 'old' economy while creating other economic opportunities ... Each artificial technology wave begins with the depression or erosion of the environment and the marginalized who are dragged under. As the wave crests, it raises up a new corporate elite. (Mooney 2006: 14)

Just as capital accumulated itself in the first industrial revolution through the immiseration of the lower classes, so do anarchists have every reason to expect contemporary waves of technology to expand state control and corporate wealth by massive dislocation, deskilling and unemployment. One does not have to be an anarchist to be a technological pessimist, but for contemporary anarchists it would seem that technological optimism is definitely not on the cards.

So much for the substance of the critique that I would propose as a basis for an anarchist politics of technology. As a sounding-board and demonstration of its application, I would like to turn briefly to what is expected to be the largest technological wave in history – one driven by the convergence of multiple technologies on the atomic scale.

THE CASE OF NANOTECH

The term nanotechnology (or 'nanotech') refers not to a particular technology but to a technological *platform* enabling the manipulation of matter at the atomic and molecular scale (1 billion nm = 1 m), literally creating new molecules from the atom up. Nanotechnology attracts massive interest and investment from the world's strongest governments and corporations, including almost all Fortune500 companies. The nano-scale has two exciting features. The first is that 'everything is the same' – on the nano-scale all you see is atoms. Molecules can be built and manipulated, and living and non-living matter behave alike. Just as genetic engineering broke through the species barrier (e.g. splicing a fish or a rabbit with a jellyfish gene to make them glow fluorescent green), nanotech breaks through the life/non-life barrier. This creates the prospect of a revolutionary technological convergence – the erosion of boundaries between materials technology, biotechnology, information technology and cognitive neuroscience. (ETC Group 2003).

More mundanely and lucratively, commercial nanotech relies on the other remarkable feature of the nano-scale: 'everything is different'. On the nano-scale, matter changes its properties (colour, strength, reactivity, conductivity) as the laws of quantum mechanics become felt. Hence the current wave of nano-materials, which take advantage of the novel properties of engineered molecules in a variety of products: paints, cosmetics, tyres, clothing, glass and computers among others. Titanium dioxide (TO_2) is widely used in sun block because it scatters UV light well. Its particles are white on the conventional scale, but artificial 20nm-wide particles of TO_2 are transparent while retaining their UV scattering properties – making for see-though sun block. Another product at the centre of attention is new carbon molecules called carbon nano-tubes, a cylindrical mesh of carbon atoms. Measuring only a few nanometres across, nano-tubes are roughly one hundred times stronger than steel and one sixth the weight, with better conductivity than copper and a huge number of commercial applications – from tyre fibres and electric conductors to receptacles for targeted delivery of pharmaceuticals into the body.

Because of their size, new nano-particles have physical properties to which biological organisms could never have adapted, and thus unexplored toxicities and environmental effects. Most nano-particles are small enough to pass through the blood-brain barrier, let alone the skin. As of summer 2007 there is next to zero regulation of nano-products. At the same time, issues like toxicity generate concerns that industry easily codes as 'risk', and often successfully placates with regulation – on which it has strong influence. The critique of technology explored above creates some more distinctly political observations about nanotechnology.

First, converging technologies have a huge potential for enhancing corporate concentration. Just as the biotechnology revolution resulted in the convergence of chemical, pharmaceutical, seed and materials interests into 'life sciences' companies such as Bayer and BASF, nan-otechnology is likely to result in even more extensive cross-sector monopolies. For example, IBM and NEC are currently competing over who has the key patents to carbon nano-tubes. Whichever company wins out will no longer be only a computer company but also one involved in materials, pharmaceuticals, etc. Technological convergence on the nano-scale is thus an obvious power-multiplier for corporations.

Alongside corporations, one of the largest single funders of nanotech research is the US Department of Defense, which is actively pursuing nanotechnology as a platform for military and surveillance technologies (there is a Centre for Soldier Nanotechnology at MIT). For example, the US government's Defense Advanced Research Projects Agency (DARPA) has set up the DARPA/MEMS program to 'develop the technology to merge sensing, actuating, and computing in order to realize new systems that bring enhanced levels of perception, control, and performance to weapons systems and battlefield environments' (DARPA 2005). One of these is known as 'Smart Dust' – tiny sensors which would pick up a variety of information from environmental conditions such as movement and light to persons' DNA signature. Entirely self-sustaining on solar energy, these sensors would be able to turn themselves on, recognise other sensors in the vicinity, and create a wireless network among themselves. This would enable the spread of a net of sensors on a battlefield, or an urban environment, which would then send comprehensive information back to a central command with enough computing power to crunch the data. The target size for Smart Dust 'motes' is 1mm cube, increasingly approximated by existing developments (cf. Warneke 2005), and it is a safe bet that further reduction and comprehensive sensing capabilities are only a matter of time.

Beyond surveillance, a point needs to be made about the novel methods of social control that converging technologies could enable, by coding property and criminal law into our physical environments. Already, 'Terminator' seeds are genetically engineered to prevent re-germination from their crop, rendering seed-saving not only illegal but physically impossible. Thus Monsanto's patent is no longer a legal chimera relying on the backing of state coercion, but a self-contained legal/coercive complex encoded into the seed itself. Nanotechnology can provide even more sophisticated mechanisms such as *conditional* termination, e.g. seeds containing a toxic layer encapsulated in a 'smart' membrane, that will release them in response to a specific remotely broadcast microwave signal (cf. Choi et al. 2002). In a similar way, pervasive surveillance combined with nano-materials and low-level artificial intelligence may well create 'smart' environments in which breaking the law is literally impossible – where materials and objects are programmed to behave in a certain way if an offence is detected.

Finally, and most fundamentally, like technological waves before it, nanotechnology will disrupt weaker economies, as major sources of export income for countries in the global South, from iron and copper to rubber and cotton, become replaced by things like nano-tubes and nano-fibres. For example, the use of carbon nano-tubes in the electronics industry looks set to render copper obsolete. The most harsh impacts of these changes will be felt not by large corporations dealing in copper (who can diversify) but by local communities who depend on copper mining from Peru to Zambia to Indonesia. This is not to say that copper mines are sustainable, or nice places to work – but their abandonment ought to be the result of social choice.

What kind of practical judgements and strategies emerge from such an approach to technology? And what could an alternative look like?

ACTUALISING THE CRITIQUE

The weaker aspect of academic writing on technology is its proposals for change. Winner suggests a process of 'technological change disciplined by the political wisdom of democracy ... citizens or their representatives would examine the social contract implied by building [any new technological] system ... [in new] institutions in which the claims of technical expertise and those of a democratic citizenry would regularly meet face to face' – presumably on equal footing. What all this amounts to is placing 'moral limits on technological civilization' by constructing a different technological constitution, 'a new regime of instrumentality' that will define socio-technological relations (2002: 55–7 and 155). As general maxims, which are by themselves reasonable, Winner proposes that technologies should be given a scale and structure of the sort that would be immediately intelligible to non-experts; that they should be built with a higher degree of flexibility and mutability; and that they should be judged according to the degree of dependency they tend to foster, with those creating more dependency being held inferior. Ideally, then, new technological forms should be developed 'through the direct participation of those concerned with their everyday employment and effects' (Winner 2002: 606).

However, it is questionable whether this process could ever take off the ground in the way Winner imagines it. Can such concessions be expected to be reached through dialogue between citizens and the states and corporations that define present socio-technical development? At a time of a general trend away from democracy in advanced capitalist societies, the prospects for the democratisation of an entirely new sphere appear very unlikely. On the other hand, thoroughgoing decentralisation and a local, self-sufficient economy would appear to be much more adequate for delivering human-scale technologies and grassroots decision-making processes about them. However, Winner rejects this position:

Given the deeply entrenched patterns of our society, any significant attempt to decentralize major political and technological institutions would require that we change many of the rules, public roles, and institutional relationships of government. It would mean that society move to increase the number, accessibility, relative power, vitality and diversity of local centers of decision making and public administration. This could only happen by overcoming what would surely be powerful resistance to any such policy. It would require something of a revolution. Similarly, to decentralize technology would mean redesigning and replacing much of our existing hardware and reforming the ways our technologies are managed ... [in both areas], any significant move to decentralize would amount to retro-fitting our whole society, since centralized institutions have become the norm. (Winner 1985: 96)

Winner's rejection of decentralist perspectives is not only due to immediate political difficulties. Today, he says, unlike under the immature industrialism that confronted figures like Kropotkin or G.D.H. Cole, it is impossible to 'imagine an entire modern social order based upon small-scale, directly democratic, widely dispersed centres of authority', unthinkable that 'decentralist alternatives might be feasible alternatives on a broad scale' (96).

The point about this argument is that it is correct. It makes perfect sense that decentralisation cannot sustain modern industrial society as we know it. It is quite impossible to imagine how the levels of coordination and precision needed for high technological exploits – from biotech to space exploration – could ever be achieved in a society that lacks centralised management and, moreover, the kind of motivations supplied by a profit economy and the arms race. In the final analysis a choice must be made between decentralisation and large-scale industrial modernity, and anarchists are going to have to bite the bullet. So I would suggest that yes, anarchism does imply a retro-fitting process of decentralisation that amounts to quite a significant roll-back of technology. There is, after all, no reason to think that technological decentralisation is any less practical than the rest of the sweeping social changes anarchists propose. It does indeed require 'something of a revolution'.

Whatever our visions of an anarchist society, however, the important question is what all this entails practically and in the present tense. In the remainder of this chapter, I would like to suggest three strands that could together express a coherent and broad-based anarchist politics of technology. While all three are already present to some degree in anarchist activities today, my goal here is to ground them in the critique of technology presented above, and to examine the possibilities and limitations of each.

Luddism

Anarchists who express critical positions on technology often find themselves on the defensive against the caricature of wanting to go 'back to the caves', resulting in statements such as this:

We are not posing the Stone Age a model for our Utopia, nor are we suggesting a return to gathering and hunting as a means for our livelihood ... Reduced to its most basic elements, discussion about the future sensibly should be predicated on what we desire socially and from that determine what technology is possible. All of us desire central heating, flush toilets, and electric lighting, but not at the expense of our humanity. Maybe they are possible together, but maybe not. (*Fifth Estate* 1986: 10)

The authors' use of a 'civilised amenities versus humanity' axis cannot be understood outside the specifics of their early anarcho-primitivist orientation (see Millet 2004). However, speaking of technology in such terms really misses the point. While the jury may still be out on flush toilets, it is clear that according to the *Fifth Estate*'s rule-of-thumb there are at least some technologies that are clearly *not* 'possible' given what all anarchists 'desire socially'. Whatever one's vision of anarchist r/evolution or a free society, it would seem beyond controversy that anarchists cannot but approach some technological systems with unqualified abolitionism. Just to take the most obvious examples, anarchists have no interest whatsoever in advanced military technologies, or in technological systems specific to imprisonment, surveillance and interrogation – the stuff of the state (cf. Rappert 1999). Additionally, anarchists will probably be unified in judging some technological systems such as nuclear power or the oil industry to be so hopelessly unsustainable from an environmental point of view that they, too, could be safely excluded from their desires for society. As a result, it should be acknowledged that on the basis of the critique formulated above, at least some measure of technological abolitionism must be brought into the horizon of anarchist politics. How extensive a technological roll-back is envisioned is beside the point: the relevant question from an anarchist perspective is not where to stop, but where to *start*.

The original Luddite campaign of sabotage against new machinery in the weaving trade began in Nottinghamshire in 1811, spreading over two years to Lancashire, Yorkshire, Leicestershire and Derbyshire until it was brutally repressed on direct orders from Parliament and the Crown. For the Luddites, the object of resistance was not framed as mere technical advance, but as technical advance promoting economic destabilisation and the erosion of livelihoods. Their declaration of war had as its target new frames and engines whereby, in their own words, 'villainous and imposing persons are enabled to make fraudulent and deceitful manufactures to the discredit and utter ruin of our trade'; breaking into factories at night, they destroyed frames that they accused of making 'spurious articles ... and all frames whatsoever that do not pay the regular prices heretofore agreed to [by] the masters and workmen' (Anonymous1 1959/1812: 531). As Kirkpatrick Sale clarifies,

It wasn't all machinery that the Luddites opposed, but 'all Machinery hurtful to the Commonality' ... to which their commonality did not give approval, over which it had no control, and the use of which was detrimental to its interests, considered either as a body of workers or as a body of families and neighbors and citizens. It was machinery, in other words, that was produced with only economic consequences in mind, and those of benefit to only a few, while the myriad social and environmental and cultural ones were deemed irrelevant. (1996: 261–2)

Writing several decades later, Karl Marx treated the Luddites with summary dismissal, seeing their struggle as an incoherent response to the introduction of machinery, while providing the pretext for state repression against the working class as a whole. 'It took both time and experience', he says, 'before the workpeople learnt to distinguish between machinery and its employment by capital, and to direct their attacks, not against the material instruments of production, but against the mode in which they are used' (Marx 1867). However, the whole point of the critique offered here is that it is not possible to distinguish between machinery and its employment by capital, since it already has the needs of capital encoded into it from the start. In retrospect, Marx was blind to the fact that machinery continues to pace the workers and circumscribe their autonomy even if they 'own' it along with its product. On such a reading, the Luddites' uprising actually represents a coherent protest against destructive industrialisation advanced under the banner of technological necessity (cf. Noble 1993, Robins and Webster 1983: 144–5).

The connection to contemporary anarchist politics of technology becomes clear when it is realised that the Luddites did not confront dislocated instances of technical change, but a technological wave that they, unlike the rich, could not foresee, shape to their interests or 'ride'. More than mere machine-breaking, then, contemporary anarchist Luddism is to be understood as a heading for all forms of abolitionist resistance to *new* technological waves which enhance power-centralisation and social control, inequality and environmental destruction.

Clearly, as far as existing technologies are concerned anarchists face certain limitations. Technological systems monopolised by the state are mostly out of reach at the moment, and others (the motorway system or the coal/oil/nuclear-powered energy grid) are so deeply entrenched in everyday life that dismantling them would require a much larger consensus than is available at the moment. However, there are many *new* technologies that anarchists would clearly reject and which are still in the process of being developed and implemented, and are thus more vulnerable to attack. Resistance can involve a diverse array of direct-action tactics – from physical destruction of products like GM crops through the sabotage of manufacturing facilities and laboratories and on to the disruption of the everyday economic activities of the corporations involved in the development of new technologies – all backed by public campaigning to expose, not only the potential risks and actual damage already caused by new technologies, but the way in which they consolidate state and corporate power to the detriment of livelihoods and what remains of local control over production and consumption. In their immediate target, then, neo-Luddite struggles are by their nature defensive or preventative. But they also contain the opportunity for finding allies and putting a radical position forward through the attachment of a thoroughgoing critique of domination to Luddite actions. A great many of these tactics have already been rehearsed in the struggles against biotechnology and GM crops, which are now joined by nanotechnology at the centre of anarchists' Luddite agendas. Note that this position is entirely separate from any ethical abolitionist arguments, such as those referring to the Promethean hubris of genetic engineering. A neo-Luddite resistance to new technologies is a second-order *political* resistance to capital's strategies of consolidation and further self-valorisation.

Hacking, cracking and e-piracy

So much for the Luddite dimension. We now arrive at the ambivalence considered at the outset: if anarchists are to take such a strong anti-technological stance, what of the fact that one of today's most advanced high-technological platforms – computer software and the Internet – draws such enthusiastic support from anarchists? And this, not only in terms of intensive use, but also to the degree that some of them participate in its very development as programmers?

On the basis of the analysis of technology offered here, it is easy to see the source of such support. Though it is an anomaly in comparison to most technological systems, there is indeed something to be said for 'libertarian and communitarian visions based on the Internet's technology, particularly its nonhierarchical structure, low transaction costs, global reach, scalability, rapid response time, and disruption-overcoming (hence censorship-foiling) alternative routing' (Hurwitz 1999: 659). Although there is another side to this coin (e-consumerism, surveillance, mediation of social relationships), it can at least be said that the structure and logic of the Internet as a technology are also highly compatible with decentralisation and local empowerment. The basic platform that the Internet is based on – the TCP/IP (Transmission Control Protocol / Internet Protocol) – is thoroughly decentralised from the start since it is computed locally in each client node. This enables a distributed network of computers to exchange packets of information with no centralised hub.

Ironically, this is one of the rare cases where a technology escapes the intentions of its progenitors. As is well known, the Internet was created by ARPA (Advanced Research Projects Agency), precursor to the very same DARPA which is now working on nanotech projects. The precursor and backbone of today's Internet, ARPANet, was created in the late 1960s with the immediate objective of enabling communication between academics, but more broadly as part of a strategy to enable US military communications to survive in the event of nuclear war. Decentralisation was introduced to prevent decapitation. However, the enduring result of ARPANet was the decentralised peer-to-peer network it created. It was TCP/IP's reliability, easy adaptability to a wide range of systems, and lack of hierarchy that made it appealing for civilian use. The hard-wiring of decentralisation into the Internet's technological platform created unintended consequences for the US government – as far as enabling groups that threaten it also to enjoy communication networks that cannot be decapitated.

Another aspect of the Internet that is attractive to anarchists is the open, non-commercial exchange of information that it enables – a modified form of a gift economy. In traditional gift economies, actors give goods or services to one another without immediately receiving anything in return. Due to social norms and customs, however, actors can expect the recipient of their gift to reciprocate, even if in an unspecified manner and at an unspecified future date. Gift economies have been extensively studied by anthropologists in the context of tribal and traditional societies, but they can easily be discerned within any extended family or friendship network (Mauss

1935/1969, Carrier 1991). Whereas traditional gift-giving is seen to take place between specific and mutually familiar actors, adapting the logic of the gift to the Internet requires a few modifications (Kollock 1999). On email lists or newsgroups, where there is direct interaction between a closed group of individuals, I may expect reciprocation for my gift, not from the individual who received it, but from a third party. When I respond to another user's request for information on an email list, for example, I reproduce the social code of gift-giving within that group. Because of this I can expect that someone – usually not the same individual – will make me a similar gift in response to a subsequent request on my behalf.

However, information contributed through an email list often has a recipient about whom nothing is known to the giver (save their email address). Internet gifts are often even made without any specific recipient in mind – posting information on to a web page effectively makes a gift of it to anyone with Internet access. With web-posting, no specific agent can be pointed to as either the recipient or the potential reciprocator. As a result, rather than a gift economy the Internet is perhaps better described as enabling a system of 'group generalised exchange' (Ekeh 1974, Yamagishi and Cook 1993). In such a system, group members pool their resources and receive the benefits that the pooling itself generates – effectively making large parts of the Internet into an 'electronic commons' (Nyman 2001). The incentive to contribute to such a public goods-based system – as both campaigners and code-hackers constantly do – can be motivated by altruism, the anticipation of reciprocity, the political will to disseminate certain information, and/or the intrinsic enjoyment of activities like programming.

The free software movement, largely self-defined as 'a-political', needs to be briefly mentioned in this context. Though it does not necessarily involve Internet applications, the networks of programmers that jointly develop free software rely on it for exchanging code. Free software could hardly have become such an extensive enterprise if this could only be done on floppies or CDs. Now what is usually meant by the notion that the software is 'free' is that its source code is non-copyrighted, and that it is distributed under a General Public License or another version of 'copyleft' legal code that gives everyone the same right to use, study and modify it, as long as they keep the source-code available to others and do not restrict its further redistribution. Many free software spokespeople repeatedly dissociate their enterprise from any non-profit connotations. Following the Free

Software Foundation (FSF1996), it is often stated that free software is 'free as in free speech, not as in free beer'. The former, we are told, entails the *liberty* to do one's will with the software provided this same right is not restricted to others. The latter applies to software distributed *gratis*. Thus, much software that is available for gratis download is still copyrighted. It is also, importantly, possible to sell free software, or to ask for payment for its development. Hence liberty is absolutely distinct from matters of price.

This is pure fantasy. Since liberty includes the liberty to redistribute a piece of software for free, then after any initial payment for programming the client can distribute the software for free, and if they do not, the programmer inevitably will. The reality is simply that the overwhelming bulk of free software packages are available for download on the Internet, for free as in 'free beer'. Since licensing rights are out of the picture, the only revenue that can be made on free software is the initial payment. There can be derivative revenues for the developers, through selling user support services and the like, but the software itself, once it enters circulation, *is* from that point on effectively gratis. This is because each actor's liberty is realised in a context that structurally encourages group generalised exchange.

The ideological truth behind the speech/beer manoeuvre is that free software spokespeople want to convince companies that they could make money producing free software. Negotiating its tense position as an alternative within the capitalist economy, the mainstream of the free software movement takes great pains to emphasise that it is not challenging profit (Victor 2003). Thus the Free Software Foundation responsibly warns that 'When talking about free software, it is best to avoid using terms like "give away" or "for free", because those terms imply that the issue is about price, not freedom. Some common terms such as "piracy" embody opinions we hope you won't endorse' (FSF 1996).

For anarchists, though, free software is attractive not because of the legal provisions of its production process, but primarily because it contains gratis, high-quality alternatives to the proprietary and monopolist software economy. The latter, already on an early critique, represents 'a special form of the commodification of knowledge ... the special properties of knowledge (its lack of material substance; the ease with which it can be copied and transmitted) mean that it can only acquire exchange value where institutional arrangements confer a degree of monopoly power on its owner' (Morris-Suzuki 1984) – i.e. intellectual property rights. One may add that these are more than mere 'institutional arrangements', since they can be encoded into the technology itself as access-codes for software packages or online content. On such an optic, the collaborative development of free software like the Linux operating system and applications such as OpenOffice clearly approximate an informational anarchist communism. Moreover, for anarchists it is precisely the logic of expropriation and electronic piracy that enables a radical political extension of the cultural ideals of the free manipulation, circulation and use of information associated with the 'hacker ethic' (Himanen 2001). The space of illegality created by P2P (peer-to-peer) file-sharing opens up the possibility, not only of the open circulation of freely-given information and software as it is on the Internet today, but also of conscious copyright violation. The Internet, then, enables not only communist relations around information, but also the militant contamination and erosion of non-communist regimes of knowledge – a technological 'weapon' to equalise access to information, eating away at intellectual property rights by rendering them unenforceable.

Do these realities of the Internet not throw a dent into the strong techno-scepticism offered above? One is tempted to think that perhaps the decentralised, liberatory logic of the Internet could be extended to other high technologies, enabling anarchists to retain an endorsement of technological advance as part of their political outlook. The answer is negative – and for a more fundamental reason than limitations such as the inequalities of access and the 'digital divide' (Winstanley 2004). What gets missed in these discussions is that although the Internet itself may be inherently decentralised, and though it may encourage liberty and gratuity, its enabling infrastructures have the more usual characteristics of modern technological systems. It is, after all, computers, ocean-floor cables and, most starkly, satellites that stand at the background of Internet communication. And these are highly centralising technologies, requiring an enormous level of precision and authoritative coordination for production, maintenance and further development. The computer industry is also one of the most resource-costly, polluting and exploitative industries in existence. The production of a single six-inch silicon wafer (one of around 30 million produced every year) requires the following resources: 3,200 cubic feet of bulk gases, 22 cubic feet of hazardous gases, 2,275 gallons of deionised water, 20 pounds of chemicals, and 285 kilowatt hours of electrical power. And for every single six-inch silicon wafer manufactured, the following wastes are produced: 25

pounds of sodium hydroxide, 2,840 gallons of waste water, and 7 pounds of miscellaneous hazardous wastes (SVTC 2005). Sending a satellite into space on a standard sized-rocket like the Zenit-3SL emits 181 tonnes of carbon dioxide (FAA 1999) – fifteen times the current yearly emissions of an average British person (UNDP 2003). The appalling conditions of employees in computer factories in Mexico, China and Thailand are well documented (CAFOD 2004).

It may well be that a large difference can be made with recycling and innovative means of wireless computer communication, but what is clear is that technological decentralisation and the lack of a capitalist system of incentives would inevitably slow down the manufacture and distribution of new computers in a major way, and certainly halt the current speed of microelectronics development that rolls out new models each year. What this suggests is that within an anarchist perspective there is a place for a disillusioned attitude towards ICTs, which would avoid casting the technology itself in an unproblematically enabling role as far as alternative social relations are concerned. However, as Barandiaran (2003) notes, this does not exclude acknowledging the technology's emancipatory potential within the confines of capitalism and extending the hacker ethic to a 'subversive micropolitics of techno-social empowerment':

We believe that it is fundamental to work explicitly on the political dimension of information and communication technologies. We cannot but consider ourselves as open subjects of technopolitical experimentation ... [affirming] the technological space as a political space, and the hacker ethic as a way to experience (collectively) the limits of the codes and machines that surround us, to re-appropriate their possible socio-politically relevant uses; inserting them into the autonomous social processes in which we situate our technopolitical practice (self-organised occcupied social centres and grassroots social movements) ... constructing and deconstructing the interfaces, the networks and the data processing tools for liberated communication and interaction, experiencing them, in an open and participatory process that seeks social conflict and technical difficulty as spaces in which to construct ourselves for ourselves.

Low-tech magic

Finally, it is possible to address the deeper core of the ambivalence framed at the outset. What is it that makes technology so popular as a cultural ideal, one into which anarchists have also been socialised? At least part of it is, quite obviously, the sense of wonder at human creativity. Technology symbolises the value people place on the uniquely human ways of influencing the material world, understanding the natural environment and fitting it to human desires. Tolkien (1964: 25) traces this impulse to the mediation of nature through language, what he calls Magic.

The human mind, endowed with the powers of generalisation and abstraction, sees not only *green-grass*, discriminating it from other things (and finding it fair to look upon), but also sees that it is *green* as well as being *grass*. But how powerful, how stimulating to the very faculty that produced it, was the invention of the adjective: no spell or incantation in Faërie is more potent. And that is not surprising: such incantations might indeed be said to be only another view of adjectives. A part of speech in a mythical grammar.

The value of this capacity, through which human beings acquire a sense of ability and mastery (effectively the actualisation of what was called 'power-to' in Chapter 3), is very hard to challenge. The issue here, however, is that the cultural ideal of technology, as it increasingly monopolises fascination with human creative power, does so while seamlessly appropriating it into a humanist Enlightenment narrative of progress. What is actually the source of fascination is *technique*, as defined above. But technology as a cultural ideal obscures this source, just as technique is materially sublimated into a *social project of rationalised surplus- and capacity-building*. It is the impulse to extract technique from its sublimation in progress, and to valorise it as an experience rather than a basis for unelected, recursive social application, that forms the basis for the 'positive' aspect of an anarchist politics of technology.

When it comes to technique, and even to its recursive application in a localised context, it is certainly possible to realise inventive/creative capabilities in a decentralised, liberatory and sustainable way. This is because there are at least some ways of intervention in the material world which anarchists *would* want to promote. As we have said, technological decentralisation is a clear aspect of any reconstruction away from capitalism and the state. Along with the move to more-or-less local self-reliance, any ecologically positive scenario for anarchists must admit that high-technological innovation would necessarily slow down.

But such a slow-down would also open a space for manifold forms of low-tech innovation in areas like energy, building and food production. This is relevant not only in terms of a 'future society', but indicative of the course that techno-critical anarchists would be encouraged to take in their creation of material alternatives in the present tense. A move to local self-reliance would mean that social transformation involves, in its material dimension, the sustained recycling or creative destruction of artificial material environments shaped by capitalism and the state. With the lack of centralised planning, ecological approaches associated with permaculture come to the fore.

Permaculture, derived from 'permanent culture', is narrowly defined as the design and maintenance of cultivated ecosystems which have the diversity, stability and resilience of natural ecosystems (Mollison 1988, Bell 1992). As a holistic approach to land use, permaculture aims for integration of landscape, people and 'appropriate technologies' to provide food, shelter, energy and other needs. A permaculture design incorporates a diversity of species and interrelations between species, weaving together the elements of microclimate, annual and perennial plants, animals, water and soil management, and human needs to generate sustainable lifestyles based on site-specific ecological conditions. Such an approach aims to work with rather than against natural rhythms and patterns, promoting attitudes of protracted and thoughtful observation rather than protracted and thoughtless action; of looking at systems in all their functions rather than asking only one yield of them, and of letting them demonstrate their own evolutions.

Permaculture is also, in its more politicised section, a worldwide movement of designers, teachers and grassroots activists working to restore damaged ecosystems and human communities. The political connection to anarchism begins from permaculture's emphasis on allowing ecosystems to follow their own, intrinsically determined course of development. The permaculture ethic of 'care for the land and the people', transposed into broader cultural terms, would involve facilitating that self-development of the plant or the person, the garden or the community, each according to its own context – working with, rather than against, the organic momentum of the entity cared for. Whereas in monoculture (or industry, or existing social relations) what is sought after is the opposite – maximal control and harnessing of natural processes and labour power. Turning away from control as a social project vis-à-vis the natural environment easily connects to the same rejection vis-à-vis society itself.

Finally, an important source for reviving decentralised, low-tech diversity is the revival of traditional knowledge. Mexican peasant movements, in planning their project of genetically modified crop decontamination, avoided the appeal for expansive and expensive scientific testing by the state. Instead, their decision was to conserve safe species which are known not to be contaminated, and to initiate experimentation intended to see if there are non-technological ways to discern whether a plant is genetically modified – observing its behaviour, cycles, etc. (Ribeiro 2003, Vera Herrera 2004). More pro-actively, the whole array of traditional plant-knowledge, artisanship and craft, could be revived for any number of everyday life applications. So could apocryphal technologies – small-scale inventions that proliferated in the early twentieth century but were sidelined by patents and monopolies. While it is likely that people will still choose to have, on however localised a level, 'technology' as the recursive application of technique and the machines that are part of it, communities will truly be able to judge whether they are appropriate on conditions such as sustainability, non-specialism, and a human scale of operation and maintenance that encourages creativity, conviviality and cooperation.

6
HomeLand

Anarchy and Joint Struggle
in Palestine/Israel

I have for many years opposed Zionism as the dream of capitalist Jewry the world over for a Jewish state with all its trimmings ... a Jewish state machinery to protect the privileges of the few against the many ... [But] the fact that there are many non-Zionist communes in Palestine goes to prove that the Jewish workers who have helped the persecuted and hounded Jews have done so not because they are Zionists, but [so] that they might be left in peace in Palestine to take root and live their own lives.

—Emma Goldman, *Letter to Spain and the World* (London, 1938)

At the crossroads of imperial conflict since the days of Egypt and Assyria, and with a central place in the cultural legacies of the three Abrahamic religions, the land between the Jordan River and the Mediterranean remains a focal point in the spectacle of world politics and a microcosm for global trends. Just as the Oslo Agreements were touted as an emblem of the 'benevolent' face of globalisation in the 1990s, so does their collapse into renewed violence parallel the transformation, since September 11, of the globalisation project into barefaced imperialism. Today, the conflict in the region which I will be calling, interchangeably, Israel/Palestine and Palestine/Israel, is a linchpin of the Clash of Civilisations ideology – and, for the same reason, a unique acupuncture point for anarchist activity.

In this final chapter I want to offer some perspectives on the politics of Israel/Palestine, where the situation raises wider questions of anarchist approaches to national liberation, international solidarity, and collective identity based on place. For one thing, I want to look at the apparent contradiction between anarchists' commitment to support oppressed groups on the latter's own terms, and those terms being – in the Palestinian case – a new nation-state. First, though, I want to focus on the joint Palestinian-Israeli struggles in which anarchist participation is prominent – pointing to the unexpected ways in which issues such as paternalism, violence and burn-out are played out in the region. Finally, I return to the broader debate on anarchism and nationalism, looking in particular at the idea of bioregionalism as an alternative form of local identity that may be more in tune with anarchist approaches.

ANARCHISM IN ISRAEL/PALESTINE

In looking at the landscape of struggle in Palestine/Israel, it should be remembered that anarchist presence on the ground is relatively small. On a generous estimation, there are today up to 300 people in Israel who are politically active and who would not mind calling themselves anarchists – most of them Jewish women and men between the ages of 16–35. However, anarchism has been a continuous undercurrent in the politics of Israel/Palestine for decades. Although they were not connected to the Yiddish-speaking Jewish anarchists abroad, the earliest Kibbutz groups in the 1920s were organised on libertarian-communist principles and their members read Kropotkin and Tolstoy. While these communards were builders and farm labourers rather than strikers and street-fighters, and while they remained largely blind to their position as pawns in an imperialist project, their form of propaganda by deed remains relevant today (see Horrox 2007). Other local dissidents were more connected to the revolutionary workers' movement, and in 1936 a number of Jewish and Arab communists and anarchists went to fight in the Spanish Civil War. After the Holocaust and the creation of the state of Israel, many Yiddish-speaking anarchists arrived in the country, among them Aba Gordin and Yosef Luden who organised the 'Freedom Seekers' Association' and published the Yiddish anarchist review 'Problemen'.

After 1968, like elsewhere in the world, there was a revival of interest in anarchism. The anti-capitalist, anti-Zionist group Matzpen saw anarchist involvement, and the anarcho-pacifist Toma Schick ran the Israeli branch of War Resisters International. The movement received a major boost in the 1980s thanks to the punk scene and the growth in army refusal during the Lebanon war and the first Intifada. The first anarchist student cells and 'zines were created in this period. The contemporary Israeli anarchist movement fused together during the wave of anti-globalisation activism at the end of the 1990s, bringing together anti-capitalist, environmental, feminist, and animal rights agendas. There was a proliferation of protests and direct actions, Reclaim-the-Streets parties and Food not Bombs stalls. The Salon Mazal infoshop and Indymedia Israel were founded. Since the beginning of the second Intifada, activities have focused on the occupation in Palestine, in particular against the building of the Apartheid Wall. Some anarchists have participated in Ta'ayush (Arab–Jewish Partnership), an initiative created shortly after the beginning of the second Intifada in October 2000. At its peak Ta'ayush had a large membership of Jews and Palestinian Arabs of Israeli citizenship, many of them students, who carried out solidarity actions in the occupied territories – bringing food to besieged cities and towns and defending farmers from settlers and soldiers as they worked their land. In 2003, the Anarchists Against the Wall initiative was founded, and the joint struggle with Palestinian villages in the West Bank continues intensively.

Among Palestinians there are a few kindred souls and many allies, but no organised anarchist movement. However, the last years have seen an alliance between Israeli and international activists and Palestinian communities renewing their own tradition of popular resistance and civil disobedience. The first Intifada (1987–89) was an uprising organised through popular committees and largely in detachment from the PLO leadership, and involved not only slingshots and Molotovs but also many non-violent actions such as mass demonstrations, general strikes, tax refusal, boycotts of Israeli products, political graffiti and the establishment of underground schools and grassroots mutual aid projects.

In addition to Israeli anarchists, many international anarchists have been present on the ground – primarily though the International Solidarity Movement (ISM), a Palestinian-led coordination which began in summer 2001 and saw its peak in the next two years. The ISM mobilised European and North-American volunteers who arrived in the occupied territories to accompany non-violent Palestinian actions (Sandercock et al. 2004). The ISM became active before the height of the Israeli state's invasions and attacks on Palestinian population centres. Its actions included forming human chains to block soldiers from interfering while Palestinians tore down military roadblocks, held mass demonstrations, or collectively broke curfews to take children to school or tend their fields. Palestinian grassroots leaders were interested in this cooperation, in the first place because the presence of internationals would hopefully moderate the reactions of the soldiers, as well as in order to influence international public opinion. Interestingly, organisers estimate that up to a quarter of ISM volunteers have been Jewish.

As the violence escalated, the ISM was driven to focus more and more on accompaniment and human-shielding, while at the same time drawing world attention to the repression of Palestinians through the 'live' presence of international witnesses. For a while, what internationals did was dictated by when, where, and how the Israeli army would attack. During the spring 2002 invasions, ISM activists stayed in Palestinian homes facing demolition, rode with ambulances, escorted municipal workers to fix infrastructure, and delivered food and medicine to besieged communities. In what was the most widely broadcast drama of this phase, internationals were holed-up for weeks in the besieged Church of the Nativity in Bethlehem with residents, clergymen and armed militants. As the violence ebbed the ISM turned proactive again, with demonstrations to break curfews and an international day of action in summer 2002.

Now while the ISM and other, unaffiliated solidarity groups on the ground are not nominally anarchist, two clear connections to anarchism can nevertheless be made. First, in terms of the personnel, international solidarity activities in Palestine have seen a major and sustained presence of anarchists, who had earlier cut their teeth on anti-capitalist mobilisations and local grassroots organising in North America and Europe. Thus, while the ISM has included participants from a wide range of backgrounds, it also constitutes the foremost vehicle for on-the-ground involvement of international anarchists in Palestine. Second, and more substantially, the ISM prominently displays many features of anarchist political culture: lack of formal membership, policy and leadership; a decentralised organising model based on autonomous affinity groups, spokescouncils and consensus decision-making; and a strategic focus on short-term campaigns and creative tactics that stress direct action and grassroots empowerment. These affinities are evinced by a statement from ISM Canada (2002) on the need to move 'from an arrogant "saviour" model of activism, to a real "solidarity" model of activism', whose emphasis on direct action contains many keywords of anarchist political language:

Solidarity means more than 'charity' work to ease our conscience. It must also do more than simply witness or document atrocities – though these tasks are also critical to our work. The ISM views solidarity as an imperative to actively engage in resistance to the Occupation, to take sides, to put our bodies on the line, and to use the relative privilege of our passports and, in some cases, colour – first and foremost, in ways that Palestinians actually request, but also in ways which help build trust and expand networks of mutual aid.

Thus, Western anarchists involved in direct action in Palestine (and in other regions, like West Papua or Colombia) often say that they deliberately participate in them as followers and supporters rather than as equals, let alone leaders. The ethos of the ISM and other solidarity groups stresses taking the lead from Palestinian community members or representatives, based on the principle that decision-making and control of actions should be in proportion to the degree to which one is affected by their potential outcome. As a result, a group of Canadian ISMers have been at pains to emphasise that 'internationals cannot behave as if they are coming to teach Palestinians anything about "peace" or "non-violence" or "morality" or "democracy", or anything else that many in the West typically (and arrogantly and mistakenly) view as the exclusive realm of Western activism and values' (ibid.). Similarly, Israeli anarchist Yossi Bar-Tal has argued that 'we're not working in Palestine to educate ... We would never hand out leaflets in Arabic explaining what anarchism is and why you should join us, because this is not our way ... we're not there to educate, because while they're being occupied by our state we have no reason to come there and preach' (Lakoff 2005).

The spring of 2003 marked a clear transition for direct action in Israel/Palestine, with the centre of gravity shifting from international volunteers in Palestinian cities to Israelis and internationals joining the popular non-violent resistance against the Segregation Barrier. The shift was accompanied by a crisis in the ISM, following a rapid succession of tragic events, notably the killing of two volunteers in Gaza. On March 16, American ISMer Rachel Corrie was crushed to death under an Israeli armoured bulldozer which she was trying to obstruct during a house demolition in Rafah. On April 11, British volunteer Tom Hurndall was shot in the head by an Israeli sniper in the same area and went into a coma, dying nine months later. While the killings raised international outcry, increased the ISM's profile and further highlighted the brutality of the occupation, they also underlined the immense risk accompanying solidarity activities in Palestine and caused many activists to think twice before going there.

This was followed by a concerted campaign of the Israeli state to associate the ISM with terrorism, justifying clampdowns on the organisation. On the night of March 27, during a period of curfew and military arrests in Jenin, a 23-year-old Palestinian named Shadi Sukiya had arrived at the ISM office in the city, soaking wet and shivering, and was given a change of clothes, a hot drink and a blanket. Soon afterwards Israeli soldiers came in and arrested Sukiya, who they accused of being a senior member of the Islamic Jihad. The army also claimed that a pistol had been discovered in the office, but later retracted the allegation. On April 25, a public memorial service for Rachel Corrie organised by the ISM was attended by two young British Muslims, Asif Muhammad Hanif and Omar Khan Sharif. Five days later, the two carried out a suicide bombing at a restaurant in Tel-Aviv, killing three people. Despite the fact that in both cases contact had been minimal and ISM volunteers had no idea about the identity of their guests, the Israeli government used these events to publicly accuse the organisation of harbouring terrorists and proceeded to repress the organisation. On May 9 the army raided the ISM media office in Beit Sahour, seizing computer equipment, video tapes, CDs and files. Though unconfirmed, it is thought that among the materials seized was a comprehensive list of past and present ISM volunteers, including their addresses and passport numbers. This enabled the Israeli security apparatus to expand its 'blacklist' of unwelcome internationals, resulting in an increase of deportations and denials of entry into Israel in subsequent months. Put together, these events placed the ISM in crisis and seriously reduced the flow of internationals into Palestine – although some continue to arrive to this day.

In the same spring of 2003, Israelis who were cooperating on direct action with ISM affinity groups and with other internationals increasingly felt the need to give more visibility to their own resistance as Israelis, by creating an autonomous group working together with Palestinians and internationals. Meanwhile, the construction of the 'Segregation Barrier' or 'Apartheid Wall' on the western part of the occupied West Bank had now begun in earnest (for details on the barrier see PENGON 2003). After a few actions and demonstrations against the barrier in Israel and Palestine, a small group started to come together and build a trusted reputation of Israeli direct-action activists willing to struggle together with local Palestinians. In March 2003 the village of Mas'ha invited the group to build a protest camp on village land that was being confiscated by the route of the fence (96 per cent of Mas'ha's land was taken). The protest camp became a centre of struggle and information against the planned construction of the barrier in that area and in the whole West Bank. Over the four months of the camp more than a thousand internationals and Israelis came to learn about the situation and join the struggle.

During the camp the direct-action group began naming itself Anarchists Against Fences and Jews Against Ghettos. In English it is normally known as Anarchists Against the Wall (the double entendre only works in English). After the eviction of the Mas'ha camp in summer 2003 amid 90 arrests, anarchists continued to participate in many joint actions across the occupied territories. With up to 50 active participants at any given time, this rapidly shifting direct-action network has been present at demonstrations and actions on a weekly basis in villages such as Salem, Anin, Biddu, Beit Awwa, Budrus, Dir Balut, Beit Surik and Beit Likia, as well as with Palestinian communities imprisoned by walls in and around Jerusalem. In some of these actions, Palestinians and Israelis managed to tear down or cut through parts of the fence, or to break through gates along it. Since 2005, the group has mainly been active in the village of Bil'in, which has become a symbol of the joint struggle.

Actions inside Israel also take place constantly, and these often display anarchism's multi-issue platform, a conscious agenda of integrating diverse struggles. By creating networks that integrate the different movements and constituencies in which they are active, anarchists can facilitate recognition and mutual aid among different struggles. In Israel/Palestine, such activities strongly connect the occupation, widening economic inequality, the exploitation of foreign and domestic workers, the status of women, racism and ethnic discrimination, homophobia, pollution and consumerism.

One example of linking the struggle against the occupation to a different liberatory agenda is the activity of Kvisa Shkhora (Black Laundry) – a direct-action group of lesbians, gays, bisexuals, transgenders and others against the occupation and for social justice. The group was created for the Pride Day parade in Tel-Aviv in 2001, a few months after the second Intifada began. Jamming the by-now depoliticised and commercialised celebration, about 250 radical queers in black joined the march under the banner 'No Pride in the Occupation'. Since then, the group has undertaken actions and outreach with a strongly anti-authoritarian orientation, which stress the connection between different forms of oppression. In recent years the radical queer community in Israel has grown in numbers and has become more strongly networked, including the organising of free public queer parties (the Queer'hana), often coinciding with official Pride Day events.

The Israeli radical queer movement has a dual role: on the one hand, promoting solidarity with Palestinians, as well as anti-capitalism and antagonistic politics, in the mainstream LGBT community; and on the other hand, stressing queer liberation in the movement against the occupation. According to one member, while many activists did not initially understand the significance of queers demonstrating as queers against the occupation, 'after many actions and discussions our visibility is now accepted and welcome. This, I can't really say about our Palestinian partners, so in the territories we usually go back to the closet' (Ayalon 2004). The latter reality has also led the queer anarchists to make contacts and offer solidarity with Palestinian LGBTs, who find even less acceptance in their society than Israeli queers do.

Connections with queer anarchists worldwide were strengthened through the organising drive towards the ninth Queeruption event – a free, do-it-yourself radical queer gathering that took place in Tel-Aviv in summer 2006, coinciding with the scheduled World Pride events in Jerusalem. The latter, however, were actually cancelled – falling victim to the Second Lebanon War, which also broke out after weeks of homophobic incitement by ultra-orthodox Jewish, Christian and Muslim leaders and the far right who formed an unholy alliance to oppose it. When the organisers of the World Pride parade called for a vigil against homophobia in lieu of the parade, Queeruption formed a significant chunk of the vigil and with flags from other countries waving, someone brought out a Lebanese flag and whole event started to become a spontaneous anti-war demo. The police immediately declared the vigil 'illegal' and all of a sudden we were surrounded by cops and being beaten. The mainstream gay community fled, and later totally condemned the actions of 'a small group of anarchists who had hijacked the event'.

Another important relationship we can mention here is that between animal liberation and anarchism. Globally the two movements clearly have shared attributes (a confrontational stance, use of direct action, extreme decentralisation, roots in the punk subculture). More recently, animal liberation groups such as SHAC have begun to target the corporate infrastructure of animal testing. While remaining a tactical choice, this also implies a deeper analysis of the connection between animal exploitation and other forms of domination – a direction explored in writing, with increasing intensity, in recent years (Dominick 1995, Anonymous8 1999, homefries 2004). Recent trends in state repression, including the narrowing of demonstration rights and legislation against economic sabotage, are beginning to generate meaningful solidarity and cooperation between the two movements, and individual activists from the animal rights movement have recently been making deliberate contacts with anarchists, a process which is beginning to create interesting cross-fertilisations.

In Israel, the small size of the radical scene has created a very large overlap between the two movements. The most prominent example has been Ma'avak Ehad (One Struggle), an affinity group combining explicit anarchism and an animal liberation agenda, whose members are also very active in anti-occupation struggles. Again this combination of agendas is there with the explicit goal of 'highlighting the connection between all different forms of oppression, and hence also of the various struggles against them' (One Struggle 2002). The group's emphasis on animal liberation again creates a critical bridge: calling attention to animal rights within peace and social justice movements, and encouraging resistance to the occupation in the vegetarian and vegan community. By operating Food Not Bombs stalls, Israeli anarchists and animal liberationists create meaningful connections between poverty, militarism and animal exploitation, which are highly poignant in an Israeli context.

Another powerful combination of agendas to be mentioned is the activity of New Profile, a feminist organisation that challenges Israel's militarised social order. This organisation does educational work around the connections between militarism in Israeli society and patriarchy, inequalities and social violence, and acts to 'disseminate and realize feminist-democratic principles in Israeli education by changing a system that promotes unquestioning obedience and glorification of military service' (Aviram 2003). Activities in this area include debates in schools that promote critical, non-hierarchical thinking and workshops on consensus, conflict resolution and democratic process for groups. In its second role, New Profile is the most radical among the four Israeli refusenik groups, and the one through which many anarchists refusing military service have organised (though the group itself is not anarchist). New Profile campaigns for the right to conscientious objection, operates a network of support for refuseniks before, during and after jail, arranges seminars for youth who are still dwelling on whether or not to refuse or evade service, and campaigns to support and recognise the struggle of women refuseniks. The group's radical feminist and anti-militarist stance, besides being an important message to society, also creates a meaningful bridge between the feminist and refusenik movements, challenging the core narratives to which most refuseniks – predominantly mainstream left-Zionist males – continue to adhere.

Direct action in Palestine/Israel raises two special points regarding political violence. The first is connected to the debates around violence discussed in Chapter 4. Now the Israeli and international anarchists take only non-violent action in Palestine. This position of non-violence plays an entirely different role in Palestine than it does in, say, G8 countries. This is because it takes place against the backdrop of a highly *violent* conflict, in which armed struggle is the norm rather than the exception. At the same time, the ISM and others recognize the legitimacy of Palestinian armed resistance, not including targeting civilians (and so does international law, for that matter). Interestingly, the endorsement of a 'diversity of tactics' places anarchists in a more comfortable position in the landscape of struggle in Palestine/Israel than it would strict pacifists. By engaging in non-violent forms of action while not denouncing armed resistance, Israeli anarchists have, after their own fashion, also adopted a diversity of tactics position. Unlike strict pacifists, they can more comfortably accept non-violent alongside armed struggle – although in this case it is they who take the non-violent option. In Palestine, then, anarchists have been squarely on the non-violent side of the 'diversity of tactics' equation, counteracting the charge that this formula is merely a euphemism for violence (Lakey 2002). Non-violence has the further goal of giving visibility to the non-violent aspects of Palestinian struggle, with which Western audiences can more easily identify.

The second point to be made here regards the uncommon degree of state violence faced by the Israeli and international anarchists, and the resultant pervasiveness of post-traumatic stress and burn-out in their ranks. While obviously amounting to very little compared to the lethal brutality directed towards the Palestinian population, the frequency of Israeli anarchists' experiences of state repression is certainly considerable in comparison to those of their European and North American counterparts. Exposure to tear-gas and truncheon blows has become a matter of weekly regularity, compounded by the use of sound grenades, rubber-coated metal bullets and even live ammunition. In one case an Israeli protester was shot in the thigh with a live bullet and almost died of blood loss, while another was shot in the head by a rubber-coated metal bullet and was also in a critical condition. In addition, there have been uncounted minor injuries sustained at the hands of soldiers and border police during anti-wall demonstrations. The army has also been using demonstrations in the West Bank as an opportunity to test novel 'less lethal' weapons such as pepperballs (a small transparent red plastic ball containing an extremely irritant powder) and the Tze'aka (Hebrew for 'scream') – a minute-long blast of deafening sound emanating from a vehicle-mounted device that causes nausea and imbalance (Rose 2006).

Beyond injuries, these experiences have led to widespread post-traumatic stress among the participants, a phenomenon which is beginning to be acknowledged and coped with in direct-action movements. In the wake of repression, people experience not only physical wounds but also anxiety, guilt, depression, irritability and feelings of alienation and isolation. Post-traumatic stress can also involve any of the following: disturbing thoughts, flashbacks and intrusive images, nightmares, panic attacks and hyper-vigilance; and physical effects including fatigue, elevated blood pressure, breathing and visual difficulties, menstrual changes and muscular tension. As a result of the accumulation of untreated stress, the Anarchists Against the Wall initiative has seen high degrees of burn-out and withdrawal from activity, creating a lack of continuity in the group. Only a handful of the founding participants remain active today, while new and younger activists join in and soon experience the same difficulties. Disturbingly, this dynamic has all too often been enhanced by the uncritical reproduction of an ethos of personal sacrifice, resilience and toughness, creating widespread reluctance to surface the psychological effects of regular exposure to repression for fear of being considered 'weak'. More recently, however, awareness of feelings is rising in the Israeli movement, and many people can more easily name what they are experiencing and feel safe to ask for support. Such developments will hopefully create a more sustainable movement and a space for the elaboration of longer-term agendas.

So much for the scene on the ground, and some of its primary issues. Now I would like to widen the debate, and approach the dilemmas anarchists confront in the course of solidarity with national liberation struggles, in particular ones that aim for establishing a new nation-state.

ANARCHISM, NATIONALISM AND NEW STATES

With the conflict in Palestine/Israel so high on the public agenda, and with significant anarchist involvement in Palestine solidarity campaigns, it is surprising that the scant polemical anarchist contributions on the topic remain, at best, irrelevant to the concrete experiences and dilemmas of movements in the region. At their worst, they depart from anarchism all together. Thus the American Platformist Wayne Price (2002) descends into very crude terms when proclaiming:

In the smoke and blood of Israel/Palestine these days, one point should be clear, that Israel is the oppressor and the Palestinian Arabs are the oppressed. Therefore anarchists, and all decent people, should be on the side of the Palestinians. Criticisms of their leaderships or their methods of fighting are all secondary; so is recognition that the Israeli Jews are also people and also have certain collective rights. The first step, always, is to stand with the oppressed as they fight for their freedom.

Asking all decent people to see someone else's humanity and collective rights as secondary to anything – whatever this is, this is not anarchism. Where does Price's side-taking leave the distinction between the Israeli government and Israeli citizens, or solidarity with Israelis who struggle against the occupation and social injustice? These Israelis are certainly not taking action because they are 'siding with the Palestinians', but rather out of a sense of responsibility and solidarity. For the anarchists among them, it is also clearly a struggle for self-liberation from a militaristic, racist, sexist and otherwise unequal society. Price's complete indifference to those who consciously intervene against the occupation and in multiple social conflicts within Israeli society rests on vast generalisations about how 'blind nationalism leads each nation to see itself and the other as a bloc'. However, people who live inside a conflict are hardly that naive – the author is only projecting his own, outsiders' black-and-white vision onto the conflict, and the side tagged as black is subject to crass and dehumanising language (see also Hobson, et al. 2001). Unfortunately, this kind of attitude has become a widespread phenomenon in the discourse of the European and American Palestine-solidarity movement and the broader left, representing what anarchist critics have been highlighting as a typically leftist form of Judeophobia or anti-Semitism (Austrian and Goldman 2003, Michaels 2004, Shot by both sides 2005).

Meanwhile, Price is so confident about having insight into the just and appropriate resolution that he permits himself to issue elaborate programs and demands, down to the finer details: unilateral Israeli withdrawal to 1967 lines, a Palestinian state and the right of return, ending up in 'some sort of "secular-democratic" or "binational" communal federation' with 'some sort of self-managed non-capitalist economy'. Meanwhile 'we must support the resistance of the Palestinian people. They have the right to self-determination, that is, to choose their leaders, their programs, and their methods of struggle, whatever we think'.

A blank cheque, then, to suicide bombings and any present or future Palestinian elite. The statement's imperative tone also begs the question: to whom, precisely, are Price's 'we' supposed to be issuing such elaborate demands? To the Israeli state, backed perhaps by the potent threat of embassy occupations and boycotts on academics, oranges and software? Or maybe to the international community, or to the American state for that matter? In all cases this would be a 'politics of demand' which extends undue recognition and legitimation to state power through the act of demand itself – a strategy far removed from anarchism.

Myopia towards what is happening on the ground is also a problem for Ryan Chiang McCarthy (2002). Though taking issue with Price's failure to distinguish between peoples and their rulers, McCarthy's call for solidarity with libertarian forces on the ground is unfortunately extended only to struggles which fall within his prejudiced Syndicalist gaze: 'autonomous labor movements of Palestinian and Israeli workers ... A workers' movement that bypasses the narrow lines of struggle ... and fights for the unmediated demands of workers'. Besides being entirely detached from reality – the prospects for autonomous labour movements are as bleak in Israel/Palestine as they are in the rest of the developed world – such a workerist fetish is also directly harmful. It reproduces the invisibility of the many important struggles in Palestine/Israel that do not revolve around work, and in which most anarchists happen to be participating. Meanwhile, stubborn class reductionism demarcates no less narrow lines of struggle than the ones which it criticises, and does the protagonists violence by forcing their actions into artificial frameworks. Thus Palestinians and Israelis are first and foremost 'workers ... manipulated by their rulers to massacre one another'; army refusal is a 'sparkling act of class solidarity carried out across national lines' (most refuseniks are middle-class, and self-declared Zionists to boot); while 'the nationalist poison ... drives Palestinian proletarian youth to destroy themselves and Israeli fellow workers in suicide bombings'. This may still be anarchism, but it is of a fossilised variety that forces obsolete formulas of class struggle on a reality that is far removed from such orientations.

The root of the problem displayed by these writings is that the Palestinian-Israeli conflict introduces complexities that are not easily addressed from a traditional anarchist standpoint. The tension between anarchists' anti-imperialist commitments on the one hand, and their traditionally wholesale rebuttal of the state and nationalism on the other, would seem to leave them at an impasse regarding the national liberation struggles of occupied peoples. The lack of fresh thinking on the issue creates a position from which, it would seem, one can only fall back on the one-size-fits-all formulae. In order to understand why this is so, let me now look at anarchist critiques of nationalism.

Prevalent in anarchist literature is a distinction between the 'artificial' nationalism constructed by the state on the one hand, and the 'natural' feeling of belonging to a group that has shared ethnic, linguistic and/or cultural characteristics. Michael Bakunin (1953: 1871: 324) argued that the fatherland ('patria') represents a 'manner of living and feeling' – that is, a local culture – which is 'always an incontestable result of a long historic development'. As such, the deep love of fatherland among the 'common people ... is a natural, real love'. However, the corruption of this love under statist institutions is what anarchists commonly rejected as nationalism – a primary loyalty to one's nation-state. On this reading, nationalism is a reactionary ideological device intended to create a false unity of identity and interest between antagonistic classes within a single country, pitting the oppressed working classes of different states against each other and averting their attention from the struggle against their real oppressors. Thus for Bakunin 'political patriotism, or love of the State, is not the faithful expression' of the common people's love for the fatherland, but rather an expression 'distorted by means of false abstraction, always for the benefit of an exploiting minority' (ibid.).

The most elaborate development of this theme was made by Gustav Landauer, who used the term 'folk' to refer to the type of organic local and cultural identity that is suppressed by state-sponsored nationalism and would return to prominence in a free society. He saw folk identity as a unique spirit (Geist) consisting of shared feelings, ideals, values, language and beliefs, which unifies individuals into a community (Landauer 1907). He also considered it possible to have several identities, seeing himself as a human being, a Jew, a German and a southern German. In his words,

I am happy about every imponderable and ineffable thing that brings about exclusive bonds, unities, and also differentiations within humanity. If I want to transform patriotism then I do not proceed in the slightest against the fine fact of the nation ... but against the mixing up of the nation and the state, against the confusion of differentiation and opposition. (Landauer 1973/1910: 263)

Rudolf Rocker adopted Landauer's distinction in his book Nationalism and Culture, where a folk is defined as 'the natural result of social union, a mutual association of men brought about by a certain similarity of external conditions of living, a common language, and special characteristics due to climate and geographic environment' (Rocker 1937: 200–1). However, Rocker clarifies that it is only possible to speak of the folk, as an entity, in terms that are specific to a given location and time. This is because, over time, 'cultural reconstructions and social stimulation always occur when different peoples and races come into closer union. Every new culture is begun by such a fusion of different folk elements and takes its special shape from this' (346). What Rocker calls the 'nation', on the other hand, is the artificial idea of a unified community of interest, spirit or race created by the state. Thus, like Landauer and Bakunin, it was the primary loyalty to one's nation-state that Rocker condemned as 'nationalism'. At the same time, these writers expected that with the abolition of the state, a space would be opened for the self-determination and mutually fertilising development of local folk cultures.

These attitudes to nationalism, however, had as their primary reference point the European nationalisms associated with existing states. The issue of nationalism in the national liberation struggles of stateless peoples received far less attention from anarchists. Kropotkin, for one, saw national liberation movements positively, arguing that the removal of foreign domination was a precondition to broader social struggle (Grauer 1994). On the other hand, many anarchists have argued that national liberation agendas only obfuscate the social struggle, and end up creating new local elites that continue the same patterns of hierarchy and oppression.

This tension comes very strongly to the fore in the case of Israel/ Palestine. The overwhelming majority of Palestinians want a state of their own alongside Israel. So how can anarchists reconcile their support for Palestinian liberation with their anti-statist principles? How can they promote the creation of yet another state in the name of 'national liberation'? The attempt to distance oneself from support for Palestinian statehood is what motivates McCarthy's workerist stance, as well as the British syndicalists of the Solidarity Federation who declare that 'we support the fight of the Palestinian people ... [and] stand with those Israelis who protest against the racist government

... What we cannot do is support the creation of yet another state in the name of "national liberation"' (Solidarity Federation 2002).

But there are two problems with such an attitude. First, it invites the charge of paternalism since it implies that anarchists are somehow better than Palestinians at discerning their real interests. Second, and more importantly, it leaves anarchists with nothing but empty declarations to the effect that 'we stand with and support all those who are being oppressed by those who have the power to do so' (ibid.), consigning anarchists to a position of irrelevance in the present tense. On the one hand, it is clear that the establishment of a capitalist Palestinian state through negotiations among existing and would-be governments would only mean the 'submission of the Intifada to a comprador Palestinian leadership that will serve Israel', as well as neo-liberal exploitation through initiatives like the Mediterranean Free Trade Area (Anarchist Communist Initiative 2004). On the other hand, by disengaging from concrete Palestinian demands for a state, the same Israeli anarchists are left with nothing to propose except 'an entirely different way of life and equality for all the inhabitants of the region ... a classless anarchist-communist society' (ibid.). This is all well and good, but what happens in the meantime?

While anarchists surely can do something more specific in solidarity with Palestinians than just saying that 'we need a revolution', any such action would appear to be hopelessly contaminated by statism. The fact that anarchists nevertheless engage in solidarity with Palestinian communities, internationally and on the ground, requires us to grip this particular bull by its horns. Here, I believe there are at least four coherent ways in which anarchists can deal with the dilemma of support for a Palestinian state.

The first and most straightforward response is to acknowledge that there is indeed a contradiction here, but to insist that in this given situation solidarity is important even if it comes at the price of inconsistency. Endorsement of Palestinian statehood by anarchists can be seen as a necessary pragmatic position. It does nobody any good to effectively say to the Palestinians, 'sorry, we'll let you remain non-citizens of a brutal occupation until after we're done abolishing capitalism'. A point to be made here is that states have a track record of hostility to stateless peoples, refugees and nomads. The Jews and the Palestinians are two among many examples of oppressed stateless peoples in the modern era. While many Jews were citizens (often second-class citizens) of European countries at the beginning of the twentieth century, an important precondition for the Holocaust was the deprivation of Jews' citizenships, rendering them stateless. As a result, anarchists can recognise Palestinian statehood as the only viable way to alleviate their oppression in the short term. This amounts to a specific value judgement whereby anti-imperialist or even basic humanitarian concerns take precedence over an otherwise uncompromising anti-statism.

A second, different response argues that there is no contradiction at all in anarchist support for the establishment of a Palestinian state. This is simply because Palestinians are already living under a state – Israel – and that the formation of a new Palestinian state creates only a quantitative change and not a qualitative one. Anarchists object to the state as a general scheme of social relations – not to this or the other state, but to the principle behind them all. It is a misunderstanding to reduce this objection to quantitative terms; the number of states in the world adds or subtracts nothing from anarchists' assessment of how closely the world corresponds to their ideals. Having one single world state, for example, would be as problematic for anarchists as the present situation (if not more so), although the process of creating one would have abolished some 190 states. So from a purely anti-statist anarchist perspective, for Palestinians to live under a Palestinian state rather than an Israeli state would be, at worst, just as objectionable. A Palestinian state, no matter how capitalist, corrupt or pseudo-democratic, would in any event be less brutal than an occupying Israeli state.

A third response, informed by Kropotkin's view mentioned above, is that anarchists can support a Palestinian state as a strategic choice, a desirable stage in a longer-term struggle. No one can sincerely expect that the situation in Israel/Palestine will move from the present one to anarchy in one abrupt step. Hence, the establishment of a Palestinian state through a peace treaty with the Israeli state, although far from a real solution to social problems, may turn out to be a positive development on the way to more radical changes. The reduction of everyday violence on both sides could do a great deal to open up more political space for economic, feminist and environmental struggles, and would thus constitute a positive development from a strategic point of view. The establishment of a Palestinian state could form a bridgehead towards the flowering of myriad social struggles, in Israel and in whatever enclave-polity emerges under the Palestinian ruling elite. For anarchists, such a process could be a significant step forward in a longer-term strategy for the destruction of the Israeli, Palestinian, and all other states along with capitalism, patriarchy and so on.

A fourth and final response would be to alter the terms of discussion altogether, by arguing that whether or not anarchists support a Palestinian state is a moot point, and leads to a false debate. What exactly are anarchists supposed to do with their 'support'? If the debate is to resolve itself in a meaningful direction, then the ultimate question is whether anarchists can and should take action in support of a Palestinian state. But what could such action possibly be, short of declarations, petitions, demonstrations and other elements of the 'politics of demand' that anarchists seek to transcend? One can hardly establish a state through anarchist direct action, and the politicians who will eventually decide on creating a Palestinian state are not exactly asking anarchists their opinion. Seen in this light, debates about whether anarchists should give their short-term 'support' to a Palestinian state sound increasingly ridiculous, since the only merit of such discussion would be to come up with a common platform. On this view, anarchists may take action in solidarity with Palestinians (as well as Tibetans, West Papuans and Sahrawis for that matter) without reference to the question of statehood. The everyday acts of resistance that anarchists join and defend in Palestine – e.g. removing roadblocks or defending olive harvesters from attacks by Jewish settlers – are immediate steps to help preserve people's livelihoods and dignity, not a step towards statehood. Once viewed from a longer-term strategic perspective, anarchists' actions have worthwhile implications whether or not they are attached to a statist agenda of independence.

For one thing, Israelis taking direct action alongside Palestinians is a strong public message in itself. The majority of the public certainly views Israeli anarchists as misguided, naive youth at best and as traitors at worst. The latter response happens because the joint Palestinian-Israeli struggle transgresses the fundamental taboos put in place by Zionist militarism. Alongside the living example of non-violence and cooperation between the two peoples, the struggle forces Israeli spectators to confront their dark collective traumas. Israelis who demonstrate hand-in-hand with Palestinians are threatening because they are afraid neither of Arabs nor of the Second Holocaust that they are supposedly destined to perpetrate. Notice how everything comes out when the anarchists are vilified by other Israelis: the fear of annihilation, the enemy as a calculated murderer, and victims' guilt expatiated through the assertion of self-defence and just war as unexamined axioms. And this is threatening on a deeper level than any hole in the fence – but then again, anarchists didn't get their reputation as trouble-makers for nothing.

ALTERNATIVES

In closing this chapter, I would like to take a more general look at the role of place-based identity and belonging in anarchist theory, and see whether any of it can apply to Israel/Palestine. While anarchists have traditionally rejected nationalism, the construction of the concept of the folk by writers such as Landauer and Rocker also has its limitations. For the idea of the folk assumes at least some degree of homogeneity, even if the term can be extended (as Rocker argues) to accommodate folk identities created by the mixing and fusion of cultures and population shifts over time. But in today's world it is questionable how useful this concept is. The idea of collective local identity based on shared culture, language and spirit is irrelevant in many regions of the world, where centuries of colonialism and immigration have created multicultural populations that share very little in these terms. Can anarchists endorse a different form of belonging that can address this situation while resonating with their broader political perspectives?

Here, the idea of bioregionalism presents itself as a promising alternative. Bioregionalism is an approach to local identity that has achieved much currency in the radical environmental movement, and is based not on ethnic or political divisions but on the natural and cultural properties of a place. A bioregion is commonly defined as a continuous geographic area with unique natural features in terms of terrain, climate, soil, watersheds, plants and animals, as well as the human settlements and cultures that have developed in response to these local conditions. A bioregion is thus also a terrain of consciousness, as can be seen in indigenous peoples' accounts of their connection to the land and in local knowledge and customs. As a result, the bioregionalist approach stresses an intimate relationship between people and their natural environment, promoting sustainability and local self-reliance instead of the alienated and monocultural lifestyles pervasive in modern industrial societies (Berg 1978, Andruss et al. 1990, Thayer 2003). According to Kirkpatrick Sale (1983),

To become 'dwellers in the land' ... to fully and honestly come to know the earth, the crucial and perhaps only and all-encompassing task is to understand the place, the immediate, specific place, where we live ... We must somehow live as close to it as possible, be in touch with its particular soils, its waters, its winds. We must learn its ways, its capacities, its limits. We must make its rhythms our patterns, its laws our guide, its fruits our bounty.

Since the early 1970s, bioregionalism has become the agenda of numerous organisations, communities, farmers, artists and writers. The Planet Drum Foundation in San Francisco was among the first pioneers of the bioregional approach, publishing literature on the application of place-based ideas to environmental practices, cultural expression and politics. Other early organisations were the Frisco Bay Mussel Group in northern California and the Ozark Area Community Congress on the Kansas–Missouri border. Currently there are hundreds of similar groups in North and South America, Europe, Japan, and Australia (Berg 2002). Since 1984, ten North American Bioregional Congresses have taken place in the US and Canada (see www.bioregional-congress.org), and there is even a popular 'BioRegional Quiz' (Charles et al. 1981), with questions like:

- Trace the water you drink from precipitation to tap.
- Name 5 edible plants in your region and their season(s) of availability.
- How long is the growing season where you live?
- Name five resident and five migratory birds in your area.
- What species have become extinct in your area?

As can be seen, the bioregional approach is mostly concerned with ecological awareness, environmental restoration, local self-reliance and similar agendas. However, it also poses a powerful alternative – at least potentially – to both nationalist and 'folkist' approaches to identity. An identity based on connection to a local area does not contain any essentialist factors – it does not stipulate anything about the content of the personal and collective identities that can flourish within and alongside it. The only requirement is that such identities should be genuinely local and that they cohere with sustainable relationships between people and the land. As a result, individuals and groups can experience bioregional belonging while still holding multiple personal and collective identities in terms of occupation, language, ethnicity, lifestyle, spirituality, cultural taste, gender, sexual preference and so on. Bioregionalism is thus in line with anarchist demands for self-realisation and for the celebration of multiple and shifting identities.

The strongly decentralist and devolutionist agendas of bioregionalism should also make it immediately attractive to anarchists. Bioregions do not recognise arbitrary political boundaries and are unsuitable for control from above. The organisation of social and economic life according to bioregional principles calls for a high degree of local autonomy, as eco-feminist Helen Forsey argues:

Community people have a common urge to make their own decisions, control their own destinies, both as a group and as individuals ... if control of decisions or resources is imposed from the outside, the balance and cycles of the community's life are likely to be disrupted or destroyed. Without implying isolation, there needs to be a degree of autonomy which will permit the community to grow and flourish in the context of its own ecofeminist values. (Forsey 1990: 84–5)

However, bioregional proposals do not imply a parochial and separatist attitude. Since bioregions do not have clear borders but flow and melt into each other, a bioregional model is more likely to promote an ethos of cooperation and mutual aid in the stewardship of regional environments, based on both commonality and diversity. Bioregionalism, in sum, offers a viable and attractive alternative to both nationalist and 'folkist' approaches to collective local identity, while strongly resonating with broader anarchist perspectives.

Can any of this be seriously applied to the situation in Palestine/ Israel? The creation of a bioregional society is difficult enough as it is, since it requires a massive transformation in the way society is organised. After all, bioregionalism is incompatible not only with war and occupation but also with capitalism, racial and religious bigotry, consumerism, patriarchy and any number of other trenchant features of hierarchical society. Like anarchism itself, full-blown bioregionalism could only come about through some form of social revolution. But the prospects look especially bleak in a context like Israel/Palestine, where decades of occupation and armed conflict have left a heavy deposit of mutual fear and suspicion that would have to be overcome before the peaceable and gentle ideals of bioregionalism could come anywhere near realisation.

Amid the daily horrors of death and humiliation, and of mutual ignorance, fear and hatred on both sides, it is tempting to say something positive about the prospects for 'real peace' in the region. Perhaps the mould of 'constructive direct action' could be extended from building alternatives to capitalism to something like 'grassroots peacemaking' – projects that build community-to-community dialogue between Israelis and Palestinians. Is this not an attractive idea? After all, even for dovish Israeli Jews the notion of peace is strongly associated with separation – 'us here, them there'. This is why the Israeli government calls it the 'separation' barrier – and most of the Israeli 'peace camp' would be satisfied if the separation were only to overlap with the Green Line. In contrast, couldn't direct dialogue and shared projects – ecological ones for example – go against the grain of separation, bypassing politicians to build peace from the bottom up?

There are already, in fact, numerous and sometimes well-funded initiatives for dialogue between Palestinian and Israeli children, shared exhibitions of Palestinian and Israeli artists and the 'Peace Team' of Israeli and Palestinian footballers that became famous for its miserable losses in friendly games against champion European clubs. Inside Israel, the network of organisations for Jewish–Arab 'coexistence' already lists over 100 organisations, from lobbying and advocacy groups through educational and artistic projects and on to local citizens' forums in mixed cities and regions.

Unfortunately, there are special complications that surround even the best-intentioned attempts of this kind. These are more serious than the fact that they can easily fall into the role of civil society initiatives which supplement rather than challenge basic political and social structures. The deeper problem, as seen by many Palestinian human rights groups and Israeli dissidents, is that such projects mask the realities of the region and present equality where there is none. In vain attempts to remain neutral, coexistence and dialogue projects end up using a language in which the situation seems to be a conflict between two peoples fighting over the same piece of land, and peace the result of a territorial compromise and safe face-to-face encounters between Palestinians and Israelis, especially youth. These coexistence initiatives, launched by Israeli NGOs and backed by international foundations, seem harmless at worst until we remember that this 'outstretched hand for peace' is coming from the citizens of the occupying power. However well-meaning, projects that aim to overcome mutual ignorance and suspicion and to heal collective traumas put the cart before the horse. They amount to a call for normalisation of relations between Palestinians and Israelis as if the occupation was already over. This is not only paternalistic, but also doomed to practical failure.

Can this Radical's Catch 22 be transcended? It would seem that the practice of joint struggle does offer an alternative to the quaint helplessness of coexistence projects. American-Israeli anarchist Bill

Templer (2003) tries to evoke one way out of the problem, in an article heavy with the catchwords of anti-capitalist language:

Reinventing politics in Israel and Palestine means laying the groundwork now for a kind of Jewish-Palestinian Zapatismo, a grassroots effort to 'reclaim the commons'. This would mean moving towards direct democracy, a participatory economy and a genuine autonomy for the people; towards Martin Buber's vision of 'an organic commonwealth ... that is a community of communities'. We might call it the 'no-state solution'.

Templer's optimism for such a project rests on the perception of a widespread crisis of faith in 'neoliberal governmentality', making Israel/Palestine 'a microcosm of the pervasive vacuity of our received political imaginaries and the ruling elites that administer them ... [but which] offers a unique microlaboratory for experimenting with another kind of polity'. While acknowledging the inevitability of a two-state settlement in the short term, he traces elements which are already turning Palestine/Israel into 'an incubator for creating "dual power" over the middle term, "hollowing out" capitalist structures and top-down bureaucracies'.

Templer's speculations may involve more than a bit of wishful thinking, but the relevant point is that unlike coexistence and dialogue for the sake of it, joint struggle does not imply normalisation. This is because it is clearly infused with antagonism towards the commanding logic of both the Israeli state, and the Palestinian parties and militias who condemn any dealings with Israelis. So while the creation and fostering of spaces which facilitate mutual aid between Palestinians and Israelis is indeed required, only such spaces which are ones of rebellion and struggle can honestly stand up to the charge of false normalisation and 'coexistence'.

The joint struggle in the villages of the West Bank not only managed to crack the unquestioned consensus around the Segregation Barrier in the Israeli public. Far more significant cracks may have appeared in the intractable image of the conflict in the eyes of many Israelis. Israeli–Palestinian cooperation in militant but non-violent action is inherently powerful because it enacts a dramatic, 90-degree flip of perspective: the 'horizontal' imagery of conflict between Israelis and Palestinians is displaced by the 'vertical' one of struggle between people and government. The Mas'ha camp was by itself an example of such a transformation. The encounter between Israelis and Palestinians engaging in a joint struggle against the construction of the segregation barrier in the village became a protracted face-to-face encounter, where members of both communities could meet each other as individuals and create a genuine, if temporary, community with no illusions about the impossibility of ending the occupation through grassroots action alone. For both sides, joint struggle can be an intense experience of togetherness, which by extension could create a model for future efforts – as these quotes from a Palestinian and an Israeli participant demonstrate (Sha'labi and Medicks 2003):

Nazeeh: We wanted to show that the Israeli people are not our enemies; to provide an opportunity for Israelis to cooperate with us as good neighbors and support our struggle ... Our camp showed that peace will not be built by walls and separation, but by cooperation and communication between the two peoples living in this land. At Mas'ha Camp we lived together, ate together, and talked together 24 hours a day for four months. Our fear was never from each other, but only from the Israeli soldiers and settlers.

Oren: The young Israeli generation realizes that the world has changed. They saw the Berlin wall come down. They know that security behind walls is illusionary. Spending some time together in the camp, has proven to us all that real security lies in the acceptance of one another as equals, in respecting each other's right to live a full, free life ... [we struggle] to topple walls and barriers between peoples and nations, creating a world which speaks one language – the language of equal rights and freedom.

In contrast to both the logic of separation and harmless dialogue initiatives, joint resistance in Palestine/Israel remains an open arena for extending and pushing the boundaries of Israeli–Palestinian cooperation, in a struggle that despite its very imperfect conditions can still momentarily manifest the hope that Jews, Palestinians and others might one day live in this land together without classes, states or borders.

Conclusion

This book has looked at contemporary anarchism, moving from an exploration of anarchist political culture and ideas to questions in anarchist theory surrounding power, violence, technology and nationalism. In mapping and assessing these issues, I have more generally attempted in *Anarchy Alive!* to show what an anarchist theory grounded in practice can look like, once it is based on a direct, partial and critical engagement with the actions and words of the living movement.

To be sure, I have not been alone in attempting this kind of endeavour. Networks of struggle against capitalism and the state have become mature and self-sustaining, and are producing fresh theory that deserves to be taken very seriously. This book joins an expanding library of writing by fellow activist-theorists and anarchademics, writing which is coming into its own as a valued contribution to the struggle. As Michal Osterweil recently noted, diverse movement networks constantly display theoretical production that attempts to 'think through, investigate and experiment with different political practices, imaginaries, as well as different analyses of the systems and sites in which we are struggling'. Moreover,

both the content of the theories, and the ways they are produced ... seem based on an ethic of partiality, specificity and open-endedness; a willingness to be revised and reworked depending on their lived effectiveness; and a sensitivity to the fact that unexpected conflicts and consequences might arise when different subjects or circumstances come into contact with them.

My own contribution to the theoretical conversation has aimed to speak in the same spirit. I hope I have managed to find the right language and concepts for addressing the 'complex, messy and unexpected elements always present in the lived realities of efforts at social change' (Osterweil 2007).

Like many others who became involved in the 'movement of movements' around the turn of the millennium, I did so with part of me believing that the global wave of struggle I was part of could accelerate in an unstoppable crescendo until genuine social transformation was achieved. It did seem like that for a while, when every mobilisation drew larger numbers and public support was rising even in advanced capitalist countries, not least as the result of police excesses. Since late 2001, however, the wave seemed to break and with energies diverting to the movement against the wars in Afghanistan and Iraq, it seemed that a downturn had arrived.

But these days anarchists and their allies are again sensing that the tides are turning. With the defeat, in Iraq and elsewhere, of the US attempt at global hegemony, things are shifting in the global system and a new surge of struggle may be on the horizon. As Kay Summer and Harry Halpin recently wrote, there are both 'terrifying and exciting' possibilities created by the spectre of collapse, as capitalism continues to approach its ecological limits. A now massively interconnected and globalised world would have to deal with a shrinking resource base and an unstable climate, potentially placing humanity in a unique moment of critical instability, a 'bifurcation point' where a phase-passage can take place from one pattern of dynamic equilibrium to another – be it gang warfare, eco-fascism or a peaceful world of self-sufficiency, freedom and mutual aid (Summer and Halpin 2007). In other words, things are going to inevitably shift – but where they go depends on us.

And so once again there are more questions than answers. Coming to the end of this particular journey, it seems that the urgency has receded away from the debates it encountered, and that new issues are taking their place. Inevitably, published books will lag behind the living movement they address – but perhaps I have succeeded in giving an adequate formal expression to some of the shared intuitions, practices and theories that anarchists and their allies have reached anyway, as a matter of organic consensus in the course of their struggles. Meanwhile, preoccupations with the purity of process, or with the boundaries of violent protest, are giving way to a certain calm determination. There are new questions for anarchists to face now – questions about winning.

Kibbutz Samar, Arava Valley
Summer Solstice 2007

Bibliography

Abramsky, Kolya (ed., 2001) *Restructuring and Resistance: Diverse voices of struggle from Western Europe* (Edinburgh: AK Distribution)

ACME collective (2000) *N30 Black Bloc Communique*; http://www.zmag.org/acme.htm

Adamiak, Richard (1970) 'The Withering Away of the State: A reconsideration', *Journal of Politics* 32.1; http://question-everything.mahost.org/Archive/WitheringAway.pdf

Adams, Jason (2002a) 'Post-Anarchism in a Bombshell', *Aporia* 3; http://aporiajournal.tripod.com/postanarchism.htm

—— (2002b) *Non-Western Anarchisms: Rethinking the global context* (pamphlet); http://www.infoshop.org/texts/nonwestern.pdf

Aguilar, Ernesto (2005) 'Breaking the Ice: Anarchist men and sexism in the movement'; http://www.infoshop.org/inews/article.php?story=2005020 1065922986

Anarchist Communist Initiative, Israel (2004) 'Two States for Two Peoples – Two States Too Many' (leaflet), in FdCA, *We are all Anarchists against the Wall*

Anarcho (undated) 'Anarchist Organisation and the Organisation of Anarchists', http://anarchism.ws/writers/anarcho/anarchism/organisationGAG.html

Anarkismo.net Editorial Collective (2005) 'Who we are and why we do it'; http://www.anarkismo.net/docs.php?id=1

Andruss, Van, Christopher Plant, Judith Plant and Eleanor Wright (1990), *Home! A Bioregional Reader* (Gabriola Island, BC: New Society Publishers)

Anonymous1 (1959/1812) 'The Declaration of the Framework Knitters', in Arthur Aspinall and E. Anthony Smith, eds, *English Historical Documents, XI, 1783–1832* (Oxford: Oxford University Press)

Anonymous2 (undated) 'What it is to be a girl in an anarchist boys club'; http://www.spunk.org/texts/anarcfem/sp000168.html

Anonymous3 (2000) 'May Day', *Do or Die 9*; http://www.eco-action.org/dod/no9/may_day.htm

Anonymous4/5 (2003) 'Lausanne Solidarity Declaration' and 'With Love from the Black Bloc'; http://indymedia.ie/newswire.php?story_id=64828

Anonymous6 (2003) 'Communiqué : face aux mensonges médiatiques, des blacks et pinks blocs témoignent et revendiquent'; http://www.ainfos.ca/03/jun/ainfos00088.html

Anonymous7 (2001) 'Some notes on Insurrectionary Anarchism', *Killing King Abacus* 2; http://www.geocities.com/kk_abacus/kka/NTINSUR.html

Anonymous8 (1999) *Beasts of Burden: Capitalism – Animals – Communism* (London: Antagonism Press); www.insurgentdesire.org.uk/beast.htm

ARA – Anti Racist Action (undated) *Points of Unity*; http://www.antiracistaction.us/pn

Armstrong, Elizabeth A. (2002) *Forging Gay Identities: Organizing Sexuality in San Francisco, 1950–1994* (Chicago: University of Chicago Press)

Arquilla, John and David Ronfeldt, eds, *Networks and Netwars: The future of terror, crime and militancy* (Santa Monica, CA: RAND Corporation); http://www.rand.org/pubs/monograph_reports/MR1382/index.html

Ashen Ruins (2002) *Beyond the Corpse Machine: Defining a post-leftist critique of violence* (pamphlet); http://www.infoshop.org/rants/corpse_last.html

ASI – Anti-Slavery International (2005) *Annual Review*; http://www.antislavery.org/homepage/resources/PDF/annualreview2005.pdf

Austrian, Guy Izhak and Ella Goldman (2003) 'How to strengthen the Palestine Solidarity Movement by making friends with Jews'; *Clamor* magazine *Communique #20*; http://www.clamormagazine.org/communique/communique20.pdf

Aviram, Adina (2003) 'Militarization of knowledge'; http://www.newprofile.org/showdata.asp?pid=347

Ayalon, Uri (2004) 'Resisting the Apartheid Wall', in FdCA, *We are all Anarchists against the Wall*

Bachrach, Peter and Morton Barratz (1970) *Power and Poverty* (New York: Oxford University Press)

Bachram, Heidi (2004) 'Climate Fraud and Carbon Colonialism: The new trade in Greenhouse Gasses', *Capitalism Nature Socialism* 15:4; www.carbontradewatch.org/pubs/cns.pdf

Bailey, Mark (2005) '"Border Thinking", the Global Justice Movement and Mythologies of Resistance'; paper at the *Second Wales and Southwest England postgraduate conference*, Cardiff University

Bakunin, Michael (2001/1866) 'The Revolutionary Catechism', in *The Anarchy Archives*; http://dwardmac.pitzer.edu/anarchist_archives/bakunin/catechism.html

—— (1953/1871) 'A circular letter to my friends in Italy', in G. P. Maximoff, ed., *The Political Philosophy of Bakunin* (London: Free Press)

Barandiaran, Xabier (2003) *Hacklabs: Ttecnologías y redes de ensamblado colectivo de autonomía digital*, v.0.9; http://www.sindominio.net/~xabier/textos/hl/hl.html

Barclay, Harold (1990) *People Without Government: An anthropology of anarchism* (London: Kahn & Averill)

Bauman, Zygmunt (1991) *Modernity and Ambivalence* (Cambridge: Polity Press)

Bell, Graham (1992) *The Permaculture Way: Practical steps to create a self-sustaining world* (Northampton: Thorsons)

Berg, Peter (ed., 1978) *Reinhabiting A Separate Country: A Bioregional Anthology of Northern California* (San Francisco: Planet Drum Foundation)

—— (2002) *Bioregionalism* (webpage); http://www.planetdrum.org/bioregionalism_defined.htm

Bevington, Louisa S. (1896) *Anarchism and Violence* (London: Liberty Press); http://www.mantex.co.uk/ou/aa810/vww-08.htm

Birnbaum, Norman (1971) *Towards a Critical Sociology* (Oxford: Oxford University Press)

Black, Bob (1994) 'The Sphincter of Anarchism', in *Beneath the Underground* (Portland, OR: Feral House); http://www.spunk.org/library/writers/black/sp001644.html (as 'My Anarchism Problem')

—— (1998) *Anarchy After Leftism* (San Francisco: CAL Press)

Black Laundry (2001) 'Nails and Feathers'; http://www.blacklaundry.org/pdfs/Wigstock_sept01.pdf

Black, Mary (2001) 'Letter from Inside the Black Bloc' *AlterNet.*, July 25; http://www.alternet.org/story/11230

Bonanno, Alfredo (1996) *The Anarchist Tension* (London: Elephant editions)

—— (1998) *The Insurrectional Project* (London: Elephant editions)

Bookchin, Murray (1972) 'On Spontaneity and Organization', *Liberation* (March)

—— (1974) *Post-scarcity Anarchism* (Montreal: Black Rose)

—— (1980) 'Anarchism Past and Present', *Comment* 1.6; in *The Anarchy Archives* http://dwardmac.pitzer.edu/Anarchist_Archives/bookchin/pastandpresent.html

—— (1995) *Social Anarchism or Lifestyle Anarchism: An Unbridgeable Chasm?* (Edinburgh: AK Press); http://www.spunk.org/library/writers/bookchin/sp001512

—— (2003) 'The Communalist Project', *Harbinger, A Journal of Social Ecology* 3.1; http://www.social-ecology.org/harbinger/vol3no1/communalist.html

Bray, Jim (2000) *(Working) Start of Critique of Black Bloc Technique* (webpage); http://www.as220.org/jb/politics/black_bloc.html

Brown, L. Susan (1993) *The Politics of Individualism: Liberalism, Liberal Feminism and Anarchism* (Montreal: Black Rose)

Buechler, Steven M. (2000) *Social Movements in Advanced Capitalism* (Oxford: Oxford University Press)

Butler, C. T. and Amy Rothstein (1998) *Conflict and Consensus* (Takoma Bay, MD: Food Not Bombs Publishing); http://www.consensus.net

CAFOD – Catholic Agency for Overseas Development (2004) *Clean Up Your Computer*; www.computertakeback.com/document.cfm?documentID=21

Call, Lewis (2002) *Postmodern Anarchism* (Lanham: Lexington Books)

Carrier, James (1991) 'Gifts, Commodities, and Social Relations: a Maussian view of exchange', *Sociological Forum* 6.1, pp.119–36

Carter, Alan (2000) 'Analytical Anarchism: Some conceptual foundations', *Political Theory* 28.2

Carter, April (1978) 'Anarchism and Violence', in J. Roland Pennock and John W. Chapman, eds, *Nomos XIX – Anarchism* (New York: NYU Press), pp.320–40

Carter, John and Dave Morland (2004) 'Anti-Capitalism: Are we all anarchists now?' in Carter and Morland, eds, *Anti-capitalist Britain* (Gretton: New Clarion Press)

Castoriadis, Cornelius (1964) 'The Role of Bolshevik Ideology in the Birth of the Bureaucracy', *Socialism ou Barbarie* 35; http://www.geocities.com/cordobakaf/castbolsh.html

Charles, Leonard, Jim Dodge, Lynn Milliman and Victoria Stockley (1981) 'Where You At? A bioregional quiz', *Coevolution Quarterly* 32 (Winter); http://www.asle.umn.edu/archive/readings/quiz.html

Chesters, Graeme and Ian Welsh (2005) *Complexity and Social Movements: Multitudes on the edge of chaos* (London: Routledge)

Choi, Sang et.al (2002) 'Microwave-driven Multifunctional Capability of Membrane Structures', *Smart Materials and Structures* 13, 38–48

Chomsky, Noam (1986) 'The Soviet Union versus Socialism', *Our Generation* 17.2; http://www.zmag.org/chomsky/articles/86-soviet-socialism.html

Churchill, Ward and Mike Ryan (1998) *Pacifism as Pathology: Reflections on the role of armed struggle in North America* (Winnipeg: Arbeiter Ring)

Class War Federation (1992) *Unfinished Business: the politics of class war* (Edinburgh: AK Press)

Cleaver, Harry (1998) 'The Zapatistas and the Electronic Fabric of Struggle', in Holloway and Peláez, *Zapatista!: Reiventing Revolution in Mexico* (London: Pluto)

Cohen, Jean and Andrew Arato (1992) *Civil Society and Political Theory* (Cambridge, MA: MIT Press)

Cohen, Joshua (1998) 'Deliberation and Democratic Legitimacy', in Alan Hamlin and Phillip Pettit, eds, *The Good Polity* (New York: Blackwell)

Cohn-Bendit, Daniel and Gabriel (1968) *Obsolete Communism – The Left Wing Alternative* (Edinburgh: AK Press)

Colectivo Situaciones (2002), *19 y 20: Apuntes para el nuevo protagonismo social* (Buenos Aires: Colectivo Situaciones)

Collins, Patricia Hill (2000) *Black Feminist Thought: Knowledge, Consciousness, and the Politics of Empowerment* (London : Routledge)

Colombo, Eduardo (2000) 'Prolégomènes à une réflexion sur la violence', *Réfractions* 5; http://www.plusloin.org/refractions/refractions5/prolegomenes-columbo.htm

Coover, Virginia, Ellen Deacon, Charles Esser and Christopher Moore (1977) *Resource Manual for a Living Revolution* (Philadelphia: New Society Publishers)

Crass, Chris (2002) '"But We Don't Have Leaders": Leadership development and antiauthoritarian organizing'; http://www.infoshop.org/rants/crass_leaders.html

—— (2004) 'Going to places that scare me: personal reflections on challenging male supremacy'; http://www.colours.mahost.org/articles/crass15.html

CrimethInc (2001) 'Alive in the Land of the Dead', in *Days of War, Nights of Love: CrimethInc for Beginners* (Olympia, WA: CrimethInc Ex-Workers Collective); http://www.crimethinc.com/library/english/alive.html

CWS organisers (eds, undated) Resources for *Challenging White Supremacy workshops*; http://www.cwsworkshop.org/resources.html

Dahl, Robert (1957) 'The Concept of Power', *Behavioral Science* 2, pp.201–15

—— with Bruce Stinebrickner (2003) *Modern political analysis*, 6th ed. (Upper Saddle River, NJ: Prentice Hall)

DARPA – Defense Advanced Research Projects Agency (2005) *Micro-Electro-Mechanical Systems (MEMS) Project website*; http://www.darpa.mil/mto/mems/index.html

Deleuze, Gilles and Felix Guattari (1987) *A Thousand Plateaus: Capitalism and Schizophrenia* (Minneapolis, MI: University of Minnesota Press)

De-Shalit, Avner (2000) *The Environment Between Theory and Practice* (Oxford: Oxford University Press)

Diani, Mario (1992) 'The Concept of Social Movement', *Sociological Review* 40.1

—— (2003) '"Leaders" or Brokers? Positions and influence in social movement networks', in Mario Diani and Doug McAdam, eds, *Social Movements and*

Networks: Relational approaches to collective action (Oxford: Oxford University Press)

DKDF organisers (eds, 2004) Readings for the *Different Kind of Dude-fest*, Washington, DC; http://differentkindofdudefest.dead-city.org/reading.html

Dominick, Brian (1995) *Animal Liberation and Social Revolution* (pamphlet)

Edelman, Lee (1993) 'The Mirror and the Tank: "AIDS", subjectivity, and the rhetoric of activism'. In Timothy F. Murphy and Suzanne Poirier, eds, *Writing AIDS: Gay Literature, Language, and Analysis* (New York: Columbia University Press)

Edwards, Paul N. (2003) 'Infrastructure and Modernity', in Misa et al., *Modernity and Technology*

Eisler, Riane (1988) *The Chalice and the Blade: Our History, Our Future* (San Francisco, CA: HarperCollins)

Ekeh, Peter (1974) *Social Exchange Theory: The two traditions* (Cambridge, MA: Harvard University Press)

Ellul, Jacques (1964) *The Technological Society* (New York: Vintage Books)

El Viejo (2002) notes to PGA 2002, *PGA Hallmarks;* http://www.nadir.org/nadir/initiativ/agp/free/pga/hallm.htm

Epstein, Barbara (1991) *Political Protest and Cultural Revolution: Non-violent direct action in the 1970s and 1980s* (Berkeley, CA: University of California Press)

ETC Group – action group on Erosion, Technology and Concentration (2003) *The Big Down – Technologies converging on the nano scale;* http://www.etcgroup.org/upload/publication/171/01/thebigdown.pdf

FAA – United States Federal Aviation Administration (1999) *Final Environmental Assessment for the Sea Launch Project;* http://www.fas.org/spp/guide/ukraine/launch/2_99Bslea.pdf

FdCA – Federazione dei Comunisti Anarchici (eds, 2004) *We are all Anarchists against the Wall* (Fano: I Quaderni di Alternativa Libertaria); http://www.fdca.it/wall/media/anarwall_EN.pdf

Feral Faun (Wolfi Landstreicher) (2001) 'The Anarchist Subculture', in *Feral Revolution* (London: Elephant editions), pp.80–97

Ferrara, Jennifer (1998) 'Revolving Doors: Monsanto and the regulators', *The Ecologist* (autumn); http://www.psrast.org/ecologmons.htm

Feyerabend, Paul (1970) *Against Method* (Minneapolis, MN: University of Minnesota Press)

Fifth Estate (1986) 'Renew the Earthly Paradise', *Fifth Estate* 322 (Winter/Spring); http://website.lineone.net/~grandlaf/Rtep.htm

Flugennock, Mike (2000) 'A16, a sort of Epilogue: Black Bloc Salute'; *MikeyZine;* http://www.sinkers.org/a16/blackbloc/

Forsey, Helen (1990) 'Community: Meeting our deepest needs', in Andruss et al., *Home! A Bioregional Reader*

Foti, Alex and Zoe Romano (eds 2004) *Precarity*, Thematic issue, *Greenpepper magazine*

Foucault, Michel (1980) 'Two Lectures', in *Power/Knowledge: Selected Interviews and Other Writings 1972–1977* (New York: Pantheon)

—— (1988) 'Technologies of the Self' in L. H. Martin et al., *Technologies of the Self: A Seminar with Michel Foucault* (London: Tavistock)

Franks, Benjamin (2006) *Rebel Alliances: The means and ends of contemporary British anarchisms* (Edinburgh: AK Press)

FSF – Free Software Foundation (1996) *Definition*; http://www.gnu.org/philosophy/free-sw.html

Freeden, Michael (1996) *Ideologies and Political Theory: A conceptual approach* (Oxford: Clarendon)

Freeman, Jo (1970) 'The Tyranny of Structurelessness', *Black Rose* 1; http://flag.blackened.net/revolt/hist_texts/structurelessness.html

—— (1976) 'Trashing: The Dark Side of Sisterhood', *Ms. Magazine* (April) pp.49–51, 92–98; http://www.jofreeman.com/joreen/trashing.htm

Freire, Paulo (1970) *Pedagogy of the Oppressed* (New York: Seabury Press)

Friends of Al-Halladj (2002) *Fawda*; http://digilander.libero.it/guerrasociale.org/fawda_ing.htm

Friends of Phil and Toby (2003) *Summit Up: Reflections on the anti-G8 actions in Lausanne*; www.nadir.org/nadir/initiativ/agp/free/evian/post_evian/0422summit_up.htm

Galeano, Eduardo (1993) *Las Palabras Andantes* (Madrid: Siglo Veintiuno)

Gandhi, Mohandas K. (1915) 'In Another's Land', in *Collected Works* (New Delhi: Publications Division, Ministry of Information and Broadcasting, Govt. of India) vol. 26

Gee, Theoman (2003) *Militancy Beyond Black Blocs* (pamphlet) (Innsbruck: Alpine Anarchist Productions)

Geertz Clifford (1975) 'Thick Description: towards an interpretative theory of culture', in *The Interpretation of Culture* (London: Hutchinson)

Gerlach, Luther (2001) 'The Structure of Social Movements: Environmental activism and its opponents'. In Arquilla and Ronfeldt, *Networks and Netwars*, Ch. 9

Gimli (2004) 'The Feral Fury Unleashed', *Green Anarchy* 16; http://www.greenanarchy.org/index.php?action=viewwritingdetail&writingId=246

Goettlich, Paul (2000) 'The Revolving Door', in *The Green Revolution: A Critical Look (website)* http://www.mindfully.org/Farm/Green-Revolution-Revolving.htm

Goldman, Emma (1917) 'The Psychology of Political Violence', in *Anarchism and Other Essays* (Edinburgh: AK Press); http://dwardmac.pitzer.edu/Anarchist_Archives/goldman/aando/psychofpolvio.html

—— (1925) 'Afterword' to *My Disillusionment in Russia* (London: C. W. Daniel); http://dwardmac.pitzer.edu/anarchist_archives/goldman/further/mfdr_12.html

—— (1989/1938) 'Emma Goldman's Views', *Letter to Spain and the World* (August). Reprinted in Vernon Richards, ed., *British Imperialism and the Palestine Crisis: Selections from the anarchist journal Freedom, 1938–1948* (London: Freedom Press), pp.24–7

Gould, Carol (1988) *Rethinking Democracy: Freedom and social cooperation in politics, economics and society* (Cambridge: Cambridge University Press)

Graeber, David (2002) 'The New Anarchists', *New Left Review* 13; http://newleftreview.org/A2368

—— (2004) *Fragments of an Anarchist Anthropology* (Chicago: Prickly Paradigm Press)

Grauer, Mina (1994) 'Anarcho-Nationalism: Anarchist attitudes towards Jewish nationalism and Zionism', *Modern Judaism* 14.1

Gullestad, Marianne (1999) 'The Politics of Knowledge', at *Advancing Cultural Studies International Workshop*, Stockholm; http://culturemachine.tees. ac.uk/Cmach/Backissues/j001/ADVCS/acs_gull.htm

Hakim Bey (1985a) 'Pirate Utopias', in *The Temporary Autonomous Zone* (New York: Autonomedia); http://www.sacred-texts.com/eso/taz.htm

—— (1985b) 'Psychic Paleolithism and High Technology: A Position Paper'; in *The Temporary Autonomous Zone*

—— (1991) 'The Willimantic/Rensselaer Questions', in Mike Gunderloy and Michael Ziesing, *Anarchy and the End of History* (San Francisco: Factsheet Five Books)

Heidegger, Martin (1977/1962) 'The Question Concerning Technology', in *Basic Writings* (San Francisco: HarperCollins)

Heinberg, Richard (2004) *Powerdown: Options and actions for a post-carbon world* (Gabriola Island, BC: New Society Publishers)

Herndon, Sheri (2001) 'Myths about Consensus Decision-making' (IMC e-list message); http://lists.indymedia.org/mailman/public/imc-process/2001-February/000463.html

Hever, Shir (2006) *The Economy of the Occupation* (bulletin series) (Jerusalem: Alternative Information Centre); http://www.alternativenews.org/the-economy-of-the-occupation/index.php

Himanen, Pekka (2001) *The Hacker Ethic and the Spirit of the Information Age* (New York: Random House)

Hobson, Christopher Z., Wayne Price and Matthew Quest (2001) 'New Intifada' (debate), *The Utopian* 2; http://www.ainfos.ca/01/apr/ainfos00225.html

Hodgson, Torrance (2003) 'Towards Anarchy'; http://www.infoshop.org/inews/article.php?story=03/01/21/7159959

Holloway, John (2002) *Change the World Without Taking Power* (London: Pluto Press)

—— (2003) 'Is the Zapatista Struggle an Anti-Capitalist Struggle?', *The Commoner* 6; http://www.commoner.org.uk/holloway06.doc

homefries (ed., 2004) *A Liberation Reader: Writings and other media connecting animal liberation and social justice*; http://www.liberationreader.blogspot. com/

Honderich, Ted (1989) *Violence for Equality* (London: Routledge)

Horrox, James (2007) *A Living Revolution: Anarchism in the Kibbutz Movement* (San Francisco: AK Press)

Hurwitz, Roger (1999) 'Who Needs Politics? Who Needs People? The Ironies of Democracy in Cyberspace', *Contemporary Sociology* 28.6, pp. 655–61

Iadicola, Peter and Anson Shupe (1998) *Violence, Inequality, and Human Freedom* (Lanham: Rowman & Littlefield)

ILS – International Libertarian Solidarity (2001) 'Declaration of the International Libertarian Meeting'; http://www.ils-sil.org/en/declaration. htm

Imarisha, Walidah and Not4Prophet (2004) 'The War of Art: A conversation', in Ashanti Alston., ed., *Our Culture, Our Resistance: People of color speak out on anarchism, race, class and gender* http://www.illegalvoices.org/bookshelf/ our_culture,_our_resistance/the_war_of_art.html

IMC – Independent Media Centre network (2001) *Principles of Unity*, http://docs.indymedia.org/view/Global/PrinciplesOfUnity

ISM – International Solidarity Movement – Canada (2002) 'History, Structure & Philosophy', http://www.ismcanada.org/en/history.shtml

Jensen, Derrick (2000) *A Language Older than Words* (New York: Context Books)

Jeppesen, Sandra (2004) 'Where Does Anarchist Theory Come From?', Insistute of Anarchist Studies *Theory & Politics* column; http://www.anarchist-studies.org/article/articleview/51/1/7/

Jordan, John (1998) 'The Art of Necessity: The subversive imagination of anti-road protests and Reclaim the Streets', in McKay, *DiY Culture*

Jordan, John and Jennifer Whitney (2003) *Que Se Vayan Todos: Argentina's Popular Rebellion* (pamphlet); http://www.nadir.org/nadir/initiativ/agp/free/imf/argentina/txt/2002/0918que_se_vayan.htm

Juris, Jeff (2004) *Digital Age Activism: Anti-corporate globalization and the cultural politics of transnational networking*; PhD thesis, University of California at Berkeley

Kaplan, Temma (1997) *Crazy for Democracy: Women in Grassroots Movements* (London: Routledge)

Katsiaficas, George (1997) *The Subversion of Politics: European autonomous social movements and the decolonization of everyday life* (Atlantic Highlands, N.J.: Humanities Press)

Kaufman, Mara (2005) 'A Hacker's Perspective on the Social Forums', http://info.interactivist.net/article.pl?sid=05/02/23/1529229

Kellner, Douglas (2001), 'Introduction' to Andrew Feenberg and Jim Freedman, *When Poetry Ruled the Streets: The French May Events of 1968* (Albany: SUNY Press)

Klein, Naomi (2000) *No Logo: Taking aim at the brand bullies* (London: HarperCollins) p.281

—— (2002) *Fences and Windows: Dispatches from the front lines of the globalisation debate* (London: Flamingo)

Kollock, Peter (1999) 'The Economies of Online Cooperation: Gifts and public goods in Cyberspace', in Smith, Marc and Peter Kollock, eds, *Communities in Cyberspace* (London: Routledge)

Kondratieff, Nikolai (1984/1922) *The Long Wave Cycle* (New York: Richardson & Snyder)

Kropotkin, Petr (1910) 'Anarchism', *Encyclopaedia Britannica; in The Anarchy Archives*; http://dwardmac.pitzer.edu/Anarchist_Archives/kropotkin/britanniaanarchy.html

—— (1916) *The Conquest of Bread* (London: G. P. Putnam's Sons)

Kunstler, James (2006) *The Long Emergency: Surviving the end of oil, climate change, and other converging catastrophes of the twenty-first century* (Berkeley, CA: Grove/Atlantic)

Lakey, George (2002) 'Diversity of Tactics and Democracy', *Clamor Magazine* (March/April)

Lakoff, Aaron and Yossi Bar Tal (2005) 'Israeli Anarchism: Being Young, Queer and Radical in the Holy Land', *Anarchist Studies* 13.2

Landauer, Gustav (1907) 'Volk und Land: Dreißig sozialistische Thesen', *Die Zukunft* (Jan. 12)

—— (1973/1910) 'Schwache Stattsmänner, Schwacheres Volk!', *Der Sozialist*
(June 10), trans. in Eugene Lunn, *Prophet of Community: the Romantic
Socialism of Gustav Landauer* (Berkeley: University of California Press)

—— (1978/1911) *For Socialism* (St. Louis: Telos Press)

Landstreicher, Wolfi (2001) 'Introductory Notes', in *Willful Disobedience:
Analysis and Theory* 2.1 (pamphlet); http://www.omnipresence.mahost.
org/wd-v2-n1–6.htm

—— (2002) 'From Politics to Life: Ridding Anarchy of the Leftist Millstone',
Anarchy: a Journal of Desire Armed 54; http://www.geocities.com/kk_abacus/
ioaa/life.html

Le Guin, Ursula (2002/1974) *The Dispossessed* (London: Gollancz)

Lenin, Vladimir Ilyich (1952/1918) *State and Revolution*; in the *Marxists Internet
Archive*; http://www.marxists.org/archive/lenin/works/1917/staterev/ch05.
htm

Levine, Cathy (undated) 'The Tyranny of Tyranny'; http://www.angrynerds.
com/tot.html

Lewis, Linda and Sally Baideme (1972) 'The Women's Liberation Movement',
in Lyman T. Sargent, ed., *New Left Thought: An introduction* (Homewood,
Ill: Dorsey Press)

Lukes, Stephen (2005) *Power: A Radical View* (Basingstoke: Palgrave
Macmillan)

Lyon, David (2003) 'Surveillance Technology and Surveillance Society', in
Misa et al., *Modernity and Technology*

Makhno, Nestor, Piotr Arshinov et al. (1926) *Organisational Platform of the
Libertarian Communists*; http://www.nestormakhno.info/english/platform/
org_plat.htm

Malatesta, Errico (1921) 'Self Defence', *Umanità Nova*, 25 August; http://
325collective.com/anok&violence_em.pdf

—— (1927) 'A Project of Anarchist Organisation', *Il Risveglio* (Geneva),
October

Marcos, Subcomandante Insurgente (1998) 'Above and Below: Masks and
Silences'; http://www.ezln.org/documentos/1998/19980717.en.htm

Marcuse, Herbert (1964) *One Dimensional Man* (Boston: Beacon)

Marshall, Peter (1992) *Demanding the Impossible: A history of anarchism*
(London: Fontana)

Martel, Frédéric (1999) *The Pink and the Black: Homosexuals in France since
1968* (Stanford, CA: Stanford University Press)

Martinez, Elizabeth (2000) 'Where was the Color in Seattle?', in Kevin Danaher
and Roger Burbach, eds, *Globalize This!* (Monroe: MN: Common Courage
Press)

Marx, Karl (1867) 'The Strife between Workman and Machine', in *Capital*
vol.1, Ch. XV, §5; in the *Marxists Internet Archive*; http://marxists.org/
archive/marx/works/1867–1/ch15.htm

Mauss, Marcel (1935/1969) *The Gift* (London: Routledge & Kegan Paul)

May, Todd (1994) *The Political Theory of Post-structuralist Anarchism*
(Philadelphia: University of Pennsylvania press)

Mbah, Sam and I.E. Igariwey (2001) *African Anarchism: The history of a
movement* (Tucson, AZ: See Sharp Press); http://www.zabalaza.net/theory/
african_anarchism/contents.htm

McBay, Aric (2006) *Peak Oil Survival: preparation for life after gridcrash* (Guilford, CT: Lyons)

McCarthy, Ryan Chiang (2002) 'Anarchists and Palestine: class struggle or popular front?', *NEFAC* website; http://makhno.nefac.net/html/drupal/?q=node/view/158

McKay, George (1996) *Senseless Acts of Beauty: Cultures of resistance since the sixties* (London: Verso)

—— (ed., 1998) *DiY Culture: Party and protest in nineties Britain* (London: Verso)

McQuinn, Jason (2002) 'The Tyranny of Structurelessness: An organizationalist repudiation of anarchism', *Anarchy: A Journal of Desire Armed* 54

—— (2003) 'Evasion of Rational Discussion in the Radical Milieu', *Anarchy: A Journal of Desire Armed* 56

—— (2004) 'Post-left Anarchy: Leaving the Left Behind', *Anarchy: A Journal of Desire Armed* 57; http://www.anarchist-studies.org/article/articleview/43/1/1

Meyers, William (2000) *Nonviolence and Its Violent Consequences* (pamphlet); http://www.sinkers.org/nonviolence/

Michaels, Lucy (2004) 'Fear and Loathing', *New Internationalist* 372 (October); http://www.jfjfp.org/BackgroundJ/michaels.htm

Michels, Roberto (1999/1911) *Political Parties* (London: Transaction)

Midnight Notes (1985) *Strange Victories: The Anti-nuclear movement in the US and Europe* (London: Elephant Editions)

Millet, Steve (2004) '*Fifth Estate*'s Critique of the Megamachine', in Jonathan Purkis and David Morland, eds, *Changing Anarchism: Anarchist theory and practice in a global age* (Manchester: Manchester University Press)

Misa, Thomas, Philip Brey and Andrew Feenberg (eds, 2003) *Modernity and Technology* (Cambridge, MA.: MIT Press)

Mitropoulos, Angela, Marina Vishmidt, John Barker, Laura Sullivan et al. (2005) *Exploring Precariousness*. Special section, *Mute* 29

Mollison, Bill (1988) *Permaculture: A designers' manual* (Tyalgum: Tagari)

Mooney, Pat (2006) *Breaking Waves: Technology Tsunamis, Globalisation and Dismemberment* (Uppsala: Dag Hammarskjöld Foundation)

Moore, John (1997) 'A Primitivist Primer', *Green Anarchist* 47–8, pp.18–19; http://lemming.mahost.org/johnmoore/

—— (1998) 'Maximalist Anarchism/Anarchist Maximalism', *Social Anarchism* 25; http://www.spunk.org/texts/misc/sp001887.html

Moore, Richard (2003) 'Will A Death in the Family Breathe Life into the Movement?', in Notes from Nowhere, eds, *We Are Everywhere*

Morris-Suzuki,Tessa (1984) 'Robots and Capitalism', *New Left Review* I/147

Mueller, Tadzio (2004) '"Will the destruction be constructive?": Anticapitalist riots in search of the radical'. Paper at the conference *Global Civil Society and Local Activism: Poststructuralism and Praxis*, SOAS, University of London

Mumford, Lewis (1934) *Technics and Civilization* (London: Routledge)

Munson, Chuck (ed., 2005) *What you should know about the WWP, IAC and ANSWER* (Web page); http://www.infoshop.org/texts/wwp.html

Newman, Saul (2001) *From Bakunin to Lacan: Anti-authoritarianism and the dislocation of power* (Lanham: Lexington Books)

Nitzan, Jonathan and Shimshon Bichler (2002) *The Global Political Economy of Israel* (London: Pluto)

Noble, David F. (1993) *Progress Without People: In Defense of Luddism* (Chicago: Charles H. Kerr)

Notes from Nowhere (eds, 2003) *We Are Everywhere: The irresistible rise of global anticapitalism* (London: Verso)

Novak, Zachary (2006) 'Communities, Refuges, and Refuge-Communities', *Transition Culture* blog; http://transitionculture.org/?p=472

Nyman, Ira (2001) 'The Gift of Generalized Exchange', *Spark* 17

O'Connor, Alan (2003) 'Anarcho-Punk: Local scenes and international networks', *Anarchist Studies* 11:2

O'Connor, Paul (2001) 'Good evening, here is the real news', *Guardian*, 20 August

One Off Press (2001) *On Fire: The battle of Genoa and the anti-capitalist movement* (UK: One-off Press)

One Struggle (2002) 'About Us'; http://www.onestruggle.org/english_frameset2.htm

Osterweil, Michal (2007) '"Becoming-Woman?" In theory or in practice?', *Turbulence: Ideas for Movement* 1 – What Would it Mean to Win? (June 2007); http://turbulence.org.uk

P.M. (1985) *bolo'bolo* (New York: Autonomedia)

PENGON – Palestinian Environmental NGOs Network (2003) *The Wall in Palestine: Facts, Testimonies, Analysis and Call to Action*; http://www.pengon.org/wall/publication.html

Perez, Carlota (2002) *Technological Revolutions and Financial Capital: The dynamics of Bubbles and Golden Ages* (Cheltenham: Edward Elgar)

Perlman, Fredy (1969) 'The Reproduction of Everyday Life'; http://www.spunk.org/library/writers/perlman/sp001702/repro.html

—— (1983) *Against His-story, Against Leviathan!* (Detroit: Black and Red); extract: http://www.primitivism.com/leviathan.htm

PGA – Peoples' Global Action network (1999), *Documents of the Second International PGA conference, Bangalore*; http://www.nadir.org/nadir/initiativ/agp/en/pgainfos/bangalore/briefreport.html

—— (2002) *Hallmarks*; http://www.nadir.org/nadir/initiativ/agp/free/pga/hallm.htm

Plows, Alex (2002) *Practics and Praxis: The what, how and why of the UK environmental direct action movement in the 1990s*. PhD thesis, University of Wales, Bangor; http://www.iol.ie/~mazzoldi/toolsforchange/afpp/plowsphd.rtf

Price, Wayne (2001) 'Anarchism and the Israeli–Palestinian War', *Barricada* 17.

Prole Cat (2004) 'Towards More Effective Political Organizations: The role of leadership in anarchist society', *The Dawn* 4; http://www.the-dawn.org/2004/10/leadership.html

Proudhon, Pierre Joseph (1847) *The Philosophy of Poverty* (Boston: Benjamin Tucker)

Purkis, Jonathan (2001) 'Leaderless Cultures: The problem of authority in a radical environmental group', in Colin Barker, Alan Johnson and Michael

Lavalette, eds, *Leadership and Social Movements* (Manchester: Manchester University Press)

Ramsey Tosh, Nancy (2001) 'Mirror Images: Wicca from the Inside Out and Outside In', in David G. Bromley and Lewis F. Carter, eds, *Toward Reflexive Ethnography: Participating, Observing, Narrating* (Oxford: JAI Press)

Rappert, Brian (1999) 'Assessing Technologies of Political Control', *Journal of Peace Research* 36.6

Reason, Peter and Hilary Bradbury (2001) *Handbook of Action Research* (London: SAGE)

resist.nl (2005) 'Morning 06.07.05 Black Block tactics in Stirling (video)'; http://www.indymedia.org.uk/en/2005/07/317377.html

Reyes, Oscar, Hilary Wainwright, Mayo Fuster i Morrell and Marco Berlinguer (2005) *European Social Forum: Debating the challenges for its future*; Project newsletter, 'Guide for social transformation in Europe: ESF and surroundings'; http://www.euromovements.info/newsletter/

Ribeiro, Silvia (2003) 'The Day the Sun Dies: Contamination and resistance in Mexico' *Seedling* (summer); http://www.grain.org/seedling/?id=292

Ritter, Alan (1980) *Anarchism: A theoretical analysis* (Cambridge: Cambridge University Press)

Robins, Kevin and Frank Webster (1983) 'Luddism: New technology and the critique of political economy', in Les Levidow and Bob Young, eds, *Science, Technology and the Labour Process: Marxist studies* (London: Free Association Books) vol. 2, pp.9–48.

Rocker, Rudolf (1937) *Nationalism and Culture* (New York: Covici, Friede)

—— (1989/1938) *Anarcho-Syndicalism* (London: Pluto)

Rosaldo, Renato (1989) *Culture and Truth: The remaking of social analysis* (Boston: Beacon Press)

Rose, Steven (2006) 'Israel's Other Weaponry', *Palestine News* (summer)

Roth, Benita (2004) *Separate Roads to Feminism: Black, chicana, and white feminist movements in America's Second Wave* (New York: Cambridge University Press)

Russell, Bertrand (1938) *Power: A new social analysis* (London: Allen & Unwin)

Sahlins, Marshall (1972) *Stone Age Economics* (New York: Walter De Gruyter)

Sale, Kirkpatrick (1983) 'Mother of All: An introduction to bioreginalism', Third Annual E. F. Schumacher Lecture; http://www.schumachersociety.org/publications/sale_83.html

—— (1996) *Rebels Against the Future: The Luddites and their war on the industrial revolution* (London: Quartet Books)

Sandercock, Josie et al. (eds, 2004) *Peace Under Fire: Israel/Palestine and the International Solidarity Movement* (London: Verso)

SchNEWS (2001) *Monopolise Resistance* (pamphlet); http://www.schnews.org.uk/mr.htm

—— (2004) 'Short Sharp Crop: How GM crop farming was killed in Britain', in *SchNEWS At Ten* (Brighton: SchNEWS) pp.171–6

Sha'alabi, Nazeeh and Oren Medicks (2003) 'The camp in the eyes of a Palestinian activist' and 'The camp in the eyes of an Israeli activist'; http://stopthewall.org.il/mashacamp/

Shepard, Benjamin and Ronald Hayduk (eds, 2002) *From ACT UP to the WTO: Urban Protest and Community Building in the Era of Globalization* (London: Verso)

Shot by both sides (2005) 'Anti semitism and the Left', Melbourne Indymedia; http://www.melbourne.indymedia.org/news/2005/02/87951.php

SVTC – Silicon Valley Toxics Coalition. Webpage: http://www.svtc.org/

Silverstein, Marc (2002) 'Breaking Free of the Protest Mentality'; http://site.www.umb.edu/faculty/salzman_g/Strate/Discus/2002–04–25Silverstein.htm

Situationist International (1959) 'Détournement as Negation and Prelude'; http://library.nothingness.org/articles/SI/en/display/315

Solidarity Federation (2002) 'Human Rights: Yes – State of Palestine: No', *Direct Action* 23; http://www.directa.force9.co.uk/back issues/DA 23/regulars2.htm

Spar, Debora (2001) *Ruling the Waves: Cycles of discovery, chaos, and wealth, from the compass to the Internet* (New York: Harcourt)

Squirrellife (2004) 'London, UK – Death Spasms of an Insurrectionary Movement'; in *Confessions of A Riot Tourist;* http://squirrellife.diaryland.com/040113_41.html

Starhawk (1987) *Truth or Dare: Encounters with power, authority and mystery* (San Francisco: HarperCollins)

—— (2002) *Webs of Power: Notes from the global uprising* (Gabriola Island, BC: New Society Publishers)

—— (2004) 'RNC Update Number Two: Power and Anarchy'; http://www.starhawk.org/activism/activism-writings/RNC_update2.html

Sullivan, Sian (2004) '"We are heartbroken and furious" (:2): Violence and the (anti-)globalisation movement(s)', *CSGR Working Paper* 133/04

Summer, Kay and Harry Halpin (2007), 'Complexity, critical instability and the end of capitalism', *Turbulence: Ideas for Movement* 1 – What Would it Mean to Win? (June 2007); http://turbulence.org.uk

Taylor, Bron (2002) 'Diggers, Wolfs, Ents, Elves and Expanding Universes', in Jeffrey Kaplan and Heléne Lööw, eds, *The Cultic Milieu: Oppositional Subcultures in an Age of Globalization* (Walnut Creek, CA: Alta Mira Press)

Taylor, Michael (1976) *Anarchy and Cooperation* (London: Wiley)

—— (1982) *Community, Anarchy and Liberty* (Cambridge: Cambridge University Press)

Taylor, Verta and Nancy E. Whittier (1992) 'Collective Identity in Social Movement Communities: Lesbian feminist mobilization', in Aldon Morris and Carol McClurg Mueller (eds, 1992) *Frontiers in Social Movement Theory* (New Haven, CT: Yale University Press)

Templer, Bill (2003) 'From Mutual Struggle to Mutual Aid: Moving beyond the statist impasse in Israel/Palestine', *Borderlands* 2.3; http://www.borderlandsejournal.adelaide.edu.au/vol2no3_2003/templer_impasse.htm

Thayer Robert L. (2003) *LifePlace: Bioregional Thought and Practice* (Berkeley: University of California Press)

Thoreau, Henry David (1937/1849) 'Civil Disobedience', in *Walden and other writings* (New York: Modern Library)

Tokar, Brian (2003) Review of Joel Kovel (2002) *The Enemy of Nature* (London: Zed) *Tikkun* 18.1

Tolkien, J. R. R. (1964) 'On Fairy Stories', in *Tree and Leaf* (London: Allen & Unwin)

Tolstoy, Lev (1990) *Government is Violence: Essays on anarchism and pacifism* (London: Phoenix)

Touraine, Alain et al. (1983a) *Solidarity: The analysis of a social movement* (Cambridge: Cambridge University Press)

—— (1983b) *Anti-nuclear Protest: The opposition to nuclear energy in France* (Cambridge: Cambridge University Press)

Unbound, Chicago anarchist bookstore (undated) *Anti-mission Statement*

UNDP – United Nations Development Program (2003) 'Human Development Indicators 19: Energy and the environment', http://www.undp.org/hdr2003/indicator/indic_182_1_1.html

Vague, Tom (1997) *Anarchy in the UK: The Angry Brigade* (Edinburgh: AK Press)

Van Deusen, David and Xavier Massot (2007) *The Black Bloc Papers* (Shawnee Mission, KS: Breaking Glass Press – www.infoshop.org)

Vaneigem, Raoul (2001/1967) *The Revolution of Everyday Life* (London: Rebel Press); http://situationist.cjb.net

Veak, Tyler (2000) 'Whose Technology? Whose Modernity?', *Science, Technology and Human Values* 25.2

Vera Herrera, Ramón (2004) 'En defensa del maíz (y el futuro) – una autogestión invisible', *Acción Ciudadana en las Américas* 13; http://americas.irc-online.org/reports/2004/sp_0408maiz.html

Victor, Raoul (2003) 'Free Software and Market Relations'; *Project Oekonux* paper; http://www.oekonux.org/texts/marketrelations.html

Wall, Derek (1999) *Earth First! and the Anti-Roads Movement: Radical environmentalism and comparative social movements* (London: Routledge)

Ward, Colin (1973) *Anarchy in Action* (London: George Allan & Unwin)

Warneke, Brett (2005) *Smart Dust* (illustrated webpage) University of California at Berkeley; http://www-bsac.eecs.berkeley.edu/archive/users/warneke-brett/SmartDust/index.html

Watson, David (1998) *Against the Megamachine* (New York: Autonomedia)

Weber, Max (1947) *The Theory of Social and Economic Organisation*. Trans. A. M. Henderson and Talcott Parsons (New York: The Free Press)

—— (1958) 'The Three Types of Legitimate Rule', *Berkeley Publications in Society and Institutions* 4.1, pp.1–11

Welsh, Ian (2001) 'Anti-nuclear movements: failed projects or heralds of a direct action milieu?' *Working Paper Series* 11 (Cardiff University: School of Social Sciences)

Williams, Raymond (1978) 'Utopia and Science Fiction', *Science Fiction Studies* 5.3; http://www.depauw.edu/sfs/backissues/16/williams16art.htm

Winner, Langdon (1985) *The Whale and the Reactor: A search for limits in an age of high technology* (Chicago: Chicago University Press)

—— (2002) 'Luddism as Epistemology', in Robert Scharff and Val Dusek, eds, *Philosophy of Technology: The technological condition* (Oxford: Blackwell)

Winstanley, Asa (2004) 'The Limits of Free Software', *Tangentium* 1.3, *Anarchism, Activism and IT*; http://www.personal.leedsac.uk/~polaw/tangentium/may04/index.html

Wittgenstein, Ludwig (1953/2002) *Philosophical Investigations* (Oxford: Blackwell)

Woehrle, Lynne M. (1992) *Social Constructions of Power and Empowerment: Thoughts from feminist approaches to peace research and peace-making* (Syracuse: Syracuse University Press)

Wolff, Robert Paul (1969) 'On Violence', *The Journal of Philosophy* 66.19, pp.601–16

—— (1971) *In Defense of Anarchism* (New York: Harper and Row)

Woodcock, George (1985/1962) *Anarchism* (Harmondsworth: Penguin)

Wu Ming (2001) 'The Magical Mystery Tour of the Fake Black Bloc in Genoa', *Giap Digest* (22 July); http://www.wumingfoundation.com/english/giap/mysterytour.html

Yamagishi, Toshio and Karen Cook (1993) 'Generalized Exchange and Social Dilemmas' *Social Psychology Quarterly* 56.4, pp.235–48

Young, Iris Marion (2000) *Inclusion and Democracy* (Oxford: Oxford University Press)

Zerzan, John (1994) *Future Primitive and Other Essays* (New York: Autonomedia)

Index